*Praise for*

# HISTORY'S 9 MOST INSANE RULERS

"*History's 9 Most Insane Rulers* is a timely and salient wake-up call. At once an entertaining history lesson and cautionary tale, Scott Rank's book chronicles a host of unhinged and megalomaniacal rulers and assesses their relative madness. Much food for thought and reflection here."

—BUDDY LEVY, bestselling author of *Labyrinth of Ice: The Triumphant and Tragic Greely Polar Expedition*

"A king who thought he was made of glass. A tsar who alternated between being a pious monk and a hedonistic mass murderer. An emperor who thought he was divine and who elevated his horse to high office. These are just a few of the fascinating (and certifiable!) rulers you will meet in *History's 9 Most Insane Rulers* by Scott Rank. Dr. Rank writes in an engaging style that will make it hard for you to put the book down. Read this book . . . you'll be glad you did!"

—JAMES EARLY, professor of history at San Jacinto College

"History is replete with unfortunate leaders who have burdened their people with their own ego, idiocy, vengeance, and madness. Scott Rank's book describes them in detail and supplies ample stories that will make you think. From a leader who turned the lights off in the capital city and demanded his people be home by curfew, to another who made the nation quit smoking because he did, to one who broadcasted names of citizens on the radio to be targeted, this book is food for thought and a chill down the spine at the same time."

—BRUCE CARLSON, host of the *My History Can Beat Up Your Politics* podcast

"Kings, princes, dukes, and presidents throughout history have been required to make decisions under the most difficult of circumstances. Pressure can force even the best leaders to falter, but what if the leader is mentally unstable? This is what Professor Scott Rank explores in *History's 9 Most Insane Rulers*. Professor Rank provides the reader with a sample of world leaders throughout history whose mental health damaged their realms. He brings alive examples from the mildly unstable all the way to purely diabolical sovereigns who massacred their populations indiscriminately. You will be shocked to discover the depths of depravity some rulers went to and the role of poor mental health in the actions of these horrible rulers."

> —STEPHEN GUERRA, host of the *History of the Papacy Podcast*

"Scott's always had a gift for making history fun, engaging, and applicable to the present. *History's 9 Most Insane Rulers* is no exception. He's done it again!"

> —GREG JACKSON, host of the *History That Doesn't Suck* podcast and assistant professor of Integrated Studies at Utah Valley University

# History's 9 Most Insane Rulers

# HISTORY'S 9 MOST INSANE RULERS

## Scott Rank

REGNERY
HISTORY

Regnery History™ is a trademark of Salem Communications Holding Corporation
Regnery® is a registered trademark of Salem Communications Holding Corporation

ISBN 978-1-68451-006-1
ebook ISBN 978-1-68451-025-2
LCCN 2019955270

Published in the United States by
Regnery History, an imprint of
Regnery Publishing
A Division of Salem Media Group
300 New Jersey Ave NW
Washington, DC 20001
www.Regnery.com

Manufactured in the United States of America

10 9 8 7 6 5 4 3 2 1

Books are available in quantity for promotional or premium use. For information on discounts and terms, please visit our website: www.Regnery.com.

*For Ellie*

*Not to imply that you will ever be on this list*

# Contents

# Introduction

Are world leaders today more insane?

    A sizable number of mental health professionals are asking this question, prompted by a global growth in populist politicians, with Donald Trump topping the list. Among other mental health problems, according to professionals, Trump suffers from narcissistic personality disorder, as evidenced by a social media logorrhea so intense that his Twitter feed alone serves as diagnostic proof.

    John Gartner, Ph.D., is the founder of Duty to Warn, an organization focused on warning the United States that Trump's alleged mental illness poses a grave threat to America. His petition has over sixty thousand signatures from mental health professionals. It seeks constitutional action:

> We, the undersigned mental health professionals . . . believe in our professional judgment that Donald Trump manifests a serious mental illness that renders him psychologically incapable of competently discharging the duties of President of the United States. And we respectfully request he be removed

from office, according to article 4 of the 25th amendment to the Constitution, which states that the president will be replaced if he is "unable to discharge the powers and duties of his office."[1]

Along with Trump, the rise of populist politicians in the Philippines, Brazil, and Italy suggests a trend of major heads of state in democracies becoming unhinged to mental health professionals. Clearly, many voters are tolerating leaders whose actions would have once been considered so outlandish as to disqualify them from office.

Rodrigo Duterte, elected president of the Philippines in May 2016, campaigned on ending endemic drug trafficking by killing thousands of criminals. But Duterte's ugly personality was made clear by his lewd approach to a reporter asking a softball question. On another occasion, he used profanity against the pope, even though the Phillipines is an overwhelmingly Catholic country. When devout voters pushed back, Duterte defended his actions and his salt-of-the-earth persona. "I am testing the elite of this country," he said. "Because we are fundamentally a feudal country."

Beyond his crudeness, Duterte rambles on in a way suggestive of schizophrenia or bipolar disorder, peppering his speeches with inscrutable jokes, wild exaggerations, and profanity, as if there are no barriers dividing his emotions, thoughts, and behavior. In an outburst against Barack Obama for the latter's criticism of the Philippines' human rights abuses, Duterte used the Tagalog phrase *putang ina,* which means, literally, "Your mother is a whore" and is also used in frustration, as in "son of a bitch."[2]

Duterte is hardly alone among boorish world leaders. Brazilian president and fellow populist demagogue, Jair Bolsonaro, has made casual jokes about racism, rape, prostitution, and torturing opponents *while on the campaign trail.* "Since I was a bachelor at the time, I used the money to have sex with people," he bragged to a Brazilian newspaper in 2018 on the usage of his congressional housing allowance. When talking about visiting a settlement of quilombos, Brazil's black slave descendants, he noted that the fittest among them weigh 230 pounds and "do nothing . . . They are not even good for procreation." In 2014, Congresswoman Maria de Rosario claimed that Bolsonaro had encouraged rape during an argument with her. He responded that Rosario was "not worth raping; she is very ugly."[3]

Perhaps the most well-known showman-turned-politician in modern European politics is former Italian president Silvio Berlusconi, whose self-descriptions suggest delusions of grandeur and exaggerated self-importance. He called himself "the best political leader in Europe and in the world . . . there is no one on the world stage who can compete with me." He was equally outrageous in deflecting questions on scandals in his private life, specifically on relations with younger women and prostitutes: "I never understood where the satisfaction [of paying for sex] is when you're missing the pleasure of conquest."[4]

Why are populists winning political offices when their actions and comments would have destroyed a political campaign not long ago? Political scientists and journalists have offered their explanations. Author Noah Millman points to Friedrich Hegel's *Anerkennung*, or "recognition." All humans seek recognition from others. In the twenty-first century, traditional societies lost a sense of recognition in the post–Cold War world of globalization and cultural progressivism. Accelerating urbanization, the collapse of traditional families, and a reduction of the labor force in relation to stock market growth have led to traditionalists turning away from elites and toward populist politicians, who recognize them.[5]

The discussion of populist rulers' sanity or lack thereof naturally led to Donald Trump in 2016. Since Trump's election, hundreds of mental health professionals have tried to diagnose him. Dozens have come together to make joint statements. Bandy Lee edited a 2017 book, *The Dangerous Case of Donald Trump: 27 Psychiatrists and Mental Health Experts Assess a President*. She and others warned that Trump was an existential threat to the United States who needed confinement, evaluation, and removal from the presidency. Contributors Philip Zimbardo and Rosemary Sword connected his impulsivity with "unbridled and extreme present hedonism."

Justin Frank, author of *Trump on the Couch*, psychoanalyzed him by looking at historical records from Trump's family, his early years, and his own public record. Other sources include Trump's personal and presidential Twitter feeds. According to his diagnosis, which Frank called "frightening," Trump desperately sought attention and approval from his family. His older brother, Fred Jr., pushed hard to succeed and follow in his father's footsteps as a businessman, succumbed to alcoholism, and died at the age of forty-three. Donald saw the chance to become the favored son and earn the approval of his father, Fred Sr., a demanding, narcissistic, and authoritarian figure. But he rebelled. Fred Sr. tried to counter Donald's rebelliousness by enrolling him in the New York Military Academy in the eighth grade. Donald never got over feelings of rejection and abandonment. To cope, professionals say he formed dangerous mental traits such as grandiosity, projection, bullying, fear of weakness and shame, lack of empathy, and habitual lying. These traits surface in the president today to counter his preternatural anxiety, which is exacerbated whenever he perceives himself inadequate.[6]

Whatever the danger Donald Trump's mental health poses to the United States and the world at large, when compared to other leaders past and present, he is not the outlier certain mental health professionals believe. As we will see, Trump's psychological well-being is no worse than that of many past leaders. Even if it were, recent precedent dictates that nobody but his own therapist should say so due to the Goldwater Rule. The American Psychiatric Association enacted that rule after mental health professionals questioned the sanity of another controversial presidential candidate, Barry Goldwater, in 1964. According to the rule, psychiatric professionals should not give an opinion on any public figure they have not examined in person.

If one looks at history, it is obvious that Trump is not even close to being one of the worst mad rulers. The truly mad rulers compete at a completely different level.

⚑

This book will look at the lives of the most insane leaders in history and how they led their kingdoms, nations, and empires with frayed connections to reality. It explores the addictive nature of power, the effects it has on those who cling to it for too long, and methods by which mad rulers lead without their full mental faculties intact. It also questions why senior government officials tolerate these leaders' actions for so long. Finally, it asks if insane rulers are relics of the past and have died out in the age of democracy.

Before venturing too far in our analysis of mad rulers, we must define what madness *is*. Doing so is challenging, as there is no universally accepted clinical definition of madness. The term covers a spectrum of abnormal behavioral and mental patterns, everything from agoraphobia to the condition formerly known as multiple personality disorder. Doctors have been arguing about the origins of madness since the beginning of medicine. Some thought insanity was a disease of the soul. Traditional societies believed the source was evil spirits that needed to be exorcised. Others thought it was a disease of the body. Ancient Greeks regarded madness as an imbalance in bodily "humors" (the four chemical systems that were thought to regulate human behavior: blood, phlegm, yellow bile, and black bile).

Social and cultural dimensions are also crucial to understanding madness. It has been recognized in every known society throughout history, but it is always filtered through that society's particular understanding of the world and its specific criteria for what makes one sane or insane. Andrew Scull, author of *Madness in Civilization*, notes that stories of madness are found in the most ancient written sources. The Old Testament is full of such stories. In one episode, King Saul, the first monarch of the Israelites, falls into madness for failing to follow God's order to destroy completely the enemy of Israel, the Amalekites. David, on the other hand, Saul's nemesis and son-in-law, feigned madness himself while seeking refuge from Saul's jealousy and growing madness in the court of an enemy king of Israel, "foaming at the mouth," according to the Bible, to escape being killed by that king too. An early record of method to madness on the part of David.

Perhaps the most famous episode of biblical madness involves Nebuchadnezzar, the Babylonian king. He conquered Jerusalem, destroyed

Solomon's temple, and took the young Daniel and other Israelites into captivity. Daniel became one of his close advisers and saw the onset of Nebuchadnezzar's madness. Nebuchadnezzar boasted obnoxiously about his power, finally moving God to act. Forced from his palace, Nebuchadnezzar went into the wilderness, his mind shriveled to the level of an ox. There he ate grass, "and his body was wet with the dew of heaven, till his hairs were grown like eagle's feathers, and his nails like bird's claws." The king remained in that state for seven years, until he acknowledged that God ruled his kingdom, not him. With Nebuchadnezzar's reason returned to him, he praised God and proclaimed that His dominion lasts forever.

Whatever the truth of this story, the Old Testament treats Nebuchadnezzar's case of madness as a divine curse, not a biological one. Other ancient accounts of madness also describe it in supernatural terms—Greece and Rome treated the mentally ill with the temple medicine of the god Asclepius and used charms, purification rites, and spells.

There has also been the idea of sacred madness. The "holy fool" played a leading role in the imagination of medieval Christendom. Like a biblical prophet who flouts society's conventions to serve a religious purpose, the "holy fool" reveals truths hidden to the wise. Most famous is Basil the Blessed, a Russian Orthodox saint known as a *yurodivy*, or "holy fool for Christ." Born in the late fifteenth century, he went naked and weighed himself down with chains to show contempt for his own flesh and to shun any recognition. But with this rejection of the world came total freedom to scorn wickedness. When Ivan the Terrible moved toward Pskov after devastating Novgorod in the sixteenth century, Basil alone stood up to him. Russian medievalist Eugene Vodolazkin recounts one legend in which Basil offered Ivan a piece of raw meat out of "hospitality." Ivan responded that he did not eat meat during the fast. Basil retorted that the tsar had done far worse by devouring the flesh of Christians. Startled, the tsar returned to Moscow without harming the people.[7]

Over time, more scientifically based methods arose to understand
and treat madness. The followers of the ancient Greek physician Hippocrates and later the Greco-Roman physician Galen considered madness to result from mental and physical conditions. As treatment
methods evolved, the public, however, clung to many old beliefs and
remained skeptical of doctors' abilities to cure madness well into the
nineteenth century. The Renaissance artist Hieronymus Bosch provides
an excellent example of this skepticism with his 1494 satirical painting
*The Cure of Folly: The Extraction of the Stone of Folly.* A doctor donning a dunce's cap uses a scalpel to draw from a patient's scalp the cause
of his madness.[8]

Because the origins of madness are so heavily disputed by mental
health experts, this book will only concern itself with the effects of
insanity, not its causes. We will use the legal term for insanity, regarding a defendant's capacity to determine right from wrong in the case
of a crime. It is defined as "mental illnesses of such a severe nature that
a person cannot distinguish fantasy from reality, cannot conduct her/
his affairs due to psychosis, or is subject to uncontrollable impulsive
behavior."[9] This is the launching point from which we will analyze the
psychosis, megalomania, and paranoia of the rulers in question.

Based on this definition of insanity, the nine leaders in this book
were chosen based on one of three criteria. The first is dissociation from
reality. France's King Charles VI thought he was made of glass and
could shatter at any moment. Ottoman sultan Ibrahim believed he was
a king from a fairy tale and ordered a massive tax to fund the decora-
tion of his palace in sable fur. The second criterion is psychopathy and
lack of remorse. Ivan the Terrible personally tortured, raped, and
murdered his subjects. Idi Amin killed up to half a million Ugandans
in the 1960s and '70s for vague political goals. The third criterion is
narcissistic personality disorder and megalomania. Caligula referred
to himself as a god and demanded to be worshipped as such. Turkmen
president Saparmurat Niyazov renamed days of the week and months
of the year after himself and his family. Kim Jong-il required his

portrait to be displayed in every North Korean home alongside one of his father's.

Each chapter in this book explores the life and reign of a different insane ruler. It asks six questions about each ruler's time in power. First, from what sort of madness did he suffer? Second, how effective was he at ruling despite mental illness? Third, was he insane before or after he started ruling? Fourth, how did his madness affect his citizens? Fifth, and most paradoxical, did any of these leaders' madness inadvertently make for greatness for themselves or their nations?

The question of insanity's inadvertent usefulness poses a sixth and last question. Against all reasonable expectations, can madness in and of itself be a source of greatness, or even genius? It is not a new question. German philosopher Arthur Schopenhauer asked it in his 1818 work *The World as Will and Representation*:

> It has often been remarked that there is a side at which genius and madness touch, and even pass over into each other, and indeed poetical inspiration has been called a kind of madness: *amabilis insania*, Horace calls it. . . . It might seem from this that every advance of intellect beyond the ordinary measure, as an abnormal development, disposes to madness.

Great statesmen and military leaders from Napoleon to Abraham Lincoln to John F. Kennedy struggled with mental illness. Nassir Ghaemi, director of the Mood Disorders Program at Tufts Medical Center, wrote in *A First-Rate Madness* that the very qualities that mark those with mood disorders make for the best leaders in times of crisis. Lincoln suffered from severe depression, as did Winston Churchill; both contemplated suicide. Removed from command over questions of his sanity, Civil War general William Sherman experienced a manic episode with paranoid delusions and wrestled with bouts of severe depression and suicidal thoughts. Martin Luther King Jr. and Gandhi both attempted suicide while adolescents.[10]

Psychological studies have shown that depression can be a source of enhanced realism and increased resilience. Well-heeled "sane" men such as Neville Chamberlain were lackluster compared to the boldness of Churchill's leadership in World War II. Abraham Lincoln used fortitude developed over a lifetime of fighting crippling depression to follow his destiny of abolishing slavery and preserving the Union. He believed that his melancholia helped prepare him for the great challenges he faced during the Civil War. The massive death tolls and horrors of the battlefield did not incapacitate him; Lincoln had spent decades learning to overcome setbacks in his own battered psychology.

Rulers who were "mad" by our definition could actually have been responding in the most reasonable way in their circumstances. They faced challenges that are unimaginable today. Ivan the Terrible killed thousands of his own subjects, but he did so (by his own reasoning) to secure the Russian Empire against external threats after the Mongols had slaughtered millions across Eurasia three centuries earlier. Caligula behaved horribly toward the Roman Senate and aristocracy, but it could have been a calculated attempt to demean them and weaken their power, elevating himself to a full monarch and thus best serving the interests of the masses by crushing corrupt politicians. From their perspectives, being mad was perhaps the most appropriate way to rule in mad times.

With these questions in mind, let us look at the nine most insane rulers in history.

## CHAPTER ONE

# Roman Emperor Gaius Caligula

## AD 12–AD 41

When Salvador Dalí set out to paint a depiction of the infamous Roman emperor Caligula in 1971, he chose to depict the thing nearest and dearest to the emperor's heart: his favorite racehorse, Incitatus. The painting *Le Cheval de Caligula* shows the pampered pony in all his royal glory. It is wearing a bejeweled crown and clothed in purple blankets. While the gaudy clothing of the horse is historically correct, the Spanish surrealist artist managed perhaps for the only time to understate the strangeness of his subject matter.

Gaius Julius Caesar Augustus Germanicus (Caligula) was born in AD 12 and reigned from 37–41. He was the first emperor with no memory of the pre-Augustan era—that is, before emperors were deified—and had no compunction about being worshipped as a god. As the object of a *cultus,* the boy emperor believed in his own semidivine status and saw no reason not to follow whatever strange desire entered his mind, such as treating his horse better than royalty. The Roman historian Suetonius writes that Caligula gave the horse eighteen servants, a marble stable, an ivory manger, and rich red robes. He demanded that it be fed oats mixed with flecks of gold and wine in fine goblets. Dignitaries bowed and tolerated Incitatus as a guest of honor at banquets. Caligula repeatedly mocked the system of imperial decorum in Roman upper-crust society. His actions would eventually lead to his violent death at the hands of political rivals.

The emperor was not called Caligula in his lifetime but instead by the formal title Gaius; the epithet Caligula ("Little Soldier's Boots"—a demeaning name from his infancy when his mother Agrippina dressed him in miniature soldiers' outfits) was used after his death. In his four years as emperor, he built a religious cult around himself, satisfied every sexual desire imaginable (and unimaginable), all while emptying the imperial treasury. Mostly, he did this to antagonize Roman senators and patricians.

More recent studies have taken a sympathetic view of his reign, suggesting that Caligula repeatedly insulted the members of the Roman aristocracy to marginalize them and return Rome to its pre–Augustan era status quo. But, as this thesis goes, he failed, and his enemies wrote the histories of this period, leading to his unfair maligning.

Other biographers take a less sympathetic view of his reign. Anthony Barrett writes that if Caligula was mad, he was not an insane ruler along the lines of Ludwig of Bavaria (an unhinged but harmless ruler who kept to his castles that looked straight out of a fairy tale), but a much more frightening, iron-fisted, Stalinesque figure, capable of rational decisions and statesmanlike acts (when it suited him), but morally cold to the financially ruinous and murderous impact his choices had on others.[1] He was a profligate spender who seized more money than any previous emperor. Only a few months into his reign, he managed to waste the entire fortune left by Tiberius, a sum it had taken the former emperor twenty-two years to collect in tribute. Caligula spent the funds on three-month-long inaugural celebrations, accompanied by over 160,000 animal sacrifices.

For Caligula to elevate himself to an object of worship was not unprecedented in the ancient world (the practice has a long history, especially in ancient Egypt and Mesopotamia). However, no previous

Roman emperor had ever claimed divinity for himself. Julius Caesar and Augustus were deified after their deaths, but Caligula fully embraced emperor worship and encouraged others to worship him as a god in his lifetime. While earlier emperors tolerated this practice, he allowed and promoted it in the Roman provinces. Caligula tried to commission a huge statue of himself inside the Temple in Jerusalem, the center of Jewish worship. This action would have nearly guaranteed a revolt from the Jews, who would have considered the construction a pagan slap in the face of their religion. Even Herod Agrippa, a descendant of the man who according to the traditional biblical account slaughtered dozens of infants in a failed attempt to kill Jesus, considered this a terrible idea and convinced the emperor to relent.

He began by likening himself to demigods such as Hercules and Bacchus, but then he went further and entered the sacred space of the supreme deities of the Roman world, claiming a seat with Mercury, Apollo, and Mars.[2] Roman historian Philo writes that Caligula convinced himself of his divinity by the bizarre rationale that as the leader of men, he was as much above them as a human shepherd was above his animal flock; it was "fitting that I who am the leader of the most excellent of all herds, namely the race of mankind, should be considered as a being of superior nature, and not merely human, but as one who has received a greater and more holy portion."[3]

Believing in his own deity, Caligula brutalized Roman citizens of high rank by sending them to prison for insulting his vanity. He once burned alive an author of Atellan farces in front of a crowded amphitheater as punishment for a double entendre he had made about Caligula. He disfigured men with branding irons and condemned them to work in the mines or build roads. He shut others up in cages on all fours like animals or had them sentenced to death by sawing.[4]

Caligula's terrible reputation made chroniclers depict him as a physically monstrous creature that was part man, part goat, a creature of uncontrolled lust and energy. Suetonius describes him as very tall and extremely pale, with an unshapely body but a thin neck and legs. His eyes were hollow, his forehead "broad and grim," his head crowned with male-pattern baldness, even though his body was hirsute. "Because of this to look upon him from a higher place as he passed by, or for any reason whatever to mention a goat, was treated as a capital offense." His outer ugliness was a reflection of his inner barbarity, and he labored to make his appearance worse: "While his face was naturally forbidding and ugly, he purposely made it even more savage, practicing all kinds of terrible and fearsome expressions before a mirror."[5]

Gaius Caligula was the third child born to Germanicus (a Roman general and adopted son of the emperor Tiberius) and a grandson of the emperor Augustus on his mother's side. He grew up around rough soldiers and stern officers; when Caligula was a small child he lived with his parents on the Rhine frontier, where his father Germanicus was forced to deal with unrest among troops. Germanicus responded to the mutiny by mass executing the ringleaders in public. Young Caligula witnessed the spectacle. He remained in the Rhine war zone until the age of four.[6]

Germanicus died three years later under mysterious circumstances, putting Caligula, his family, and his mother Agrippina at the mercy of his adoptive grandfather, Tiberius. They were now one coup away from losing their protection and having an enemy political faction kill them. Shortly after Germanicus's death, Caligula went to live with his great-grandmother (and Tiberius's mother) Livia. When she died two years later, he went to live with his grandmother, Antonia. Caligula's absence from the court of Tiberius was a blessing, as his family was mostly exiled and killed; his brother Nero (not the emperor) died in exile, and his other brother, Drusus Caesar, was imprisoned on charges of treason.

When the emperor Tiberius took ill and secluded himself on the island of Capri in AD 31, he remanded Caligula to help him on the island. Meanwhile, his mother and brother Drusus had died in prison. Suetonius claims that Caligula showed no remorse at the death of his family and remained opportunistically obedient to Tiberius—noting that "no one had ever been a better slave or a worse master."[7] Tiberius granted him an honorary quaestorship, or public office, in AD 33.

An observer said that even in his illness, Tiberius could tell that Caligula, whom he had appointed joint successor in AD 35 along with his grandson Tiberius Gemellus, was not suitable to reign. The emperor later referred to him as a viper unleashed on Rome. When Tiberius died in AD 37, Caligula and Gemellus received his estate and titles in order to serve as joint heirs of the Roman Empire. Factions quickly formed. The Praetorian prefect Macro, who led the imperial guard, sided with Caligula. He had Tiberius's will nullified to remove Gemellus, ironically on grounds of insanity. Caligula assumed sole powers of the principate, a term for the early Roman Empire, and triumphantly entered Rome.

Crowds received their new emperor with open arms, based on affection for his father Germanicus. Philo of Alexandria described Caligula as the first emperor beloved by "all the world, from the rising to the setting sun." The people were hopeful for a ruler who would demonstrate more warmth and charity than Tiberius had. Tiberius was a gifted military commander but a poor politician and a paranoid loner who used charges of treason to exile or execute anyone he suspected of disloyalty.

The beginning of Caligula's rule went well. He tried to right the wrongs of Tiberius and ended the deceased emperor's treason trials that were still open. He paid off all the former emperor's debts. He recalled all those whom Tiberius had exiled and compensated those whom he thought had been wrongly taxed. To shore up political support, Caligula gave the Praetorian guard, the city troops, and the army outside Italy all a significant bonus. He also honored his slain family by retrieving their bodies and giving them a proper Roman burial in the tomb of Augustus.

Not long into his reign, however, he fell ill and slipped into a coma. When he awoke, he was a completely different man. Roman biographers mark his awakening as a turning point in his reign. His narcissism grew and his empathy diminished. Whatever concern Caligula had for the welfare of his empire, it was swallowed by his vanity. He began to treat the state treasury like his own personal expense account. One biography of the emperor estimates that when Tiberius passed away, the treasury held approximately 2.7 billion *sesterces*, or five to six years of revenue.[8] These funds were depleted before the end of Caligula's first year of rule.[9]

Caligula quickly ratcheted up his honorary titles, accumulating more than a Hapsburg count who ruled kingdoms, territories, and duchies. He began with *Pius* (Pious), *Castrorum Filius* (Child of the Camp), *Pater Exercituum* (Father of the Armies), and *Optimus Maximus Caesar* (Greatest and Best of Caesars). These excessive titles were soon not enough. Caligula, as Suetonius notes, overheard several kings who had come to Rome to pay their respects to him. At dinner, they disputed the nobility of their descent. Caligula cried, "Let there be one lord, one king." He began from that time to claim kingship and divine majesty. Caligula ordered that Greek statues of the gods famous for their sanctity or artistic merit, including one of Jupiter of Olympia, be moved to Rome, have their heads removed, and have his put in their place. To religious Romans, this would be equivalent to a modern-day Catholic seeing a new pope declare that icons of saints should have their heads destroyed and replaced with his own.

The young emperor also transformed other Roman holy items to bear his likeness. Suetonius writes that Caligula extended a part of the palace as far as the Roman Forum and turned the temple of Castor and Pollux, a sacred site built to commemorate a 484 BC military victory, into a vestibule. He often took his place between statues of the demigod sons of Zeus to be worshipped. To make matters worse, he set up a temple solely for worship of himself, attended by priests. In the temple was a life-size statue of him in gold.[10]

The grossest display of Caligula's twisted sense of grandeur came from his attempt to mimic Xerxes's Pontoon Bridges. Greek historian Herodotus describes this "bridge" in his *Histories* as a row of ships that allowed the Persian ruler to cross the Hellespont, the strait separating Anatolia from Greece, which he did in 480 BC during the second Persian invasion of the Greek peninsula. Caligula, as recounted in the works of Suetonius and fellow historian Dio, decided to copy Xerxes's legendary crossing to project the image of a conquering hero to his subjects. He ordered the construction of the Bridge of Baiae, by which the gap between the mole of Puteoli (a pier formed of large stones and earth) and the Gulf of Baiae, a distance of three miles, was bridged by bringing together merchant ships and anchoring them in a double line, heaping a mound of earth on them and fashioning the structure in the style of the Appian Way, a major Roman road. Caligula rode over this bridge back and forth for two successive days. On the first day, he rode a richly decorated horse, himself adorned with a crown made of oak leaves, along with a buckler, a sword, and a cloak made of golden cloth. On the second day, he wore the dress of a charioteer in a vehicle drawn by a pair of horses, carrying before him a hostage boy from the Parthian Empire, Rome's eastern enemy.

On the bridge were rooms and even whole houses with drinking water in them. While Caligula rode across these ships in his gorgeous raiment, he gave a banquet to his men but in the end hurled many guests off the bridge into the sea; many drowned. The entire Praetorian guard was called to attend this spectacle, along with a company of his friends in Gallic chariots. Caligula believed himself to have outdone Xerxes, since the Hellespont was much narrower than the gap between Baiae and the mole at Puteoli. Caligula may have also done this to inspire fear in the northern European provinces of Germania and Britannia (ancient analogues to Germany and Britain), which he had designs to conquer, by demonstrating his construction abilities and showing off his "military prowess."

Classicist M. P. Charlesworth doubts Dio's and Suetonius's accounts of the Bridge of Baiae. He considers the latter prone to basing his stories on the wildest gossip about Caligula (including stories of Caligula committing habitual incest with all three of his sisters, or wallowing in gold, or planning for universal poisoning). Simple physics also refutes the boat bridge story. Bridging the three-mile distance between Puteoli and Baiae would be impossible due to the number of ships needed. Deploying so many ships would bankrupt the empire. Dio at least acknowledged the complications of this shipping project; he wrote that so many boats were requisitioned that it disturbed the Mediterranean importing of grain from Egypt to Italy, triggering a famine. Different writers also place this story at separate times in Caligula's reign: Josephus and Seneca place the story a few months before Caligula's assassination; Dio and Suetonius put it two years into his four-year reign. While it is plausible that Caligula was mad enough to try to outdo Xerxes with a boat bridge, the fantastic details make the facts of the story unlikely.[11]

Whatever the historicity of Caligula's Bridge of Baiae, Suetonius rattles off other examples of Caligula's "innate" madness and brutality. Gladiatorial shows were notably violent under his rule. For the spectacle wild beasts were fed cattle, but the emperor thought the livestock too expensive, so criminals were devoured instead. He reviewed the line of prisoners without examining any charges and took his place in the middle of a colonnade, commanding them to be led away "from bald head to bald head."

As a newly coronated emperor, Caligula sought glory in battle and the status of a *dux bellorum* (war leader). Rather than achieving real victory, he went through the motions of a military campaign and borrowed the symbols of victory without earning them. Caligula launched only one campaign as emperor, and it originated from what appeared to be a sudden and irrational impulse. Having gone to visit the springs at the river Clitumnus in modern-day Umbria, Italy, he remembered the need to recruit Batavian bodyguards, the Germanic foreign-born soldiers who traditionally protected the emperors. Caligula then had the idea of an expedition to Germania. The emperor assembled legions and auxiliaries, exacted levies, and raised vast amounts of money to fund the campaign while collecting provisions on a scale that made Julius Caesar's Gaul campaign appear modest.

He made the march so hurriedly that the Praetorian cohorts had to suffer the shame of laying their standards on pack animals (an insult to their dignity as elite soldiers). But Caligula rode around in a litter carried by eight bearers, ordering townspeople to sweep the roads before him and sprinkle water to settle the dust. The officers and soldiers held Caligula in barely concealed contempt for forcing them on such a hurried march while he traveled in ease, but he was oblivious to their hatred. On reaching his camp, to show his vigilance as a commander, he dismissed the generals who arrived late from the far-flung provinces. While reviewing troop strength, he canceled the pensions of many of the chief centurions—some of whom were only a few days away from retirement—or reduced the rewards given on completion of full military service to six thousand *sesterces*, or about four years' worth of salary.

The "victory" that resulted from this unnecessary campaign was the surrender of the exiled Briton chieftain Adminius, who had been banished by his father, Cunobeline (Shakespeare's Cymbeline), and deserted to the Romans with a small force. Caligula, with typical theatrics, treated the surrender of this band of exiles as if the entire British island had surrendered to him. He dispatched a letter to Rome to announce the small achievement, demanding couriers to ride at full speed to the Forum and the Senate. Despite the "surrender," Caligula found nobody to fight with on the European continent or a battle that would allow him to boast of victory. If a real conquest was not possible, then a fake one would have to do. He ordered Germans from his Batavian bodyguards to be taken across the river and concealed there. They were ordered to bustle around as if they were enemy scouts or a vanguard. His ruse, Suetonius writes, worked: word came to him that an enemy force was nearby. On the news, he rushed out with a part of the Praetorian cavalry to the woods to do battle with imaginary foes. After cutting a few tree branches, he returned by torchlight, mocking those who had not followed for their "cowardice." He presented his companions and the partners in his "victory" with crowns ornamented with figures of the sun, moon, and stars, called *exploratoriae*.[12]

Finally, as if he were drawing this "war" to a close, Caligula drew up a line of battle on the shore of the English Channel and arranged his ballistas and other artillery. No one could have imagined his next action. He suddenly ordered his troops to collect shells and put them in their helms and folds of their gowns. The shells were "spoils from the Ocean, due to the Capitol and Palatine." He then promised the soldiers a hundred denarii each as a gratuity, as if he had been exceedingly generous up to this point. "Go your way happy; go your way rich," Caligula said.

After the campaign, Caligula purportedly crafted a victory parade that took far more effort than the original military action. He wrote to his financial agents to prepare for military triumph at the smallest possible costs but for the victory celebration on the grandest scale possible. The Romans showcased a cast of defeated enemies. Caligula, as if he were a casting agent, selected the tallest of his troops and reserved them for his parade. The emperor compelled them to dye their hair red and let it grow long, learn the Germanic language, and take barbarian names to appear as if they were conquered Batavians.[13]

The ersatz triumph and forced celebrations were another occasion for Caligula to show disrespect for the Senate. His dealings with senators were a break in protocol from the reign of the seclusive Tiberius, during which the Senate had done most of the decision-making on its own. Caligula did what he could to shame, embarrass, and humiliate senators, individually and collectively. To do so he treated his horse, Incitatus, with more respect than he treated them. In addition to Incitatus's fine garments, he also served as a royal host. When invitations were sent from the palace, they were in the horse's name, and Incitatus could dine at the emperor's table. Roman historians claimed Caligula tried to make Incitatus either a senator or a priest before the emperor's death.

Modern classicists have argued that Caligula was not intentionally malicious but a victim of his own cult of personality. Early twentieth-century British historian J. P. V. D. Balsdon blames the manipulative Senate for stoking Caligula's arrogance, leading to his belief in his divinity so that he could be better controlled. Caligula accepted honors without reservation and removed or executed advisors who could have helped him in dealing with flatterers. Wealthy citizens fed his cult of personality to secure well-compensated priesthood positions in his new cult.[14]

The most toe-curling acts of Caligula's madness concern his incestuous relations with his sisters. Suetonius claims Caligula lived in habitual carnal relations with all of them but had special affection for Julia Drusilla, whom he may have violated when he was still a minor. Although she became the wife of consul Lucius Cassius Longinus, Caligula took her from him and openly treated her as his lawful wife, even making her heir to his property and the throne. When she died in 38, Caligula appointed a season of public mourning, declaring it a capital crime to express merriment or to feast with one's parents, wife, or children. Consumed with grief at Drusilla's death, Caligula fled Rome, went to Syracuse, and returned in a disheveled state, refusing to cut his hair or shave his beard—a shameful look for an emperor. From that moment onward, Suetonius states that Caligula never took an oath on important matters, even in public assemblies before soldiers and citizens, except by the godhead of Drusilla.

Historians have tried to make sense of Caligula's madness since the Roman Empire. Firsthand biographical accounts come from six Roman sources. Two writers—Philo of Alexandria (*On the Embassy to Gaius*) and Seneca the Younger (*Various Writings*)—knew him personally. Two other writers, Tacitus (*Annals* and *Histories*) and Josephus (*Antiquities of the Jews*), were born too late to know him but had access to Roman politicians and courtiers who did know Caligula. The final writers were the historians Suetonius (author of *Lives of the Caesars*) and Dio (*Roman*

*History*), who penned their works generations after the death of Caligula, 80 and 190 years later respectively. The further removed in time the writers were from the emperor, the more outlandish the stories became. The scribes may have let their imaginations get the best of them, or perhaps because they were not under any threat from partisan hatchet men, as Seneca and Philo had been, they were free to write critically. The earlier generations of writers offered balance to the story of Caligula's reign; the latter accounts turn him into a sort of monster from a Brothers Grimm tale.[15]

These historians thought that Caligula's madness resulted from two faults: extreme assurance and excessive fearfulness. They described him as hating and fearing the gods to such a degree that he shut his eyes and covered his ears at the slightest thunder and lightning, terrified at the wrath of Zeus. If the storm increased, he leaped from his bed and hid under it. In a similar incident on a journey through Sicily, he mocked so-called miracles attributed to the gods. And yet, he became panic-stricken one night when Mount Etna, a Sicilian volcano, erupted, spewing smoke.

Mortal threats equally terrified Caligula. When he rode in a chariot on the far side of the Rhine river, it was said there could be mass panic if the enemy appeared anywhere. With speed he would mount a horse and escape to the bridges. When a lengthy line of camp servants and baggage prevented his crossing, soldiers moved the emperor hand-to-hand over the crowd. On learning of a rebellion in Germania, he prepared to flee Rome and readied his ships for this purpose.[16]

New methods of psychological analysis developed in the last century have allowed historians to diagnose Caligula with every mental illness for which professionals have a name: schizophrenia, psychopathy, epilepsy, bipolar disorder, or more simply, garden-variety megalomania. Some think that his madness came on suddenly with an illness in AD 37, while others think it had to do with childhood trauma and parental abandonment. Still others say that his madness was never as bad as our historical record claims; his crazed actions never happened and are only a fictional account created by chroniclers who had something to gain by demonizing Caligula and making their own political faction appear better by comparison.[17]

German scholar H. Willrich wrote in 1903 that the emperor was not simply mad, but rather there was a system (or method) to his alleged madness, and he suffered a breakdown from the stress of his duties as an emperor.[18] A recent biography by Aloys Winterling argues that Caligula may have been manic, because his behavior matches symptoms of the illness.[19] Others say he was a product of the Roman imperial system, whose worship of the emperor and indulgent lifestyle could turn anyone insane with delusions of grandeur. Others do not reach for a complex explanation and write him off as a sociopath who had no concern about the effect of his monstrous actions on others. But without the ability to perform a psychiatric assessment on Caligula, reaching firm conclusions is ultimately impossible.[20]

Accounts written decades after someone's death, especially by political enemies, are suspicious and lack objectivity. An examination of Caligula's turbulent childhood might be more relevant in explaining his adult behavior. Arther Ferrill, a modern-day biographer of the emperor, argues that his path to megalomania began early in his life and witnessing the execution of mutinous soldiers when he was only a toddler triggered a lifelong fear of a mutiny of his own, making him paranoid of conspiracy and all too happy to execute anyone perceived as disloyal.[21]

Roman accounts of Caligula's abnormal behavior suggest an anxiety disorder. He is often described as petulant and excitable, even in normal situations. His condition, therefore, was likely triggered by the stress of the imperial office.

He was especially tormented with sleeplessness; for he never rested more than three hours at night, and even for that length of time he did not sleep quietly, but was terrified by strange apparitions. For example, he once dreamed that the spirit of the ocean talked with him. Weary of lying in bed wide awake during the greater part of the night, he would not sit upon his couch, but would wander through the long colonnades, crying out from time to time for daylight and longing for its coming.[22]

Infant separation anxiety could have caused Caligula to deliberately remove himself from men who represented father figures. This disorder could explain his lack of close relationships in general and the distance he put between himself and senior advisors, such as the Praetorian prefect Macro and his father-in-law Marcus Junius Silanus.[23] After Germanicus's death, Caligula may have rejected anyone who might have filled the void of a father figure in order to protect himself from another abandonment. Separation anxiety could further explain why Caligula kept competent advisors and respectable politicians at a distance while filling his court with flatterers and disreputable figures.[24]

On the other hand, several analysts believe his behavior is better explained by a thyroid disorder. Robert S. Katz, a medical expert and classicist, argues that although Caligula was far from normal, he was too consistent in his behavior to be described as mentally ill and was more likely affected by a biological condition. The emperor may have suffered from hyperthyroidism, a glandular disturbance, which accelerates the body's metabolism and causes nervousness, anxiety, and irritability.[25]

But Caligula's narcissism, promotion of emperor worship, and violent temper are hard to explain by a simple glandular disorder. One of the most common diagnoses of the emperor is sociopathy. Caligula's callous disregard for the suffering of others (apart from a select few close to him) suggests he was mostly incapable of empathy. He constantly made impulsive decisions without concern for the harm they caused to others—whether it was Roman peasants, soldiers, aristocrats, or senators. He had no remorse about hurting a stranger. This explanation is reasonable, but there are reasons to doubt this diagnosis. The emperor did care about others' opinions of him, even if he had a warped sense of public taste and what would appeal to the masses. He loved to showboat in front of politicians and the public.

As such, he was a gauche figure who defied custom in his dress and personal appearance. He did not follow the style preferred by other upper-crust Romans in his clothes, shoes, or the rest of his attire, not even that "of a man or even an ordinary mortal." Caligula often appeared in public in embroidered cloaks covered with precious stones, with a long-sleeved tunic and bracelets, even sometimes in silk and a woman's robe and low shoes. Other times Caligula looked like a poorly dressed theatre performer attempting to portray a god: he presented himself with a golden beard, holding in his hand a thunderbolt, a trident, or a caduceus. Sometimes he would even appear in the garb of Venus. He frequently wore the ceremonial dress of a triumphant general, even before his campaign, and sometimes the breastplate of Alexander the Great, one of the holiest relics in Roman martial culture, which he had taken from the Macedonian's sarcophagus.[26]

J. Lucas believes that Caligula suffered from psychopathy, a more severe form of sociopathy in which one cannot form deep bonds with others. While a sociopath can form deep bonds with family or close friends, a psychopath does not show love, empathy, or remorse for *anyone*. Other national leaders thought to be psychopaths, such as Fidel Castro and Muammar Gaddafi, match Caligula's love of endless speechifying; they all thought nothing of subjecting their countrymen to four- or five-hour harangues. Caligula was ready to give a speech at a moment's notice, particularly if he had an occasion to make a charge.[27]

While this view does explain Caligula's propensity for imprisoning and torturing Roman officials, it does not explain the few cases where the emperor did show a strong emotional attachment, particularly to his sister Drusilla.[28] He doted excessively on his sister and elevated her to the level of goddess after her death in AD 38. He gave her the honorary title *Thea Nea Aphrodite Drusilla* or *Diva Drusilla, Panthea*. Caligula decreed that she be worshipped in Italy and the provinces.[29]

Vin Massaro and Iain Montgomery examined the literary sources on the life of Caligula, listed out the symptoms of mental illness, and tried to interpret them through modern psychological, psychiatric, and medical frameworks. According to them, Caligula suffered from anxiety brought on by stress associated with traumatic events in his life and by early separation from his immediate family. These stresses then led to various chronic phobias.[30]

Massaro and Montgomery believe he suffered from anxiety or mania. The latter requires (according to the American Psychiatric Association's Diagnostic and Statistical Manual of Mental Disorders) three of the following symptoms for a minimum of one week to fit the diagnostic criteria: inflated self-esteem/grandiosity, decreased need for sleep, more talkative than usual, flights of ideas, thoughts racing, distractibility, increase in goal-oriented activity; and excessive involvement in pleasurable activities that have a high potential for painful consequences.

If the above criteria were a test, then Caligula would score perfectly.

Caligula was not always evil. Suetonius begrudgingly admits that he did complete public works that remained unfinished by his predecessor Tiberius. He completed the Temple of Augustus and the Theatre of Pompey. He also commissioned an aqueduct in the region near Tibur (which was finished by his successor Claudius) and an amphitheater beside the Saepta, a building where the *comitia tribuna*, an assembly of the people, would gather to cast its votes. He repaired the city walls at Syracuse, which had fallen into ruin, and the temples of the gods there. Caligula intended to rebuild the palace of Polycrates of Samos, a sixth-century BC tyrant revered in Rome; to finish the temple of Apollo at Didyma (the fourth-largest sanctuary in the Greek world); to establish a city high in the Alps; and to dig a canal through the Isthmus of Corinth that would have increased Aegean commerce by connecting the Gulf of Corinth with the Saronic Gulf (building something like a Panama Canal of the Greek peninsula). He sent a chief centurion to survey the work, but nothing came of it. The project was eventually completed in 1893.[31]

One of the most charitable views of Caligula's actions is that there was a reasonable explanation for them, even if he was mad. Caligula performed acts so bizarre they were downright theatrical, but they were done with a political purpose in mind. Aloys Winterling argues in his 2011 biography of Caligula that he specifically wanted to humiliate the senatorial aristocracy. Emperor Augustus had created an ambiguous system of communicating with the nobility to bridge the gap between the facade of trying to restore the Roman Republic and the reality of the Roman Empire. Because of Augustus's position of power, senators automatically obeyed him in a thoroughly opportunistic manner. The withdrawn Tiberius, however, could not sustain Augustus's model of indirect communication, so the aristocracy ended his reign with treason trials that led to his removal from Rome.[32]

Caligula's troubled upbringing and abuse by Roman politicians meant he would never conform to their system. His only amicable relations with them were at the beginning of his reign in AD 37. Conspiracies led by senatorial aristocrats to overthrow Caligula began in AD 39. According to Dio, the emperor accused senators of "hypocrisy, deception, and lies" for heaping honors on the late Emperor Tiberius and his confidant Sejanus. He then reopened treason trials that had begun under Sejanus, aimed at senators and wealthy property owners of Rome to remove those who could oppose his power and extend the imperial treasury. "Caligula had not only stripped the mask from the face of aristocracy," Winterling notes, "he had also given a name to what lay behind it: their resentment of imperial rule, their hatred of the emperor, and their readiness to attack him whenever a favorable opportunity presented itself . . . by rebuking the Senate for the way it communicated with the emperor, Caligula had rendered it incapable of communication."[33]

So, Caligula began a process of humiliating the senatorial aristocracy. He sought their financial ruin by requiring enormous sums for his own travel and entertainment when visiting them, along with sponsoring public games and spectacles. He lived in obnoxious splendor to flaunt his social status. Caligula's plan to bankrupt the senatorial aristocracy even offers a sort of logic to his strange relationship with his favorite racehorse, Incitatus, and to his equipping the horse with a palace and staff of servants, along with his plans to name him to a consulship, an office for which all senators vied.

Caligula ratcheted up his garish displays of wealth and power every time he experienced opposition, whether it was criticism or a conspiracy to depose or assassinate him. After crushing a third conspiracy against him, Caligula allowed slaves to bring legal charges against their masters in another ploy to financially cripple the aristocracy. He further humiliated them by abolishing reserved seating for senators and elite soldiers at the theatre, and insulted their forefathers by removing the statues of great men of the Republic from the Campus Martius where Augustus had collected them. The purpose of all this, Winterling argues, was to destroy the aristocratic hierarchy and expose it to ridicule.[34]

Perhaps Caligula's sin, then, was not playing Augustus's game, by which the latter pretended that emperors were not autocrats, and to which the Senate responded by bestowing lavish praise on him. Caligula caused this ambiguous communication system to collapse, which had up to then been a crucial means of avoiding the paradox of the simultaneous existence of a monarchy and a republic. A bell was rung and nobody could silence it.[35]

In the four years of Caligula's reign, the aristocracy hated him so much that the Roman Senate considering abolishing the empire and returning to a republic due to the stain on the office of Augustus.[36] His consistent and unrelenting disrespect eventually led to his murder. The attack was likely conducted by two tribunes of the Praetorian guard, with help from centurions. They struck enough fear into the Praetorian prefects and Caligula's adviser Gaius Julius Callistus to discourage them from warning the emperor or doing anything to stop them.

In AD 41, in a secluded hall in the basement of the palace, they stabbed Caligula thirty times. A Praetorian guard named Cassius Chaerea, whom Caligula had humiliated on multiple occasions, led the attack. Cassius Chaerea hit him with a violent blow first, but it was not fatal. His failure was likely intentional, as some say it was his plan to kill Caligula not with one strike but by many wounds. He may have done so as a vengeful end to an emperor who had killed so many. Watching Caligula's lingering death with joy gratified the guard's moral sense. In the end, Caligula met the same terrible, prolonged death he perversely enjoyed inflicting on others. By the time his guards found Caligula, the conspirators were long gone, and he eventually succumbed to his injuries. Dio writes that when Caligula lay dead "the bystanders recalled how he had once said to the people 'Would you had but one neck,' and they showed him now that it was he who had one neck while they had many hands."[37]

Whatever the merits of the theory that Caligula was eccentric but not mad, problems still abound in trying to evaluate his mental health. Many of the sources which recount his deeds are so biased, and the nature of his mania so unpredictable, that the precise nature of his mental illness may never be determined.[38] From a clinical perspective, diagnosing an emperor who died two thousand years ago is nearly impossible. Establishing a disorder solely based on biased accounts written by authors who were neither contemporaries of the subject nor the era is unreliable. Any court of law would reject such a psychiatric evaluation with extreme prejudice. A psychological diagnosis would need to depend on statistical analysis of contemporary data to achieve generalizations. The most likely conclusion, history professor Barbara Sidwell writes, is that Caligula suffered from a personality disorder that caused dysfunction, and the most likely trigger was his troubled upbringing and relationship with his family. He was an autocrat who let the power go to his head, not a delusional madman.[39]

Whatever the nature of his madness, Caligula appears in the chronicles as an ancient equivalent to a character in a 1961 episode of *The Twilight Zone*, "It's a Good Life." In this episode, six-year-old Anthony Fremont holds godlike powers and terrorizes his hometown, his family, and, most of all, his parents. Forced to obey the petulant brat, everyone must constantly think of happy thoughts. If they do not, Anthony destroys them or transforms them into hideous creatures. All fear him, endlessly praising his actions as good, since anyone who disagrees is banished. Anthony has never been disciplined, and does not even understand that his actions are monstrous. Perhaps the only difference between Anthony and Caligula, at least as he is described in the Roman chronicles, is that in the end the emperor received a form of justice from his assassins.

CHAPTER TWO

# King Charles VI
# of France
## 1368–1422

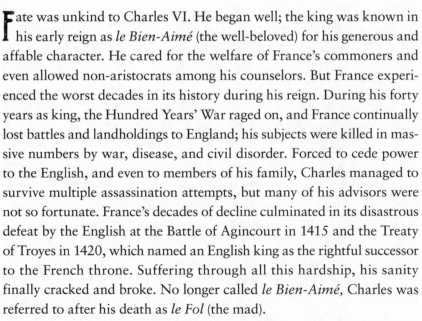

Fate was unkind to Charles VI. He began well; the king was known in his early reign as *le Bien-Aimé* (the well-beloved) for his generous and affable character. He cared for the welfare of France's commoners and even allowed non-aristocrats among his counselors. But France experienced the worst decades in its history during his reign. During his forty years as king, the Hundred Years' War raged on, and France continually lost battles and landholdings to England; his subjects were killed in massive numbers by war, disease, and civil disorder. Forced to cede power to the English, and even to members of his family, Charles managed to survive multiple assassination attempts, but many of his advisors were not so fortunate. France's decades of decline culminated in its disastrous defeat by the English at the Battle of Agincourt in 1415 and the Treaty of Troyes in 1420, which named an English king as the rightful successor to the French throne. Suffering through all this hardship, his sanity finally cracked and broke. No longer called *le Bien-Aimé,* Charles was referred to after his death as *le Fol* (the mad).

France had a long history of mentally unstable monarchs, going back to the kingdom's founding in the fifth century. Its first mad king was

Clovis II (633–657). Medieval monks considered him a *roi fainéant* ("do-nothing king"), declared him insane, and attributed the "stupidity of his descendants" to him. The story is that he went mad after stealing the arm of a dead martyr.[1] His great-grandson Childeric III (717–754), known as "the Idiot," was even more feebleminded. He was the last king of the Merovingian line before Pepin the Short, father of Charlemagne, deposed him.

By the time Charles became king, France and the rest of Europe had hit another low point. The fourteenth century was perhaps the most unstable period in Europe since the Roman Empire's collapse eight hundred years earlier. The Great Famine of 1315–1317 left millions to starve, with countless children abandoned by parents who could no longer support them. Sources claim the starving turned to cannibalism. A few decades later, the Black Plague killed one-third of Europe. In 1360, Giovanni Boccaccio wrote in *The Decameron* that Europe had fallen into near-apocalyptic conditions: "Such terror was struck into the hearts of men and women by this calamity, that brother abandoned brother. . . . what is even worse and nearly incredible is that fathers and mothers refused to see and tend their children, as if they had not been theirs."

Crowned in 1380 at the age of eleven on the heels of this continent-wide chaos, Charles's uncle, Philip, ruled as regent from Charles's ascension to the throne until he fully assumed power in 1388. Charles ran state affairs with the aid of his brother, Louis of Orleans, but the realm was in a poor state. Philip had raised taxes and depleted the treasury to fund war with England. French peasants revolted in response. Despite these challenges, the young king was lucid in the first decade of his reign and calmed domestic disorder by curbing nepotism at the royal court. Advisors were traditionally blood relatives, but Charles broke with this precedent by appointing intelligent advisers who were neither princes nor civil servants. He dismissed his uncles, bringing political and economic stability to the French kingdom. This break with the status quo, however, triggered intense competition in his court. Princes of blood—mostly

Charles's uncles—vied with this close-knit group of advisers (whom they called the "marmousets," or "monkeys," a term at the time for the English).

In another kingdom, Charles might have remained a figurehead and left the work of governance to a patchwork of lords and landowners. However, France was a centralized state in which a successful king actively ruled and did not delegate duties to an aristocratic oligarchy. But family members continued to vie for power, particularly his brother, Louis of Orleans, and John the Fearless, duke of Burgundy. Chaos and conflict engulfed France for the rest of Charles's reign. He died in October 1422, leaving behind a severely weakened kingdom on the verge of catastrophic defeat by the English.[2]

The France of Charles VI's early reign was a disaster area. Those who weren't killed by plague or famine fell to irregular soldiers and brigands. During the decades of war with the English, France's armies and their mercenary allies sacked towns and plundered the countryside. Unprotected peasants and townsfolk were robbed of harvests and left to starve. Charles's father pursued a policy of reconstruction and entrenchment against future attacks. But France could not mount an effective military response to the English because of its squabbling political factions.

Despite the turmoil in the background, Charles was coronated in full medieval splendor. Crowned in Reims, he traveled there in the middle of an entourage of princes and knights. Described as beautiful, he was a blond boy with freckles, and tall for his age. He held his place in the cathedral at the center of a grand troupe. The following Sunday, the king made his entry into Paris. Tapestries billowed down from windows. Fountains of wine and milk were set up in the squares, with scenes organized by the city's middle classes. The crowd acclaimed the child with cries of, "Noel! Noel!" Feasts, dances, and jousts followed his entry.[3]

Behind the scenes, however, his uncles were already scheming to expand their landholdings at the expense of the French crown. Before Charles ruled independently, Philip the Bold, the duke of Burgundy, created a semiautonomous appanage in the county of Flanders. He had nearly enough territories and power to rival Charles. Louis I, the duke of Anjou, wanted to acquire the kingdom of Naples, the homeland of his mother from whom he had inherited a claim to that land. John, duke of Berry, ruled the province of Languedoc and heavily taxed it to fund the war effort against the English, leading to a peasants' revolt. Charles, nevertheless, paid no mind to these intrigues during his minority. He sought pleasure in hunting and jousting, taking part in a tournament soon after receiving the holy unction at his coronation. He even rode at a tournament held to celebrate the double marriages of the son and daughter of the duke of Burgundy.[4]

A stronger distraction came in the form of a Bavarian lady of royal background. Charles was a lusty and energetic young man with strong "carnal appetites." They surfaced in 1385, when his uncles introduced him to Isabeau of Bavaria, great-granddaughter to Wittelsbach Holy Roman Emperor Louis IV. His uncles suggested a political marriage to create an alliance with the House of Wittelsbach. The two royals were sixteen years old. For the youths, it was love at first sight—and it could have been little else, because she did not speak French and he did not understand German. Despite the language barrier, Charles was instantly smitten. On their first meeting, Charles felt "happiness and love enter his heart, for he saw that she was beautiful and young, and thus he greatly desired to gaze at her and possess her." He demanded they be wed immediately, and they were three days later.[5] "And if," court historian and royal chronicler Jean Froissart commented, "they passed that night together in great delight, one can well believe it."

The young couple did spend their early marriage in happiness. They feasted together on many occasions and held lavish festivals that lasted for days. For their first New Year together in 1386, Charles gave her a red velvet palfrey saddle, lined with copper and adorned with an intertwined K and E (for Karol and Elisabeth—the German renderings of their names), among many other gifts.[6] Charles's power grew as his uncles' waned. He took personal rule in 1388, relieved his uncles of their duties, and restored the advisors of his father, the "marmousets." They reorganized the French court, declaring the king responsible for leading a new council with honest and capable administrators, including a few non-aristocrats. Their goal was to purge the corrupt court of the royal uncles and revive the administration of Charles V.

However, the happy years of his reign ended, as did his mental well-being, when these plans failed. His decline is described in detail by court chronicler and eyewitness Jean Froissart, a historian patronized by aristocrats in England, France, and the Low Countries. Three events occurred in 1392–93 that triggered Charles's madness. The first was a severe fever that occurred during the launch of a military campaign. On Easter Day 1392, the king insisted on an expedition to Brittany despite the objections of his uncles and advisors over his illness. During the king's stay at Le Mans, he labored hard and assiduously in the council despite having little help and not yet being restored to health. He had been "the whole summer feeble in body and mind, scarcely eating or drinking any thing, and almost daily was attacked with fever, to which he was naturally inclined, and this was increased by any contradiction or fatigue."[7] Charles began acting crazed.

Onlookers were shocked. They could not explain what had come over the king, who until then had appeared mentally stable. Because his madness came suddenly and unexpectedly, Charles's uncles first ascribed it to bewitchment or poison. In response, the king's physicians announced he had suffered from an unknown disorder due to his weakness of intellect. Others thought that environmental triggers set off the frenzy. Whatever the reason, the king convalesced and eventually appeared to be restored to health.[8]

The second event that triggered his madness was an attack on his faithful advisor, Olivier de Clisson, constable of France, by Pierre de Craon, a debauched aristocrat who had been expelled from the French court. Craon was a protege of Charles's enemy, John IV, duke of Brittany. Their plan was to assassinate Clisson en route to his lodgings in Paris after he dined with the king at the Hôtel Saint-Pol, a royal residence. On June 13, 1392, Craon and his men waylaid him in a narrow Parisian street. Stabbed (but not fatally due to his chainmail coat), Clisson staggered into the doorway of a baker's shop and was rescued. Craon thought Clisson had perished. He fled Paris and made his way to friendly territory in Brittany. When learning that the assassination had failed, Craon told the duke, "It is diabolic. I believe all the devils of hell to whom the Constable belongs, guarded and delivered him out of my hands, for he suffered more than sixty blows by swords or knives and I truly believed him dead."

Charles was outraged when he heard the news. He unleashed his fury on all who had aided the attempted murder of his constable. He ordered the execution of his steward, two squires, and a page. Charles then sought swift revenge. He planned an expedition to Brittany while still suffering bouts of fever and incoherence. Michel Pintoin, known as the monk of St. Denis, who wrote a history of Charles VI's reign and was with the king at the time, reported that during the course of Charles's journey to the southwest he spoke nonsense and made rude gesticulations. Charles suffered from a "strange and hitherto unheard of disease" in which he was doubled over with a high fever and lost his hair and nails. The symptoms suggested typhoid, cerebral malaria, or encephalitis (it has been said he suffered from syphilitic meningitis, but this is improbable, as syphilis was a New World disease and unknown in Europe in the early fifteenth century). Charles returned to Paris to convalesce and prepare again to lead his army against the Breton duke, but his royal physician opposed the expedition.[9]

His doctor suspected Charles suffered from the same mental illness as his mother, Joanna of Bourbon, who had experienced a complete nervous breakdown after the birth of her seventh child in 1373. The king spent a month recuperating and eventually recovered. Froissart thought that the rising of heated humors to Charles's brain created a pathology (the ancient Greek theory of humoral medicine still lingered in Europe). The diagnosis has a hint of truth, as a heat stroke or an attack of hypothermia could have damaged his brain. Other historians have suggested schizophrenia, arguing that Charles had a predisposition to mental illness from his mother's side and this incident was merely one of the many schizophrenic episodes that occurred throughout his life.[10]

Other contemporaries thought the king's madness had a supernatural origin. The chronicler known as the monk of St. Denis believed Charles's madness was triggered by a prophecy that caused him to fall into a state of psychosis. This prophecy was revealed on August 5, 1392, a scorching summer's day, as the king and his entourage approached the borders of Brittany. Charles had consumed a considerable quantity of wine and wore a black velvet jacket, a cuirass (an armor breastplate and backplate fastened together), and a hat of scarlet velvet. In the morning he traveled through the forest near Le Mans. By midday the king left the forest and entered a sand plain, where the sun was blazing. Everyone suffered from the heat. The princes trailed behind the king to minimize the dust and avoid dirtying his garb.

The expedition neared a leper colony. One leper dressed in a raggedy white smock stepped from behind a tree and appeared to be raving. The leper rushed up to the retinue and seized the bridle of Charles's horse. The men-at-arms forced him away from Charles and sent him on his way. Any other French subject would have been arrested or struck down for such reckless actions toward the king, but they thought him to be a madman and released him. The leper, however, was unfinished. He followed the king and cried out: "Ride no further, noble king! Turn back! You are betrayed!" An escort beat the leper back, but again no arrest. He continued to follow the procession for an hour with his cries. As he returned eventually to the colony, the leper's cries of betrayal echoed from the forest. This disturbed Charles.[11]

Later in the day, one of the king's pages, half asleep from the merciless heat, dropped the king's lance. It clattered on the steel helmet of his companion, startling the king. Charles, catching the glimmer of light as the sun reflected off the lance, spurred his horse and drew his sword. He cried out: "Attack! Attack the traitors! They want to deliver me!" He ran with his sword to the duke of Orleans to strike him. The duke escaped, but Charles killed four in the ensuing scuffle before his officers restrained him. One of those killed was a knight of Gascony. The duke of Burgundy exclaimed, "The king is out of his mind! Hold him someone!"[12]

Guillaume Martel, lord of Bacqueville, finally managed to seize the king from behind. Others grabbed his broken sword from the scuffle. Disarmed, Charles was pulled from his horse and gently laid on the ground, prostrate and speechless. His eyes rolled strangely in his head. The king recognized nobody and said nothing.[13] Charles then fell unconscious, his body became cold, and his pulse weakened. He lost all sensation in his limbs. His attendants placed him in an oxcart and returned him to Le Mans.[14] The king could not speak for two days and, after regaining consciousness, was unable to recognize anyone, including his uncles and brother. Some thought his illness was God's punishment for heavy taxes or insufficient support of the Church. Others thought sorcery had been at work. Pity for the king's condition quickly morphed into opportunism. The royal uncles made a power play during the king's convalescence and reclaimed their roles as advisers. They marginalized the marmousets for a time, but the two factions continued to struggle throughout Charles VI's reign.[15]

Although Charles regained lucidity for four months, he then experienced a third event triggering his complete fall into madness. It was by far the most frightening in his life. On January 28, 1393, Isabeau arranged for one of her ladies-in-waiting to marry a prominent gentleman. Held in her honor was a costume party—later known as the Bal des Ardents (Ball of the Burning Men). The celebrations included a masquerade, which induced five young noblemen to appear as near-naked savages. (One account notes: "Such was the indelicacy of the times.") The king decided to join his friends in the incognito group. Their dress was made of linen cloth soaked in tar to appear shaggy from head to foot and designed to sit close to their bodies. The costumes were highly flammable, a considerable risk in a palace illuminated with torches. No one could guess the identity of the wearers.[16]

At one point in the ball, the duke of Orleans arrived with friends. He feigned running a lighted torch against one of the savages. But the fire came too close and ignited the costume's incendiary materials. Flames erupted, which quickly spread to the rest of the group. The party fell into chaos. Isabeau and the duchess of Berry were the only two besides the costumed noblemen who were aware the king was in one of the costumes that had just been set on fire. During their torments, the costumed men called out, "Save the king! Save the king!"

The queen fainted. The duchess saved Charles's life by wrapping her robes around him to extinguish the flames. Another member of the group leaped into a cistern of water. The four others were not so lucky. Terribly burned, they succumbed to their injuries over the next two days. A frightened Charles suffered a complete mental breakdown.[17]

Later, the king was "covered by such heavy shadows" that he flew into a rage at anyone who tried to help him. When physicians came to treat him and deliver his food, Charles would claw and bite those who entered his private apartment. He denied that he was the king, and he could not recognize Queen Isabeau. Charles declared he was not married and had never had children. He even destroyed objects displaying the fleur-de-lis, the symbol of the French monarchy. The king could be lucid for brief intervals, but his general madness continued for six months. Charles only appeared to recover, according to his own reckoning, after making a pilgrimage to Mont Saint-Michel.[18]

Madness ran in the king's bloodline due to centuries of intermarriage among European royal houses. Kingdoms paired their children as stratagems to inherit territories. England and France demanded each other's land in the Hundred Years' War because their royal lines intertwined to the point that the English could rightfully claim the crown of France.

This intertangled circumstance of familial-cum-political warfare was not unique to English and French rivalry. All European royal dynastic lines had equally intermingled. The result was internecine family struggles, but also genetic defects, hereditary diseases, and madness.

Mental illness came from Charles's mother, Joanna of Bourbon, and passed through him to his daughter, Catherine of Valois. Others in the Bourbon dynasty were also affected by mental infirmities; Joanna's brother, Louis II of Bourbon, suffered from acute depression. The English line was similarly affected when King Henry V married Catherine to conquer France as part of his growing kingdom. Unknowingly, he opened the door for madness to affect his bloodline too.

Charles had a total of forty-four psychotic episodes throughout his reign. These lasted up to nine months in duration, followed by short spells of clarity. Between psychotic episodes, Charles was mentally healthy and capable of leadership. He offered no resistance to resuming his royal duties. Only one chronicler, Enguerrand de Monstrelet, who wrote his history after the death of Charles, suggested that the king's mental health had steadily degenerated over the years and he had never really recovered. But even Monstrelet acknowledged that the king appeared to return to health after his first breakdown: "Nevertheless, by the grace of God, he recovered his health, and his sense, [although] not as soundly has he possessed them before this accident."[19]

Over time, periods between recovery and relapse shortened. Hope for Charles's full recovery declined along with his health. Even during times of clarity, his memory was weak. In later years, he was unable to take part in decision-making except for casting the deciding vote for imperial matters between his uncles and brother, Louis of Orleans. During bouts of madness, he could not govern responsibly or keep up the facade of leadership.[20]

Opportunists took advantage of the king's condition, especially when Charles fired staff members and had vacancies in his court for anyone who could earn his favor. During a manic episode in 1395, Charles treated those close to him with suspicion and distrust, particularly his physician, Renauld Fréron, whom he exiled from Paris along with twenty-two doctors, two surgeons, and an apothecary.[21] Charlatans came to the court, claiming they had the power to heal the king through magic. One was Jehan de Bar, a "physician" accused of practicing sorcery in 1398, for which he was executed in Paris. In his formal confession, Jehan de Bar acknowledged invoking demons, devil worship, and consecrating swords, steel mirrors, and rings to summon dark spirits. He also created necromantic images of Charles and the duke of Burgundy, trying to gain power over them.[22]

By 1396, Charles exhibited the full signs of what some believed to be chronic schizophrenia, which in its more acute form caused hallucinations and even acts of violence. Sometimes he was listless and prostrate. Other times he was excitable, running to the point of exhaustion, claiming to be chased by enemies. Accounts record him damaging royal property. In late 1397, Charles asked that all knives be taken away from him and his courtiers. In another episode, he feared himself bewitched and begged that those who had enchanted him would let him die.[23]

In 1405, another fit of "frenzy" that lasted for six months caused the king to display himself in a filthy state. He neglected his hygiene and refused to have his bed linens changed. He had hallucinations and thought himself breakable, and that a thousand lead needles were pricking him. Charles tore his clothing, threw the apparel into the fire, and urinated on his *houppelande*, a medieval outer garment.[24] He refused to bathe or shave and was afflicted by lice. The court physicians decided the king could only be cured by shock treatment (in the sense of surprise, not electrical stimulus). In November, a group of ten men with blackened faces entered the royal apartments to frighten him. It worked. Charles agreed to be cleaned.[25]

The most well-known story of Charles's insanity involved bouts with "the glass delusion." The psychiatric disorder caused sufferers to believe themselves made of glass and susceptible to shattering into pieces at any moment. The king refused to allow others to touch him and required them to don protective clothing to prevent them from fracturing him. To keep a perfectly serene environment, he required all the windows in his palace to remain shut. Anyone who approached him had to do so on tiptoe. The future Pope Pius II claimed Charles inserted iron rods into his clothes for added protection from a deadly fall.[26]

Petteri Pietikäinen writes in *Madness: A History* that the glass delusion was a subset of melancholy. Sufferers feared that exposure to others or even to the sun could cause them to break. Some believed themselves to be oil lamps or some other object made of glass. Others thought themselves imprisoned in a glass bottle. Medieval and Renaissance physicians saw this illness in other patients, notably noblemen and scholars, and wrote accounts of it. It became associated with a more well-known affliction called "scholar's melancholy."[27]

Sixteenth-century Dutch physician Levinus Lemnius (1505–1568) chronicled cases of this disorder. He had a patient who refused to sit, fearing his glass derriere would break. To accommodate his fragile hindquarters, he stood while defecating. These "glass people" could also believe they were chamber pots. This fixation with urine could have come from the Greek theory of the four humors, in which the dark color of urine was associated with melancholy (perhaps meaning they were psychologically conditioned to accept a prognosis that made sense within the medical knowledge of their society). Miguel de Cervantes in all likelihood knew these accounts when he wrote his short story "The Glass Graduate" in 1613, the story of a madman who thinks himself made of glass. He fears physical contact and only drinks out of his cupped hands.

Why did Charles and certain other nobles and scholars believe themselves to be made of glass? This disorder is mostly nonexistent today, having disappeared after the early modern age. If the glass delusion does still exist, it is not widely known (two rare modern examples are twentieth-century pianists Vladimir Horowitz and Glenn Gould, who both feared their fingers would be damaged). Petteri Pietikäinen speculates that the delusion came from confusing a metaphor about physical and spiritual health with a statement of fact. Medieval Europeans were preoccupied with the union of body and soul. Their theory of medicine dictated that their "vital life forces" were contained in the fragile "vessels" of their bodies. Theology of the time borrowed this imagery, in which sinfulness was associated with a broken vessel, while glass was associated with cleanliness and purity. Pietikäinen argues that the glass delusion is an overlap between beliefs and values, and a result of the afflicted taking literally the metaphors of glass as a container for pure bodies and souls.[28]

The legacy of Charles VI lives on in literature and film that follows his tragic descent into insanity. Notable examples include *The Night of Queen Isabeau*, a 1920 German silent film, and *The Notebooks of Malte Laurids Brigge*, an early twentieth-century German novel by Rainer Maria Rilke that influenced French philosopher Jean-Paul Sartre. Charles's larger legacy was probably genetic. It is likely that he directly affected the neighboring realms of Europe after his death by spreading his mental illness to the rulers of those kingdoms through intermingled bloodlines. Due to the same policies of royal intermarriage that brought madness to Charles, he passed on mental illness to his grandson, Henry VI of England. Henry's own battle with insanity and inability to govern England led to the dynastic struggle of the Wars of the Roses.

Beyond Charles's genetic influence on Europe's future monarchs, the king's fits of madness disrupted his kingdom, sent it into violent domestic turmoil, and weakened France to the point of its disastrous defeat in the Battle of Agincourt in 1415, and its near total defeat in the Hundred Years' War. As a result, England took over more and more land on the European continent. England controlled much of northern France by 1420. Henry VI was crowned king in Paris in 1431. The English remained in Normandy until 1450.

In an accidental but happy turn of events from Charles's mental illness, his inability to govern may have accelerated France's transition from feudalism to the early modern era. The late fourteenth century brought political changes to feudal society in which the king's direct power could be obstructed. His ability to rule his kingdom directly diminished due to duchies evolving into kingdoms. They had their own governmental, administrative, and judicial institutions which ran with near independence. A duke could rule his realm with little interference from the king while still offering feigned allegiance. These rival administrations may not have been a direct threat to the crown, since his lordship was acknowledged along with the king's right to levy feudal contingents and collect taxes. But these rights were slowly annihilated. This process of power moving out of Paris had already started before the reign of Charles VI, but it accelerated due to court turmoil.[29]

Although France was slowly evolving from a kingdom into a modern administrative state, French subjects suffered from Charles's inability to enforce justice. The worst power struggles were between Louis I, duke of Orleans, and John the Fearless, duke of Burgundy. In 1407, John kidnapped Charles's eldest son, the heir to the throne; the queen later recovered him. At this time, Louis I effectively governed France and was rumored to be the queen's lover. Not only that, he also tried to seduce the duke of Burgundy's wife. She refused Louis, so he then tried to rape her. Personal and political grudges boiled over. The duke of Burgundy decided to be rid of Louis. On November 23, 1407, Louis was riding back from Isabeau's house in Paris with ten guards in his retinue. Suddenly, seven or eight masked, armed men rushed the guards, shouting "Kill him! Kill him!" They cut off one of his hands and sliced his head in two. Louis lay battered to death on the street.

Suspicion quickly fell on the duke of Burgundy, who ended all doubt by admitting he had ordered the murder. He issued a justification in 1408, saying that he had ordered the killing for "the general good of the realm" as an act of tyrannicide: Louis had oppressed the people of Orleans through excessive taxation and by preventing reform.[30] He even accused Louis of trying to bring about Charles's death by black magic. John the Fearless fled Paris shortly after the assassination, not out of fear of Charles but for the safety of his own territory. The king, in fact, accepted the justification and issued a formal pardon. A ceremony of reconciliation between the duke of Burgundy and Louis's son was held in Chartres Cathedral. But the assassination of the king's brother demoralized the French government. Moreover, the knowledge that there was considerable public support for the duke's deed prolonged and deepened the court's inaction.[31]

Charles's response to the assassination, and his failure to punish John and his henchmen, was inadequate. The faction allied with Louis resented that justice was not served. The event became the catalyst for internecine war and widened the rift between supporters of the two dukes. Violence between the two factions grew as they relentlessly sought revenge.[32]

Chroniclers no longer looked at Charles as a well-intentioned king sabotaged by his own poor mental state. They considered him a tyrant plunging the kingdom into civil war. According to the Westminster chronicle, Charles played "the despot over his people more savagely than he ever had done in the past, according to report—or rather according to true and established fact."[33] Other advisors and officials thought him more powerless than tyrannical. They thought of invoking the Church law tenet of *rex inutilis*, or "useless king." This tenet originated with bishops who were too infirm to perform their duties, but in the thirteenth century, it was applied to incompetent lay rulers. Kings deposed under this tenet included Sancho II of Portugal (1209–1248), who let his kingdom fall into ruin due to his "idleness," "timidity of spirit," and "simplicity."[34]

France's neighbors took advantage of the chaos. What followed was the greatest military disaster in medieval French history. In 1415, English king Henry V landed near the Norman seaport of Harfleur with thirty thousand men. He captured it after a five-week siege. France countered with fifty thousand troops led by Constable Charles d'Albret. He destroyed the fatigued English force. Henry offered to surrender his conquest of Harfleur for a safe passage to Calais. Rejected by the French, Henry determined to force his way through. Half of his exhausted force returned to England, leaving him only fifteen thousand men. The French force consisted of sixty thousand, headed by the Dauphin, Charles's son, and all princes of royal blood.

The resulting conflict was the Battle of Agincourt, the most significant English–French battle of the fifteenth century. English longbowmen famously mowed down French forces, especially the cavalry, who were impeded by the clay ground softened by the rain. Few victories were ever more complete than this. The English lost as few as one hundred men. The French lost Constable Charles d'Albret and seven princes. Over ten thousand French died, many just left on the battlefield.[35]

France's losses in battle and internal turmoil incited Paris to revolt. The duke of Burgundy captured the city in 1418 and stoked this anger, leading Parisians to force open the city prisons, murder the jailers and guards, make the prisoners walk out one by one, and massacre them all without distinguishing by age or gender. Some prisoners ascended the towers to repel the mob, resulting in the strange sight of prisoners keeping a siege. They couldn't hold back the mob, and the prisoners were forced to throw themselves from the towers onto the pike-filled streets below. One account claims the mob stood up to their ankles in human blood.

In the end, the English pressured Queen Isabeau to persuade Charles to sign the disastrous Treaty of Troyes in 1420. Under the terms, Charles disinherited his offspring and named the king of England as successor to the French throne. The treaty arranged for the marriage of Charles's daughter, Catherine of Valois, to Henry V, who became regent of France and heir to the French throne. The Dauphin, Charles VII, was for a time disinherited from succession, along with his offspring. Isabeau agreed to oust her son in the hope of ending the war with England and returning France to prosperity under the rule of a capable king.

Overall, Charles's story of madness stands out in the historical record because of the impact that his poor mental health had on the lives of thousands of French subjects. At his death in 1422, independent France was whittled down to its heartland of Orleans and cities along the Loire River. Paris itself lay deep in English territory. Charles VII established a makeshift court at Chinon. The French were without hope until a young maid from Orleans named Joan arrived at the court and made the pre-posterous claim of having been sent by God to liberate France. Her story is well told, but the miraculous rescue of France by a seventeen-year-old peasant girl, Joan of Arc, would have never been necessary if not for the disastrous reign of Charles.

## CHAPTER THREE

# Russian Tsar Ivan the Terrible

## 1530–1584

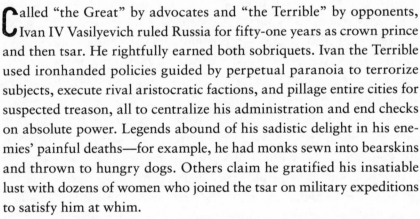

Called "the Great" by advocates and "the Terrible" by opponents, Ivan IV Vasilyevich ruled Russia for fifty-one years as crown prince and then tsar. He rightfully earned both sobriquets. Ivan the Terrible used ironhanded policies guided by perpetual paranoia to terrorize subjects, execute rival aristocratic factions, and pillage entire cities for suspected treason, all to centralize his administration and end checks on absolute power. Legends abound of his sadistic delight in his enemies' painful deaths—for example, he had monks sewn into bearskins and thrown to hungry dogs. Others claim he gratified his insatiable lust with dozens of women who joined the tsar on military expeditions to satisfy him at whim.

Yet even Ivan's strongest detractors do not deny he was also Great. The Russia of Ivan's youth was the Duchy of Muscovy, a minor Eurasian state at the mercy of more powerful European and Central Asian empires. At first, he ruled fewer than three million subjects and warred constantly with the Golden Horde, a successor state of Genghis Khan still active three centuries after his death. Muscovy had continued to swear fealty to the Mongols up until Ivan III (the Great's grandfather) renounced allegiance in 1480. Russians were under perpetual risk of being captured in raids and sold in the Central Asian slave markets. But by the end of Ivan's reign, his duchy had been transformed into the Tsardom of Russia, absorbing the Horde's successor states of Kazan, Astrakhan, and Siberia, with complete control of the Volga River and access to the Caspian Sea. The population under his rule doubled. Through these acquisitions, he turned Russia into a multi-religious, multi-ethnic empire. Ivan abandoned the customary title of Grand Duke and declared himself Tsar (Caesar).

Ivan was the son of Vasily III Ivanovich by his second wife, Helena Glinskaya. Vasily died when Ivan was three years old. Proclaimed grand prince of Moscow, Ivan found himself in the middle of a contentious and ongoing grab for power among relatives and noble families. His mother Helena Glinskaya ruled in his stead and fended off claims from Ivan's uncles, Yury Ivanovich and Andrey of Staritsa. She enacted minor monetary reforms in her reign, negotiated peace with Lithuania, neutralized Sweden, and constructed defensive walls around Moscow. However, she died in 1538—it is rumored by poisoning. The Shuisky family boyars, the feudal Russian aristocracy one rank below princes, followed her as regent. Quarreling boyar families vied for the regency in the following years.[1]

Shuisky and Belsky boyars mistreated young Ivan. He claimed in one letter that a drunk boyar placed his dirty boots on the prince's bed; in another letter he wrote he was denied garments and food. Accounts claim the unsupervised child developed sadistic tendencies. Ivan stood at the top of the high ramparts of the Kremlin and hurled cats and dogs from the roof. Other accounts say that at age thirteen he ordered his mentor beaten to death.[2]

From here narratives of Ivan's life hopelessly diverge, depending on whether his conquests or his madness are emphasized. The charitable interpretation depicts him as a sixteenth-century Charlemagne, a leader who completely subdued enemies in battle and extended the borders of his state far beyond its traditional domains. He reduced the role of the traditional aristocracy and made reform possible in his backward state, allowing for the Westernization and Europeanization programs of Peter and Catherine, both also called the Great, two centuries later. The pessimistic take on Ivan depicts him as a Robespierre, who was the leader of the Reign of Terror after the French Revolution and executed anyone who disagreed with his uncompromising vision or threatened his national goals. Ivan curtailed the traditional powers of the elites and created the despotic, tsarist autocracy that came to define the Russian state. He was perfectly willing to execute enemies in his attempt to radically purify politics. Humans were not humans to Ivan; they were either tools for or hindrances to his purposes.

Nothing is known of the education of Ivan except by inference. Ivan grew up in a multilingual environment, as his mother was of Serbian and Lipka Tatar descent—a Turkic group that originated in the Crimea. Among his playmates was a cousin, Prince Vladimir Andreyevich, whom he later often left in charge in Moscow whenever he had to leave the capital.

Ivan's interests included watching the court cohort of dwarfs and fools, minstrels, clowns, and buffoons. As an adolescent Ivan spent increasing time on the chase, hunting bears and other wild animals. Records of his travels show hunting expeditions with cousin Vladimir and his brother Iuri in 1544, 1545, and 1546. He grew up religious, a tendency that never ebbed even during his violent purges of so-called traitors; perhaps his religious displays were motivated by subconscious remorse. During his trips, Ivan went on pilgrimages to monasteries, including the Troitsky monastery north of Moscow. He attended services at the Russian Orthodox Church and gave alms to the poor.[3]

Crowned "Tsar and Grand Prince of All Russia" in 1547, he wed Anastasia Romanovna the next month. Power at the time rested with his Glinsky uncles on his mother's side. His first action as tsar was to contest the boyars for control of Muscovy. As the boyars' power was hereditary and defined by a legal code from 1497, they were not constitutionally constrained, and the feudalistic autonomy of their principalities remained a threat to national sovereignty. The murderous scheming of the Russian court made Ivan suspicious, distrustful, self-defensive, and cruel. No adult male in his entourage supplied guidance in this transitional period of bringing the court under control. He had confidants, including Macarius, Metropolitan of Moscow (a position similar to a Catholic bishop); statesman Aleksei Adashev; and his brother, Iuri. Among Ivan's most positive influences was the Orthodox priest Sylvester, a stern but loyal figure who became a court favorite. Ivan made decisions on his own, however. He had a keen sense that power was his and he should exercise it freely and ruthlessly.

N. M. Karamzin, nineteenth-century author of the twelve-volume tome *History of the Russian State*, described Ivan at this stage as an unbridled colt who capriciously used his powers as tsar to disgrace and grant rewards. Also, he had a preference for noisy festivities and idleness. Ivan was light on his feet "like a leopard," and a tall, powerful man, in every way like his grandfather Grand Prince Ivan III. From the beginning, Ivan managed complaints from subjects with total tactlessness. In 1547, seventy-five residents of Pskov complained in Moscow against their governor. Ivan did not heed them. Karamzin claims that instead, seething with rage, Ivan poured boiling wine over them, singed their hair and beards (a mark of shame for a Russian man), and ordered them stripped and laid on the ground. The Pskovites expected death to come. At that moment, the bell in Moscow rang and Ivan rushed to see what had occurred, forgetting about the poor subjects' fate. Karamzin's interpretation of the story is that neither marriage nor sovereignty restrained Ivan's impulsiveness and unpredictability, but only magnified his innate cruelty.

Another event in Ivan's early reign made him suspicious of his own people. A fire started in Moscow on June 24, 1547, leaving an estimated 2,700–3,700 people dead and over 80,000 homeless. Muscovites looked for a scapegoat. They claimed the cause of the fire was the witchcraft of Princess Anna Glinskaya, Ivan's grandmother. According to rumors, she stripped the hearts out of the dead bodies and soaked them in water, then sprinkled the dried remnants on the streets of Moscow. Two days later, a mob marched to where Ivan had taken refuge with his family. They demanded that Anna, her family, and her servants be handed over. The boyars and men-at-arms managed to protect the princess and put down the revolt. The confrontation deeply affected young Ivan, likely causing him to become more callous toward his subjects. The mob's demand that he hand over his grandmother showed complete disregard for his authority. Already, Ivan's propensity for cruelty had started. From then on, he became afraid and outraged whenever a feeling of powerlessness overwhelmed him, triggering paranoia that expressed itself in a growing number of political killings and executions.[4]

Historians point to 1553 as the year in which he began showing signs of mental deterioration. According to the Book of the Tsar (*Tsarstvennaya Kniga*), the primary chronicle of Ivan's reign, the tsar suffered from a "fiery sickness" in March and could not recognize others. Questions of succession arose in case of his death. All sides stepped forward, ready to take power. Ivan told the boyars to swear fealty to his only son, Tsarevich Dmitrii, who was only five months old. Disagreements arose among them for fear that the infant king's rule would lead to a power grab from Ivan's wife's family, the Zakharin-Yuriev clan. Others wanted to place Ivan's cousin, Prince Vladimir Andreyevich, on the throne. But the tsar, still aware, considered such flippant talk about his ensuing death treasonous. With his remaining strength he cursed them with rage and forced their oath of allegiance. Ivan recovered the next week but vividly remembered the "treachery" for the rest of his life. He never stopped suspecting his cousin Vladimir of plotting to remove him as tsar.

Ivan's sanity also suffered a crippling blow at the death of his wife Anastasia. In July 1560, fires again consumed Moscow. That same year three thousand Crimean Tatars raided the capital, hauling Muscovites into slavery. The tsar removed Anastasia to his country palace in

Kolomenskoye, a royal estate southeast of Moscow, but she died in August from the effects of smoke and shock. Ivan later accused state minister Aleksei Adashev and the priest Sylvester of contributing to Anastasia's death by urging Ivan not to take her on pilgrimages to visit holy shrines and relics, which he believed would have enabled her to recover. Russian historian Karamzin succinctly says that, at this point, a good and an evil Ivan existed. Anastasia's death marked "the end of the happy days for Ivan and for Russia; for he lost not only his wife, but his better nature."[5]

Many believe Ivan's violent outbursts and change of character rose from psychological shock at the death of Anastasia. The tsar's sense of vulnerability was renewed, and memories of his grandmother being wrongly accused of witchcraft resurfaced. Ivan became possessive and distrustful of princes and boyars. He forced them to pay bonds as guarantees that they would not flee Moscow, and he exiled generals who failed him on the battlefield. All these actions can be psychoanalyzed as Ivan acting out for the loss of Anastasia, but from a political perspective they can also be explained as the tsar consolidating power and eliminating the Russian aristocracy by marginalizing those who did not recognize his authority.

Only a week after Anastasia's death, Metropolitan Macarius, the bishops, and the boyars appeared before Ivan with an unexpected petition. They begged him to stop grieving and place his hopes in God, to remember that he should not put off remarrying, because he, a thirty-year-old, had not yet reached the years when he could live without a spouse. He should therefore marry quickly in order not to suffer from privation. Ivan was taken aback by this bold statement but took the advice. Almost at once, he announced that he would take a new wife and forgo a traditional period of mourning.[6]

In the 1560s, Ivan's opponents saw a "great persecution," as described by Andre Kurbsky, a friend of Ivan and later a leading political rival. Ivan marginalized his former court favorites, Adashev and Sylvester, no longer listening to their admonishments or advice. It was as though he suddenly released himself from their moral guidance. He danced with his male friends, wore masks (a practice forbidden by the Russian Orthodox Church), and was served by *skomorokhi*, the disreputable wandering clowns, minstrels, and jugglers who entertained the lower orders. Older, more conservative boyars were horrified. Others feared for their lives. Ivan killed the incautious Prince Dmitri Obolensky Ovchinin when he reproached Fedor Basmanov, the tsar's new catamite. Obolensky Ovchinin proclaimed, "We serve the tsar in useful ways, and you in your filthy sodomitical affairs." Basmanov complained to Ivan, who responded by pouring a boiling hot dish all over Obolensky Ovchinin. He then stabbed him.[7]

In 1565, Ivan isolated himself from much of his empire and created what he referred to as the *oprichnina*, or "separate estate." He also had a set of advisers called the *oprichniki*. The oprichnina was a group of specific territories within his domain whose reassigned revenues underwrote his new lifestyle. He broke with most of the remaining power of the Muscovite boyars, exiling them to Siberia. The oprichnina kept its own army. Its primary goal was to maintain Ivan's power, whether through standard military action or through shock campaigns of intimidation through looting, rape, torture, and killing with Ivan's permission. The oprichnina committed notorious atrocities during Ivan's reign. While the Russian council was still in charge of the daily administration of the empire, those outside of the oprichnina, the *zemshchina*, could not contact Ivan except in the most urgent circumstances. Speaking against the oprichnina was a punishable offense, and in certain situations a capital one. Ivan's growing isolation gave members of the oprichniki freedom to act with impunity against most who were not within Ivan's inner circle.

Ivan's conception of his role as tsar and that of the court and the upper ranks of the military clashed at a meeting in July 1566. The gentry openly denounced Ivan's oprichniki for their thuggish behavior. Never had so many subjects so openly challenged Ivan. Letters to Kurbsky indicate Ivan's pure belief in his unlimited, divinely ordained power and his right to punish at will all who disobeyed his orders or failed in their duties on the battlefield or to the Russian Orthodox Church. Ivan considered his sovereign power to extend far beyond the traditional power of the duke of Muscovy; he was an absolute monarch at the level of Charlemagne or Justinian of Byzantium, not hemmed in by obligations to aristocrats or a constitution. This collective demonstration therefore shocked the neurotic and apprehensive Ivan, who saw no checks on his rule.

Yet Ivan's mind also began to fill with doubt. In May 1567, he went on a pilgrimage to a monastery in Aleksandrovskaya Sloboda, a town seventy-five miles northeast of Moscow. There he held long talks with the abbot and elders, speaking openly of his wish to become a monk. In the meantime, he compelled members of his oprichnina to live a modified monastic rule. They wore monkish garments and followed the prayers of the hours, a set of prayers marking the day recited by monks and other clergy, beginning at 4:00 a.m. when a bell was rung for matins, the morning prayer. The tsar enforced strict discipline, keeping the hours throughout the day. Ivan functioned as abbot, Prince Afanasy Vyazemsky as the cellarer, and Malyuta Skuratov as the sacristan. Having summoned his "monks" to the refectory, Ivan would remain standing while the others ate and only sit down to eat when they had finished. He went to bed about nine o'clock at night, when three old blind men would tell him stories, tales, and fantasies about the past. Senior boyars questioned Ivan's sanity and wondered if the tsar was considering abdicating.[8]

Ivan's ascetic period did not last long. He returned to his autocratic ways with the Massacre of Novgorod, one of the most well-known demonstrations of the tsar's mental instability, paranoia, and brutality. In 1570, Ivan attacked Novgorod and Pskov (the neighboring territory to the west) for fear they would side with Poland during his ongoing wars with that nation, along with Sweden and Lithuania. During this time, he executed anyone who he even *thought* might commit treason or plot to have him deposed. He had taken a similar action the year before by executing more than one hundred members of the boyar council and their families.

The massacre occurred against the backdrop of the Livonian War. Russia fought a coalition of Denmark–Norway, Poland, Lithuania, and Sweden from 1558 to 1583 for control of Old Livonia, found in present-day Latvia and Estonia. Ivan invaded Livonia in the hopes of crushing its weak protectors, the Teutonic Order, which was made up of Catholic knights. They had invaded the region in the Middle Ages to Christianize the Baltic pagans but remained long after to keep up their feudal levies. Ivan wanted to conquer Livonia to access the Baltic Sea and build up a Russian naval presence north of Europe. In the first period of the war, Russia conquered Livonian fortresses and negotiated peace with the belligerents. But renewed fighting occurred in the 1560s after peace treaties expired. The stronger Baltic powers pushed Russia back.

Ivan suspected a treasonous plot by Novgorod's leadership, led by the city's Archbishop Pimen, to surrender to the Polish-Lithuanian commonwealth. While concrete evidence of such plans is nonexistent, other events aroused the tsar's paranoia. He believed the city to have rebellious elements. His cousin, Vladimir Andreyevich, was accused of high treason in 1569 and killed along with his family. Many of Vladimir's retainers and supporters still lived in Novgorod. In December 1569, the tsar set out on a punitive expedition accompanied by a large band of the oprichnina, his son Ivan, and many nobles. The goal was massive bloodshed.[9]

The tsar's retinue set out on the 350-mile expedition northwest from Moscow to Novgorod. The ancient city was one of the oldest in Russia, dating back to 862, and was the center of its own republic that had maintained its independence until Ivan's grandfather annexed it in 1478. The city was one of the few Russian regions to escape Mongol conquest in the 1200s. It and nearby towns finally faced conquest, subjugation, and destruction at the hands of Ivan. On their way to Novogrod his band slaughtered inhabitants of the town of Klin. The oprichniki were free to rape, murder, rob, and burn. Streets filled with corpses, among them women and children. The butchers moved to surrounding villages. At the provincial city of Tver, Ivan prayed five days in a monastery while his executioners roamed from house to house, murdering wantonly. From Tver to Novgorod, the tsar and his oprichniki ravaged with fire and sword. On January 2, 1570, Ivan and the oprichniki arrived at Novgorod. He laid his plans for the massacre of the city. They built a high timber rampart around Novgorod to prevent anyone from escaping; churches were locked to prevent victims from seeking refuge; and monks were removed from monasteries to prevent them escaping to obscure cells or through underground passages. Rich merchants and leading citizens had their dwellings padlocked with inhabitants left inside. Ivan had officials and clergy arrested and bound. He closed the market. Church bells did not ring. A dreadful calm hung in the air.

There was a delay in the expected massacre as Ivan entered the city and met Archbishop Pimen and his clergy. The tsar marched with them to the church to attend Divine Service. He and his company then dined with Pimen at his palace. According to some accounts, the tsar entered a trancelike state and his eyes suddenly blazed with a meteoric light. He stopped eating, turned to the princes and boyars at the table, and let out an inarticulate howl of rage. His bodyguard understood the howl as a signal to seize the archbishop, bind him, and place him in a dungeon. His guard rushed off to sack his palace and remove everything of value. Ivan, meanwhile, continued his dinner.[10]

Ivan declared his plans for punishment. Each day a few thousand inhabitants would be tortured to death in the presence of the tsar and his son. The torture was as cruel as it was varied. Husbands and wives were mutilated in each other's presence. Children were ripped from their mothers' arms before flogging. Holes were drilled in the frozen river and victims pushed under the ice. One account claims these mass tortures and executions continued for five weeks. Along with the killing of Novgorod's population, Ivan's oprichniki plundered the city. Once all valuables were taken, his guard rode to nearby farms, destroying livestock. Then they fell upon monasteries and seized any gold they found. The clergy was put to the sword.

On February 12, Ivan ended the bloodbath and acted the role of munificent king, absolving the people of their "crimes." He gathered the remnants of the population and proclaimed mass amnesty. Ivan barely made eye contact with the stragglers who were rounded up to hear his pardon. The tsar's eyes, it was written, were dull, the rage in them extinguished. He then spoke to them in a faint voice.

"People of Novgorod still living. Pray God to bless our rule as Tsar; pray for the Christ-loving army that it may conquer all its enemies both seen and unseen. May God judge that traitor to me, your Archbishop Pimen and his evil advisors. Theirs is the responsibility for the blood which has been shed. May the wailing and crying cease in the city! Forget your wrongs! Live and prosper! I leave with you my new governor Prince Peter Danielovitch Pronsky. Go now in peace to your homes!"[11]

Estimates claim sixty thousand perished. Kurbsky wrote that the tsar killed fifteen thousand in one day alone. Taube and Kruze, two Germans at the court, claim twenty-seven thousand. Whatever the total number, the Massacre of Novgorod permanently crippled the city. Russians had not seen destruction of this scale since the Mongolian invasions by the descendants of Genghis Khan in the thirteenth century. Inhabitants left after the massacre died from terrible living conditions, leading to epidemics. The burning of 90 percent of nearby arable land triggered famine. Novgorod had once rivaled Moscow as Russia's premier city. It was now degraded to a "run-of-the-mill provincial town."[12]

Ivan returned to Moscow in the spirit of a triumphal entry, as if he were on a victory march from a great battle. He paraded along at the head of his oprichniki. He then prepared the trials of numerous accomplices in the "crimes" for which he had punished Novgorod and Pskov. On June 25, 1570, he summoned his subjects to the city square to attend the public execution of suspects who were found guilty. They totaled three hundred, already mutilated and at the point of death from the pain of the torture chambers. Ivan prepared instruments of more torture—stoves, red-hot pincers, iron claws, needles, cords to rip bodies into two halves, and cauldrons full of boiling water. Sir Jerome Horsey, a sixteenth-century English adventurer, produced a detailed eyewitness account of Muscovy. He gave hideous examples of the executions he claims he saw. One man—Prince Boris Telepniev, whom he calls Teloupa—was impaled and remained on the stake for close to sixteen hours, while his own mother was repeatedly sexually assaulted in front of him until she died. Horsey's claims should be treated with skepticism; he also claimed that seven hundred thousand had been massacred at Novgorod, which would place Ivan beyond the body count of Caligula or Nero.[13]

Ivan met sizable challenges in the 1570s. Most had to do with the Crimean Tatars, a semi-nomadic Muslim population that inhabited the Crimean Peninsula on Russia's southern border. They had raided Russia for centuries to capture slaves, exporting thousands to Ottoman slave markets in Istanbul. In May 1571, the leader of the Crimean Tatars, Devlet I Giray, and his army raided Moscow during the Russo-Crimean Wars. Only six thousand Russian troops stood against them due to the manpower requirements of the ongoing Livonian War. Up to eighty thousand Muscovites were killed; many were kidnapped and enslaved. On May 24, Giray set fire to Moscow's suburbs. The city, the palace, and suburban wooden dwellings burned completely in six hours. Because Ivan's oprichniki did not repel these forces, he officially disbanded *them*.

While his capital lay in smoldering ruin, Ivan focused on his ravenous sexual appetite. Toward the end of 1574, he had grown tired of his young wife, Anna, and was displeased by her barrenness. Ivan regarded the lack of fecundity in their union as a sign of God's displeasure with the marriage. He blamed the archbishop of Novgorod, installed after the massacre, who had made the marriage possible by absolving the tsar from the Russian Orthodox Church's customary prohibition against marrying beyond a third wife. Ivan summoned the prelate to Moscow, tore his vestments with his own hands, and, as sensational accounts claim, had him sewn up in a bearskin and given to dogs to be torn to death.

The event, if true, occurred in early 1575. A convent and austere cell were selected for Anna in exchange for her tsaritsa's palace. She became Sister Darya and remained so for fifty-one years until her death. Once Ivan had put Anna away, he bedded another commoner, Anna Vasilchikova, whom some referred to as Ivan's fifth wife, athough they consummated their union without a church-sanctioned wedding. But even before he had disposed of Anna Vasilchikova and removed her to a convent, the tsar took a beautiful widow, Vasilisa Melentyeva. If these unions count as marriages, Ivan was a bigamist who was married to his fifth and sixth wives concurrently.[14]

What sort of madness did Ivan suffer? Are the wildest stories of Ivan true? Did he engage in orgies? Deflower hundreds of maidens? Force noble ladies to leave their carriages and raise their skirts as he and his men-at-arms jeered? Did Ivan travel with fifty ladies to satisfy his carnal desires? Did he have corpulent priests sewn up in bearskins and thrown to the dogs? Such stories almost invariably come from foreign sources. Englishmen such as diplomat Jerome Horsey provide shocking accounts, along with Livonian authors who wrote in German, such as Taube and Kruse, and the Germans Schlichting, Staden, and Oderborn. Illustrations of Ivan's cruelty are mostly from books printed in German kingdoms or the Netherlands, and foreign bias does call them into question.

Scholars have tried to address the historicity of these claims and, by determining their truth, offer an analysis of the tsar's psychological state. Ivan's record is distorted by various accounts. A good example is the alternate takes on Ivan and his son's 1578 raid on a Moscow suburb inhabited by ethnic German craftsmen and traders. One account states that inhabitants there were beaten and stripped of their clothes and possessions, due to Ivan's edict to plunder but not kill them.

Another account given by the Lutheran pastor Paul Oderborn, who was not an eyewitness and lived in the city of Riga in modern-day Latvia, describes Ivan mocking unfortunate people of the suburb, mostly women and children. "The tyrant, blind with rage, driven by barbaric savagery and maddened with hatred for the German race" moved among them. When young maidens protested sexual abuse, Ivan ordered that they be beaten, have their nails pulled out, their tongues removed, and be run through with glowing stakes. This all occurred as the maidens beseeched Christ for deliverance. English ambassador Jerome Horsey writes that Ivan set a thousand gunners on the young women to strip them naked and then kidnap or rape them. Horsey, no stranger to histrionics, functioned as the chivalrous hero, rescuing and clothing women who escaped with him to an English house.[15]

Accounts are muddled, as are theories of Ivan's madness. Charles Halperin, a historian of medieval Muscovy, has compiled a full survey of academic theories on Ivan's mental health. There was not, and is not, a consensus: "There seems to be greater agreement than there was some decades ago that [Ivan] was not always completely sane, but exactly what and to what effect is still in dispute."[16] Many contemporary historians accept stories of young Ivan throwing animals from towers, pointing to signs that by 1547 he suffered from "uncontrollable savage impulses" and "incipient paranoia" infused with his innate cruelty.[17] The opposition in 1566 to the oprichnina may have further unhinged Ivan's mental stability, challenging his fantasy political world of absolute authority. Isabel de Madariaga, a biographer of Ivan, concludes that he had "no outstanding abnormality" until Anastasia's death triggered a breakdown, causing "incipient acute paranoia."[18]

Halperin notes how other scholars of the tsar have described Ivan: "madman," "pathologically afflicted," "a warped mind," "insane," "paranoid," guilty of sadism, debauchery, erotomania, severe persecution delusions and a diseased imagination, delusions of grandeur, paranoid, "totally insane" and employing mass terror. Some wrote that his marital discord was an outflow of his diseased mind. However, the lack of sources makes a definitive psychological profile of Ivan difficult. Many accounts come from foreign contemporaries of Ivan, who present near-Freudian theories of Ivan's insanity and diagnose him with a medieval version of paranoia, but not extreme schizophrenia-paranoia, since Ivan evidenced no hallucinations and continued to function in his political and diplomatic duties.[19]

Most foreigners did not categorize Ivan as mentally ill, no matter how brutal they considered him to be. The Polish could not have thought him insane if they proposed to "tame" him once he was declared king of Poland. Broadsheets produced in Poland, Livonia, and Germany during the Livonian War portrayed him as bestial, cruel, and inhuman, but fully in control of his mental faculties, however cruel he was. Halperin notes contemporary criticism of Ivan relied on political theology, arguing that Ivan was the Antichrist (mere demonic possession would have been beneath his dignity). Such time-appropriate conceptions avoid the issue of Ivan's mental health entirely. There are many superlatives to describe the Antichrist, but insanity is not one of them. And fellow rulers of the sixteenth century were certainly not paragons of mental health. Monarchs in the European houses of Tudor, Stewart, Valois, and Hapsburg also showed signs of mental instability, neurosis, paranoia, melancholy, sadism, perversion, and depression, all without being dethroned.[20]

That Ivan alone has the moniker "Terrible," while no other contemporary European rulers do despite committing similar acts of brutality, calls again into question the type of sources that color modern opinions of Ivan. Halperin explored the Russian-language word choices used to describe Ivan. Many did dub him mad, but only in the sense of a terrible fury, not in a modern psychological, sociological, or anthropological sense of mental illness. If the only qualification for Ivan's madness was the desire to inflict pain on others, then rulers across history, occupying thrones from the ancient Assyrian to the Ottoman empires, were also "mad." Furthermore, not every form of cruelty is a mental disorder. If it were, all of the premodern European monarchs were mentally ill, as they conducted warfare at a time without international criminal courts and human rights activists. Poor political judgment may be evidence of stupidity, and a violent outburst completely disproportionate to real or imagined threats could be a sign of inexperience, but labeling every such action madness does nothing to separate demagoguery from delusion.[21]

Ivan was born into a world of scheming and court intrigue, but so was every medieval and Renaissance-era monarch, from English king Henry VIII to Peter the Great; it was an occupational hazard of the profession. None of these royals have had their paranoia labeled as madness, at least not in accounts that formed conventional narratives of their reigns. Halperin believes that to characterize Ivan as insane is an admission of failure to understand the rationality of his actions. One needs to understand the historical context, motivations, and impetus for his barbarity—no matter how cruel it appears to contemporary eyes. Furthermore, calling Ivan mad absolves him of moral responsibility for his terrible actions.[22]

Yet the tsar still shocked observers with his use of violence. While Ivan likely had full use of his facilities, he was still insane in the sense that he was completely indifferent to the suffering of others.

Russia suffered under Ivan's madness, but his mental condition may also have been a source of his greatness. Researchers and historians have argued as such as far back as the early nineteenth century, the dawn of the field of psychiatry. Revelle-Parise (1834) and Schilling (1863) tried to prove genius is a form of neurosis, and very often of madness. Argentine psychiatrist Ramos Mejia argued in his 1885 work *Neuroses of Famous Men in History* that all great men of the Argentine Republic had been drunkards, neuropathic subjects, or madmen. Italian criminologist Cesare Lombroso and his disciples believed that Napoleon's genius was a phenomenon produced by epileptic neurosis. While such hypotheses are interesting, they do not explain Ivan. Whatever common mental illness suffered by Napoleon or Ivan, a massive gulf exists between their cruelty and barbaric actions. Ivan's fury, according to the Russian chroniclers, would fit in well with Norse chronicles describing the Vikings' plundering raids of Irish monasteries and Merovingian estates. Ivan was not a calculated despot, like a Napoleon or a Frederick the Great. He was akin to Genghis Khan, holding a rational mind but perfectly able to murder as many as it took to achieve an objective, with pity or empathy being no check on this impulse.[23]

Nevertheless, Ivan's madness-as-greatness theory holds when one considers what he achieved in his long reign. He expanded Russia eastward. Kazan, Astrakhan, and Siberia all came under Imperial Russia's control. The greatest beneficiary of Ivan's eastern conquests of Kazan and Astrakhan, east and south of Moscow, respectively, was the Russian Orthodox Church. Gourii, first archbishop of Kazan, made converts among the Muslim Tatars. In terms of religious reform, Ivan was no Peter or Catherine; his attempts were perfunctory at best and produced little noticeable effect.[24] In terms of political reform, however, he was a rousing success. Ivan weakened the Russian aristocracy and the landed gentry. With the creation of the oprichnina, Ivan sidestepped Russia's feudal hierarchical system that held aside government posts for boyars and instead gave positions to his supporters. Locally and centrally appointed officials staffed the empire's administration.[25]

Despite all his faults, cruelty, vices, and criminal behavior, Ivan remained popular among Russian subjects. These popular sympathies have endured, earning him the moniker "Great" among the descendants of his subjects. Though he killed disloyal villagers and rebellious Tatars by the thousands, raped and pillaged his enemies, and executed boyars on the suspicion of treason, his violence was seen as a necessary end to further Russian might and transform it from duchy to empire. He extended Russian cultural, trade, and political connections to Europe, which in the eighteenth century made it a European great power, not a Eurasian backwater. Ivan's worst actions, if they indeed happened, either were excused or ignored by his strongest supporters.[26]

Ivan committed many terrible acts, but like many of the other brutal leaders in the late medieval/early modern period of history his legacy is indissolubly connected with the modern nation that descended from his rule. A stronger, centralized rule enabled the Russian Empire to seize control over its far-flung landholdings, which by the nineteenth century stretched to the Pacific Ocean, encompassed all of Central Asia, and went down into Eastern Europe. That the Russian tsars were able to control such vast landholdings before railroads, modern communications, and anything more than primitive technology would have been impossible without the political infrastructure created by Ivan.

His brutality, however, was only possible because of the loyalty of his poorer subjects. His violent acts were mostly committed against the aristocratic boyars, who exploited the peasants, and against the Tatars, who threatened them with their frequent raids. Kazimierz Waliszewski explains in his 1904 biography of Ivan that despite all his faults, crimes, weaknesses, and failures, Ivan was popular. When he indulged in savage acts of violence over the corpses of the vanquished Tatars or handed one of his boyars over to the executioner on the smallest suspicion of treason, the Russian people were on his side. They applauded the carnage, Waliszewski argues, and rejoiced in their master's joy. Even when they could not applaud, they shut their eyes respectfully, religiously, and cast a mantle of fictional decency over acts that were appalling.

Ivan's belief in violence as a means of purging his people of the sin of disloyalty led to the tsar justifying his brutality as a means of God punishing the unjust who dared to question their sovereign. He needed such a system of self-delusion, and he upheld it in letters to his advisors. Writing to his friend-turned-political-opponent Andrey Kurbsky, Ivan said: "If you are so righteous and pious . . . why have you feared an innocent death? . . . that is the will of God—doing good to suffer. If you are so righteous . . . why do you not permit yourself to accept suffering from me, your forward master, and so inherit the crown of life?"

It was also Ivan's firm conviction in his God-given duty of rewarding and punishing his people that induced in them obedience to the divinely powerful tsar, to whose judgement they submitted as though it were the final judgment of God on all humanity. In his power to decide their fate, Ivan acted as if he were God, or at least an instrument of God's righteous justice. To his victims, though, he was an Antichrist, sent to torment them out of a twisted belief in his own righteousness, but mostly for his sadistic pleasure.

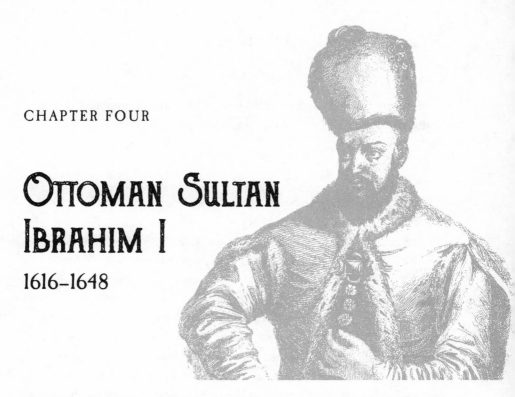

## CHAPTER FOUR

# Ottoman Sultan Ibrahim I

### 1616–1648

**N**o prisoner ever enjoyed luxury to the extent that Sultan Ibrahim I of the Ottoman Empire did. He lived in the Topkapi Palace of Istanbul, the wealth center of the largest empire in Europe and the Middle East. His harem overflowed with concubines selected from the empire's far-flung provinces purely for their beauty. He decorated the palace with sable fur and scented rooms with expensive amber. The sultan believed himself to have total power over his subjects' lives; so much so that he may have influenced the absolutist governing style of Louis XIV.[1]

But he spent the first two decades of his life in "the Cage," a harem quarter of the palace designed to imprison Ottoman princes and prevent them from scheming to capture the sultanate. Ibrahim never left the palace grounds until he became sultan himself in his twenties. In both periods of his life the fear of political assassination relentlessly haunted him. Paranoia and seclusion damaged his sanity, which broke completely when he ascended the throne. As a narcissistic hedonist who put his own pleasure before the needs of the empire, the harm that Ibrahim caused in his eight-year reign drained state coffers, alienated the military and political classes, led to a disastrous war with the rival Republic of Venice, and nearly brought down the House of Osman, the dynasty that had ruled the Ottoman Empire for over three hundred years.

Before exploring Ibrahim's life, it is necessary to delve into the reasons that a royal would spend his youth in a gilded prison. The Cage was an imperfect solution to the even worse fate that met earlier Ottoman princes. For three centuries, the choice of the next Ottoman sultan worked according to a simple but Darwinian system. Young princes were sent to distant provincial cities to rule as governors, learn politics and administration, and build alliances with soldiers, advisors, and religious scholars. Ottoman dynastic succession allowed any son of the sultan to be next in line for the throne, as they did not practice primogeniture—the right for the firstborn son to automatically become ruler. Sons of the sultan knew from childhood that they would have to fight for the throne upon their father's death.

At the sultan's passing, the princes would race home to Istanbul to rally their factions. With enough support from the most powerful officers, bureaucrats, and judges, an Ottoman prince formed his own coalition and took power. Any son, regardless of age, could become the sultan, but any brother of the current sultan could take his throne if he could force him out of it. A new sultan was aware of this perpetual danger, which Ottoman historian Donald Quataert describes as "survival of the fittest, not eldest, son." If his brothers lurked around the empire, the sultan faced the possibility of removal. Anyone who reigned long enough was bound to offend a part of the population, who in turn could throw their support behind a challenger.[2]

Ottoman sultans accounted for this threat in the beginning of their reign in the most draconian manner possible. On accession to the throne, they had all their brothers and pregnant concubines killed to remove possible claimants to the throne. It was done by "the silk rope" of strangulation (due to the belief that royal blood was sacred and shedding blood of members of the dynasty must be avoided).

Sultan Mehmet III (r. 1566–1595) killed an estimated twenty-seven of his preteen brothers. The practice was considered barbaric by the public and condemned. However, according to the political logic of the Ottoman dynasty, it was an act of mercy to society and saved thousands of lives. It prevented the empire from plunging into civil war every time a claimant to the throne battled the sitting sultan for power (as had happened in 1403, 1509, and 1559).[3]

This all changed with the reign of Sultan Ahmet I, who ruled from 1603 to 1617. He had an insane brother, Mustafa, on whom he took pity and did not consign to execution. But he could also not let him live freely, since an enemy faction could revolt against him and place Mustafa on the throne. Ahmet struck a balance and sent him to live in confined quarters of an ornate section of the harem. Mustafa stayed in this luxurious but restrictive apartment until his death. These quarters became known as "the Golden Cage." It was so effective in ending the threat of a dynastic rivalry that the Cage became precedent among sultans.

Soon young princes were not sent out to the provinces but placed in these quarters. They remained there from their birth until their accession to the throne. If they did not win the throne, they stayed there throughout their lives under strict conditions, unless they became heir presumptive. A life in the Cage could leave them insane and incapable of ruling, and, if by chance they did reign, rival factions quickly crushed them. Mustafa I, Ibrahim's mentally ill uncle, was dethroned in 1618, reinstated by supporters, and dethroned again in 1623 by a rival faction. His older brother Osman II was murdered while still a sultan, the first member of the dynasty to be killed while on the throne. Another older brother, Murat IV, ruled from 1623–1640 by asserting his rule through violent measures to crush opposing political factions.[4]

Ottoman dynastic politics did not victimize Ibrahim alone. He also suffered from power struggles within the imperial harem. Due to the strange nature of Ottoman slavery, concubinage, and harem life, women in the empire gained enormous political power in the seventeenth century. Ibrahim's mother, Kösem, was the de facto leader of the empire for decades, and she ruled through weaker sultans. These included Ibrahim's father, Ibrahim himself, his brother Murat, and eventually his son Mehmet. She was also responsible for his survival into adulthood and his eventual downfall.

Kösem was born on the Greek island of Tinos in 1590, at the time a province of the Ottoman Empire. The Christian daughter of a Greek Orthodox priest and born with the name Anastasia, Kösem was bought as a slave by a high-ranking Ottoman official. Noting her beauty, the official sent her to Istanbul to join a cohort of other slave girls marked by their striking appearance or intelligence to be trained in the palace as an imperial court lady. She was fifteen when she was brought to the imperial harem, a section of private apartments on the grounds of Top-kapi Palace consisting of more than four hundred rooms.

When Anastasia arrived, she met dozens of other intelligent young concubines. They came from the Middle East, the Balkans, or the Crimea, and had either been captured in war or recruited within the empire for the harem. Compelled to convert to Islam, Anastasia took the name Mahpeyker Kösem. "Mahpeyker" meant "moon-shaped" in Persian, a period-appropriate compliment to the celestial nature of her beauty. "Kösem," given to her later by Sultan Ahmet I, meant "leader," "free," or "independent," and shows that she had already gained a reputation for her shrewd character. Placed into the harem's rigorous education system, she and other inductees learned the disciplines of the palace. She took lessons in theology, mathematics, embroidery, music, and literature.

Placed at the lowest rung of a viciously competitive hierarchy, harem "cadets" earned a promotion by attracting the attention of the sultan. Kösem began as a concubine unable to leave the palace without permission of the queen mother (valide sultan), the reigning sultan's mother and a former concubine herself. If she managed to share a bed with the sultan, which Kösem did with Ahmet I, she became a gözde (the favorite). If she continued to curry his favor, then she became *ıkbal* (the fortunate). A woman to whom the sultan wanted a permanent union would become one of his four wives (*kadın*). If she bore him a son who went on to become sultan, she became the next queen mother. Through a combination of her intelligence, beauty, and attractiveness to Sultan Ahmet I, she quickly ascended the hierarchy and leapfrogged over more senior wives.

When Ahmet died in 1617, the twenty-eight-year-old widow arranged for Ahmet's mentally ill brother, Mustafa I, to rule. She exercised effective power in the empire during his three-month reign. Her adversaries then deposed him in a palace coup d'etat and placed his nephew, the child Osman II, on the throne. She lacked a close connection to him and lost her position in the court. A setback for Kösem, officials kept her under custody in the Old Palace in the Beyazit district of Istanbul until the seventeen-year-old Osman was deposed and executed by enemy factions in 1622. Her eleven-year-old son, Murat IV, became the sultan in 1623 and his mother the official regent. She was finally able to exercise control over the empire.

When Murat came of age, Kösem became the queen mother. She obtained this title at a time when the position was stronger than the sultanate itself due to a string of weak sultans who were too young or too incapable to lead the empire. This time was known as the Sultanate of Women, a 130-year period in the Ottoman Empire in which the wives and mothers of the imperial harem held extraordinary levels of political power.[5] Although the queen mothers had already gained influence in the court, they had always ruled in an informal fashion as de facto advisors or administrators. Her stewardship of the empire, however, was the first time in Ottoman history that a *valide sultan* was chosen to be the official regent of her son. Kösem met with foreign ambassadors and discussed international treaties. She appointed political posts and had responsibility for maintenance of the state's administration. Kösem made alliances with statesmen, judges, and other figures in the court; she effectively ran the empire for three generations through her husband, then her sons, and then her grandchild.[6]

And Ibrahim was unfortunate to be in the middle of this political war zone.

Ibrahim spend his childhood and young adult life watching his siblings gain power, take the throne, execute rivals, and then face execution themselves by usurpers. His older brother, Murat IV, for example, ordered the execution of his other brothers Beyazit, Süleyman, and Kasim. The young prince Ibrahim couldn't help but wonder when he would be strangled too—the preferred method of execution according to Ottoman interpretations of Islamic law.[7] Ibrahim had been a prisoner during Sultan Murat's reign, and the eight-year period until he became sultan carried the daily expectation of death.

By 1640, Murat IV was terminally ill by cirrhosis of the liver. In the final days of his reign, the sultan's dying wish was to have Ibrahim killed. Even though the House of Osman was moribund, Murat IV didn't want a madman as sultan. But his order was not carried out. While the Ottoman court knew of Ibrahim's tenuous connection to reality, the consequences of the collapse of the Ottoman line would be far worse. The Middle Eastern political tradition of the time emphasized pedigree as one of the most important factors of whether one was fit for command. An ambitious upstart descended from another illustrious Islamic or Central Asian ruler, such as Genghis Khan or Timur the Tatar, would have a strong claim to rule the empire.[8]

Court officials spared the life of Ibrahim. The paranoid young man could hardly believe his stroke of good fortune. When the grand vizier Kemankeş Kara Mustafa Pasha, the empire's chief administrator, hurried to his apartment to announce the death of Murat and proclaim him sultan, the terrified Ibrahim thought his executioners were coming. He barred the door. Ibrahim refused to believe his brother had died. He was only convinced when Kösem ordered the body of her dead son to be showed to Ibrahim.[9]

Ibrahim took power with no brothers or nephews to contest him and so enjoyed a respite from possible execution by a rival political faction. He produced nine male heirs, three of whom went on to become sultans themselves, including Mehmet IV (1648–87), Süleyman II (1687–91), and Ahmet II (1691–95). But despite lacking a male challenger, Ottoman court scheming never ended. Only eight years after becoming sultan, a dethroned Ibrahim was murdered.[10]

A palace shut-in with no political experience, Ibrahim was poorly prepared to lead a global empire that spanned three continents. Nevertheless, the young sultan did his best in the early years of his reign. Ibrahim kept Murat's grand vizier, Kemankeş Kara Mustafa Pasha, and chief legal scholar or *şeyhülislam*, Zekeriyazade Yahya Efendi. Both remained in office until 1644. The grand vizier was allowed to take the lead in governance and competently carried over the reform policies from the previous administration. He achieved such political successes as negotiating peace with Iran, the traditional foe on the Ottoman Empire's eastern border.[11]

Ibrahim ruled at the height of Ottoman land possessions. The empire stretched from Istanbul to Hungary in the west, all along North Africa, down into the Arabian Peninsula, and up into the Caucasus mountains and modern-day Ukraine in the east and north. But it was also a time of growing foreign challenges to Ottoman supremacy. The Cossacks fought for possession of the Crimean Sea fortress Azov. Local revolts sprang up across Anatolia in 1643 before suppression. Dozens of fortresses were captured along the empire's border with the Hapsburg Empire. Meanwhile, eighty Venetian ships patrolled waters in the Dardanelles, the strait that connected Istanbul to the Mediterranean Sea and the blockade of which could cripple the Ottoman economy.

As these challenges grew, Ibrahim began abusing his office to seek out pleasure wherever he could find it, making up for years of freedom lost in the Cage. His long imprisonment and deprivation of the delights of the outside world made his greed override his timidity. Nineteenth-century Austrian historian and diplomat Joseph von Hammer-Purgstall, a pioneer of Turcology in the West who spent decades in the Ottoman archives, looked on Ibrahim's avarice with particular distaste: "Under Ibrahim the worst evils that had prevailed in the time of [Sultan] Murat's weakest predecessors were speedily revived; while the spirit of cruelty, in which Murat had governed, continued to rage with even greater enormity."[12]

Like the Romanovs falling under the spell of Rasputin, a mystic and self-proclaimed healer, Ibrahim's poor mental health left him susceptible to scammers and quacks. He found a spiritual advisor in Karabaşzade Hüseyin Efendi, nicknamed Cinci ("Demon-chaser") Hoca. Cinci Hoca was a spiritualist and fraud who worked his way into the palace under the invitation of Kösem to cure Ibrahim. He rose rapidly in the palace. Ibrahim appointed him judge and administrator over Istanbul's Galata district in 1643. The next year he became *kazasker,* one of two chief military judges in the Ottoman Empire. Other officials were furious.

Cinci Hoca supplanted the *şeyḫülislam* as the foremost authority on spiritual matters for the sultan, among other things. He had a terrible understanding of theological matters and an even worse understanding of politics. In 1644, a group of Maltese pirates attacked a small fleet of Ottoman ships that happened to be carrying pilgrims to Mecca. Among the crew was the "chief black eunuch," the head of the imperial harem and one of the most important administrators in the empire. The pirates carted off the treasure to the Republic of Venice. Istanbul considered Venice and the pirates to be working together and the kidnapping to be an act of war on the part of Venice. Cinci Hoca pushed for going to war over this incident, and he was joined by other bellicose members of the Ottoman imperial council. They got their wish in 1645 with the beginning of the Ottoman–Venetian War, the fifth conflict between the two states in their centuries of rivalry for naval superiority in the eastern Mediterranean. War raged on intermittently until 1669, crippling the economies of Venice and Istanbul.[13]

However, the war went well at first. In 1645, the Ottoman armada arrived off the contested island of Crete and conquered the fortress city of Candia on the northern coast. In keeping with classical forms of Islamic warfare, they transformed the primary cathedral of the city into a mosque and named it after Ibrahim. But whatever favor these advisors thought they would curry with Ibrahim for going to war ended up being short-lived. The commander, Silahdar Yusuf Pasha, faced criticism when he returned to Istanbul for his handling of the siege and for returning with so little plunder. Ordered to return to Crete, Yusuf Pasha refused, as the winter months made for dangerous sailing on the Mediterranean. Ibrahim ordered his execution.[14]

The Siege of Candia dragged on for two decades. Ottoman shipping was attacked in the Mediterranean. From 1648 to 1649, Venetian forces blockaded the Dardanelles, Istanbul's main shipping line, preventing Ottoman fleets from sailing into the Aegean. Supplies could not reach the city. The Ottoman treasury dried up as war dragged on with Venice. Unrest grew in the provinces, as enough troops could not be fielded to maintain order due to lack of funds. Unchecked groups of brigands harassed peasants. And against the backdrop of all this domestic turmoil, Ibrahim occupied himself in the harem, caring little about the domestic and international threats outside the walls of his palace.[15]

Ibrahim tried to fashion himself as a ruler from antiquity, directly out of legend. Ottoman citizens looked upon the behavior of their sultan with a mix of contempt and fear that Ibrahim was invoking God's wrath. Hammer-Purgstall writes that Ibrahim appeared in public with his beard adorned with jewels, an embellishment that according to folk tradition was only worn by the pharaoh in the Old Testament story of the Exodus. Precious stones encrusted one of his chariots. Enormous sums were spent on a skiff that bore the sultan along the Bosphorus, the strait that separates the European and Asian sides of Istanbul.[16] As a self-anointed marksman, he practiced archery on subjects within his range. Ibrahim's power had always been heavily circumscribed, but episodes such as these convinced military leaders and palace officials that his rule must be curtailed.[17]

Ibrahim treated the hundreds of concubines in his harem with contempt (at least those who did not manipulate him); to him they were nothing more than objects to satisfy his carnal desires. Moldovan statesman Dimitri Cantemir wrote, "In the palace gardens he frequently assembled all the virgins, made them strip themselves naked, and neighing like a stallion ran among them and, as it were, ravished one or the other, kicking or struggling by his order."[18] When he met the daughter of the şeyḫülislam, he proposed marriage. The şeyḫülislam knew Ibrahim well and told his daughter to refuse. Ibrahim responded by having the girl kidnapped. He ravaged her for days and then sent her back to her father.

Ibrahim, who had developed a craze for scents and furs, sought to decorate his palace in expensive pelts, inspired by stories from his palace court members of legendary princes who covered themselves, their furniture, and their entire palaces in pricey furs. He called on his imperial council, the *ulema*, and military officials to collect furs throughout the empire to make this dream a reality. To be able to buy these luxury items in abundance Ibrahim sold offices of the state in the administrative and military branches to the highest bidder. He also created two new taxes: the fur tax and the amber tax.

One morning he went to the imperial council and demanded that it send letters to all provincial governors, commanding them to collect and forward to Istanbul a certain number of sable skins. He made a similar request to heads of the religious, civil, and military branches of the government. Some responded with anger. Mehmet Çelebi, the judge of the Istanbul district of Galata, appeared before the grand vizier wearing the humble garb of a religious mystic. He reproached him for the foolishness of the government. Mehmet Çelebi demanded an audience with the sultan: "There can but happen to me one of three things. You may kill me; and in that case, I shall think myself fortunate in being made a martyr. Or, you may banish me from [Istanbul], which will not be unpleasant, as there have been several shocks of earthquake here lately. Or, perhaps, you will deprive me of my employments. But in that I have saved you the trouble. I have appointed my deputy, and have changed my judge's robe and turban for the dervish's gown and cap." The vizier looked at him with amazement for his boldness.[19]

Rank-and-file Ottomans reacted to the new fur taxes with equal amounts of rage but far less diplomacy. A commander of the Janissaries (elite infantry soldiers) named Kara Murat returned from Crete around 1646 in the course of the Ottoman–Venetian War. A treasury official, who met him on arrival, had the unfortunate responsibility of explaining to him the sultan's fur tax. The imperial council demanded of him sable skins, a fixed quantity of amber, and a sum of money. His eyes "bloodshot with wrath" at the news of the tax, the commander growled, "I have brought nothing back from [Crete] but gunpowder and lead. Sables and amber are things I know only by name. Money I have none; and if I am to give it you, I must first beg or borrow it." When Ibrahim couldn't raise enough funds for his indulgences, he turned to confiscation of heritable property.[20]

Ottoman chroniclers blame Ibrahim's downfall primarily on powerful women of the harem. Elevated by him to the position of royal consort (*haseki*) were eight of his concubines, a position previously held by one woman. They received a daily stipend of one thousand silver coins, higher than that of leading officials. Ibrahim allowed his favorite concubines to take what they pleased from the shops and bazaars without payment. One of these ladies complained to the sultan that she disliked shopping by daylight. According to one account, Ibrahim mandated that merchants and shopkeepers of the capital keep their businesses open all night and supply sufficient torchlight for shopping. The cost for other gifts provided to harem concubines further drained the treasury.[21]

Palace officials looked at the favoritism with loathing. Naima, a bureaucrat and historian of the period, wrote with venom against the concubines of Ibrahim and even against the queen mother herself for not maintaining order in the harem; discretion normally prevented court chroniclers from directly criticizing her or any other royal family member (although European accounts happily noted the hostile barbs directed by Ottoman statesmen against queen mothers and their favorite concubines). Naima noted the frustration of Ibrahim's grand vizier when, in 1648, the sultan petulantly threatened to stuff his skin with straw if he did not recover from the holy city of Medina all the precious items sent by earlier Ottoman sultans. Naima records the angry complaint of the vizier: "It is at the instigation of a pack of mentally deficient slave girls, daughters of Russian, Polish, Hungarian, and Frankish infidels, that I am subjected to such violent propositions."[22]

The traditional Ottoman account of Ibrahim depicts his concubines as conspiring to oust the competent Grand Vizier Kemankeş Kara Mustafa and replace him with a yes-man. The pretense that the court ladies used against Kemankeş Kara Mustafa was a petty disagreement over firewood. One of them asked that he supply five hundred carts of firewood for use in the harem. At the same time Kemankeş Kara Mustafa received word of problems in an Ottoman province that required immediate attention. He neglected to send the firewood. A few days later, while presiding over the imperial council, he received a message from Ibrahim commanding him to dismiss the meeting and appear before the sultan.

The grand vizier obeyed and appeared before Ibrahim. "Why have not the five hundred loads of wood for the harem been supplied?" he asked. "They shall be sent," replied the vizier. Then, stepping closer to softly reproach the sovereign, Kemankeş Kara Mustafa said, "My padishah, is it wise or proper for you to call on me to break up the divan and to confuse and delay the weightiest affairs of state for the sake of attending to five hundred loads of wood, the whole value of which does not amount to five hundred silver pieces? Why when I am before you do you question me about firewood, but say not a word about the petition of your subjects, the state of the frontier, and of the finances?"[23]

He had taken a step too far. A court official warned the vizier to be more careful in the future and treat nothing in which Ibrahim took an interest as unimportant. Kemankeş Kara Mustafa replied, "Is it not doing the sultan good service to tell him the truth? Am I to turn flatterer? I had rather speak freely and die than live in servile falsehood." He would soon get his wish. Ousted on January 31, 1644, he was executed not long afterwards.

Sultanzade Mehmet Pasha became the new grand vizier in 1644. He was an experienced statesman, but he could not counter the palace intrigues of the charlatan Cinci Hoca. Not wanting to meet the same fate of the prior grand vizier, Sultanzade Mehmet flattered Ibrahim at every opportunity and considered no desire of the women of the harem to be too trifling. He was, as Hammer-Purgstall notes, ready to accommodate every desire of the sultan, "whose immoderate appetite for sensual pleasures, and savage fondness of ordering and of witnessing acts of cruelty, now raged without stint or shame." Ibrahim remembered the check that Kemankeş Kara Mustafa had put on him and seemed determined to spite such limits by living in wild excess.[24]

Sultanzade Mehmet even shocked Ibrahim in his propensity for shameless flattery, praising all his actions as the right ones, no matter how absurd. One day he asked his grand vizier, "How is it that you are able always to approve of my actions, whether good or evil?" "My padishah," he replied, "You are Caliph; you are God's shadow on earth. Every idea which your spirit entertains is a revelation from Heaven. Your orders, even when they appear unreasonable, have an innate reasonableness, which your slave ever reveres, though he may not always understand." This answer seemed enough to Ibrahim and may have given him the self-righteous assurance that God sanctioned whatever strange desire entered his mind.

From that point on he spoke of himself as a divinely inspired agent, while engaging in obscene levels of vice and consumption. Contempt from former allies arose. Other women of the harem murmured against him. Even his mother reproached him for his beastly conduct. But Ibrahim responded back with the words of his grand vizier.

Ibrahim's belief that every carnal pleasure of his was the inscrutable wisdom of God whispering in his ear inspired other pleasure-seeking monarchs. French historian Pierre Daru argues in *Histoire de la République de Venise* that Ibrahim directly influenced the grandiose delusions of French king Louis XIV. The Sun King heard of Ibrahim's assertions of absolute power over his subject's lives. The Count de Cezy had been French ambassador in Istanbul and claimed to have seen Ibrahim stab a minister accused of misconduct without bothering to hear a trial. When the count returned to Paris, he told Louis of the sultan's peculiar belief that a monarch's desire for wealth was divinely approved. This may have inspired Louis XIV's solipsistic belief, *l'état, c'est moi* (I am the state).[25]

The most notorious member of Ibrahim's harem was a concubine named Şekerpare. Ibrahim had a preference for full-figured women and commissioned his advisers to find for him the largest woman in his realm. Dmitri Cantemir tells the story of how Ibrahim gave his heart to the most corpulent female in the empire. According to his tale, Ibrahim once viewed the genitals of a large cow. He had them molded and sent copies across the empire with orders to inquire whether a woman made in this manner was available. Such a woman was, in fact, found in Armenia. She weighed over three hundred pounds, an enormous size in the seventeenth century. Ibrahim called her Şekerpare (sugar cube).[26]

Ibrahim became obsessed with her. She held considerable influence over Ibrahim in political matters, to the dismay of Kösem. Şekerpare began as the treasurer of the imperial harem. She soon became mistress housekeeper and escaped Ibrahim's periodic purges. Şekerpare was a member of the faction that eventually deposed Grand Vizier Kemankeş Mustafa Pasha. Her political power expanded after her 1647 marriage to Grand Vizier Kara Musa Pasha, whom she had helped appoint to the position of grand admiral of the Ottoman navy. As part of the Ottoman practice of wealthy members of the royal family patronizing public architecture, Şekerpare endowed a fountain in 1648 and commissioned the building of her own mausoleum in the Istanbul neighborhood of Eyüp.[27]

Şekerpare launched purges against rival consorts. She told Ibrahim a rumor that an outsider had compromised one of his concubines, but she knew nothing more. The sultan raged. The chief black eunuch tried to find the concubine's identity. According to one account, Ibrahim then had his entire harem of 280 women thrown into the Bosphorus, tied up in weighted sacks. The only survivors were Şekerpare, Turhan Hatice (the mother of his first son, Mehmet), and a third concubine who was insufficiently tied. Şekerpare's power grab was stopped finally by Kösem, who quickly counterattacked. Şekerpare was marginalized and then exiled to Egypt after Ibrahim's death.[28]

At the same time, Ibrahim's position as sultan had become far less secure. His concubines had given birth to sons, which meant the Ottoman lineage could live on without him. Ibrahim was now expendable. He had few supporters due to his neglect of office and increasing of taxes to crushing levels to support his extravagant tastes.

Rival political factions, who had conspired to remove Ibrahim at the very beginning of his sultanate, now prepared to strike. Kösem had tried to protect him, but he was too weak to avoid manipulation by sycophants and opportunists. By 1647, the year before his death, plots to dethrone the sultan became coordinated and well planned. After the deposition of the obsequious Sultanzade Mehmet Pasha, the new grand vizier Salih Pasha conspired with Kösem and Abdürrahim Efendi, the şeyhülislam, to depose Ibrahim and replace him with one of his sons. The plot failed and Abdürrahim Efendi was executed. A coalition of provincial governments then launched their own rebellion against the sultan, but they were crushed in May 1648.[29]

The failure of these insurrections only delayed the inevitable. All factions in Istanbul agreed by 1648 that Ibrahim needed to go. Even his mother agreed that the mad sultan was a threat to the empire. She was weary of his volatile nature and extravagant spending, as was the rest of his circle. Advisors tired of fearing that displeasing him meant their immediate execution. Kösem wrote to the new grand vizier, Ahmet

Pasha: "In the end he will leave neither you nor me alive. We will lose control of the government. The whole society is in ruins. Have him removed from the throne immediately."[30]

It was the military and religious leaders who finally deposed the mentally unstable sultan. His fiercest antagonists were Ottoman cavalry regiments and the Janissaries. They saw themselves as guardians of the state and held the sultan personally responsible for the troubles in the empire. They went again to the *şeyhülislam* to obtain a formal ruling declaring his deposition legal.[31]

The *şeyhülislam* then deferred to Kösem in the matter of her son's deposition, aware that she needed to be consulted before any final decision was made. They told the queen mother that all agreed he must go. They were prepared to swear allegiance to Ibrahim's son Mehmet, the eldest prince. But Kösem hesitated, likely out of maternal instinct. She begged the coconspirators to consider leaving her son in possession of the throne under the guardianship of the *şeyhülislam* and the grand vizier. This was not a good solution to the problem, since partisans could then return Ibrahim to the throne. Hanifezade, an Ottoman judge, appealed to her not as a mother but as a stateswoman:

> Oh, royal lady, we have come hither, fully relying on your grace, and on your compassionate solicitude for the servants of God. You are not only the mother of the sultan; you are the mother also of all true believers. Put an end to this state of trouble; the sooner the better. The enemy has the upper hand in battle. At home, the traffic in places and ranks has no bounds. The Padishah, absorbed in satisfying his passions, removes himself farther and farther from the path of laws. The call to prayers from the minarets of the Mosque of Aya Sofia is drowned in the noise of fifes, and flutes, and cymbals from the palace. No one can speak counsel without danger to the speaker: you have yourself proved it. The markets are

plundered. The innocent are put to death. Favorite slaves govern the world.[32]

Still, Kösem did not understand how deposing Ibrahim and giving the throne to his son, a seven-year-old, would solve any problems of Ottoman governance. How could a child rule the empire? Hanifezade had a ready answer: "In the opinion of our wise men of the law, a madman ought not to reign, whatever be his age; but rather let a child, that is gifted with reason, be upon the throne. If the sovereign be a rational being though an infant, a wise vizier may restore order to the world; but a grown-up sultan who is without sense ruins all things by murder, by abomination, by corruption, and prodigality."[33]

Finally, she agreed to meet with them in the palace. In the company of the statesmen she appeared disgusted at the attempted regicide: "For so long you have permitted whatever my son wished [and] proved your loyalty; not once has any of you admonished him or not wished him well. Now you wish to reverse the situation and criticize such an innocent one. This is an evil act."

Discussion went on for two hours. She despaired at the end: "All are united in the opinion that the Sultan must be deposed; it is impossible to do otherwise. You tell me that if I don't hand over the Prince, they will enter the palace and take him by force."[34] Kösem finally relented. She agreed to fetch her grandson Mehmet and have the turban placed on his head. Nobody stood by Ibrahim when the time for his deposition came. The şeyhülislam announced to him that, by order of the religious scholars and the chief dignitaries of the empire, he was to retire the throne.

"Traitor!" cried Ibrahim. "Am I not your Padishah?"

"No," replied Abdürrahim. "You are no Padishah, for as much as you have set justice and holiness at nought and have ruined the world. You have squandered your years in folly and debauchery; the treasures of the realm in vanities: and corruption and cruelty have governed the world in your place."

Finally deposed, Ibrahim was returned to the Cage, his childhood home. His wails were heard all over the palace and outside its walls. On August 18, 1648, ten days after his gilded prison reunion, the grand vizier, *şeyhülislam,* and two executioners came to the Cage.

There they found Ibrahim reading the Qur'an. He recognized the chief executioner, who had served him well over the years. The sultan exclaimed, "Is there no one among those who have eaten my bread who will take pity on me and protect me? These cruel men have come to kill me. Mercy! Mercy!" When the executioners grabbed Ibrahim to strangle him with a bowstring, pleas for mercy turned to curses against his subjects for infidelity to their sovereign.[35]

Not all historians are convinced of Ibrahim's villainy, believing he was unfairly maligned in the earliest accounts. While a childhood and adolescence spent in solitary confinement could damage the mental health of anyone, not to mention someone who saw all his siblings executed by political assassination, Ibrahim may have been passively ineffective rather than stark raving mad. Abdülkadir Dedeoğlu argues that political opponents spread rumors of the sultan's insanity. They looked to justify their scheming by impugning Ibrahim as a pleasure-seeking lout who deserved his fate. These stories trickled down to Ottoman chroniclers and Western diplomats who wrote the surviving accounts. European authors then seized on the most sensational moments of Ibrahim's madness to make their works of orientalist history as exotic as possible.[36]

Yet Ibrahim's weakness and personal indulgence damaged the office of the sultan at a time of major political and foreign crisis. Built on an imperial ideology of state building and expansionism, the Ottoman Empire needed a strong sultan. Weak leaders such as Ibrahim created a power vacuum filled by queen mothers, harem eunuchs, grand viziers, and other Ottoman court factions. The empire suffered major territorial losses in the forthcoming decades to the Hapsburgs, Russians, and Iranians.

In the story of the Ottoman Empire, Ibrahim left behind little mark besides being known for his epithet "The Mad." Buried in the Aya Sophia mosque next to his equally mad uncle, Mustafa I, no crowned sultan was ever named Ibrahim again.

# CHAPTER FIVE

# King George III of England

## 1738–1820

Americans might have been tempted to schadenfreude, a peculiar German-origin term that means pleasure from another's misery, after learning the fate of British king George III (also of German origin and also peculiar). The villain of the American Revolution spent the final years of his life insane. He experienced five extended bouts of madness in his life, with the final one lasting until his death in 1820. They consisted of anxiety, hallucinations, insomnia, and manic and depressive periods. During this time, George suffered from poor medical care that was designed to cure his madness but only worsened it. Medicine was primitive, and his physicians did not know that treatments such as blistering, binding him in a straitjacket, chaining him to a chair, or prescribing high doses of arsenic would damage his mental state.

The schadenfreude, however, is undeserved. George was, by most accounts of those who knew him personally, an unfailing gentleman. Only in revisionist American popular accounts, written in the patriotic Reconstruction period of the nineteenth century, does the image of the villainous tyrant George survive. This image lingered among those who only knew of him from descriptions in the Declaration of Independence as a tyrant who sought to suffocate the noble American experiment in its cradle. "He has refused to assent to laws . . . necessary for the public Good . . . He has abdicated Government here . . . He has dissolved Legislative Houses repeatedly . . . He has plundered our Seas, ravaged our Coasts, burnt our Towns, and destroyed the lives of our People," says the unequivocal Declaration. Historians are less abusive toward George but still question his effectiveness as a king, and many in Britain remember him as a mad monarch or fool; nevertheless, he was beloved by his subjects and mourned at his death.

George's reign encompassed far more than the Revolutionary War. He ruled in the most difficult decades of the emerging British Empire. Domestic and foreign challenges threatened its destruction. Across the channel, the French monarchy fell. Napoleon Bonaparte rose through the ranks during the French Revolution and conquered France afterwards, ruling it as emperor. He then turned his eye on Great Britain, which became engulfed in the Napoleonic Wars from 1803 to 1814. France embargoed the island and instituted a naval blockade. If there ever was a time when Great Britain needed a king to shore up its resolve, George's long reign was that time. He did so despite battling with degenerative mental health.

George William Frederick was born on June 4, 1738, to Frederick Louis, Prince of Wales, and Princess Augusta of Saxe-Gotha (who had arrived in England two years earlier, speaking no English). His education was fitting for a British royal. The young prince was the first British monarch to receive a systematic scientific education. Early in his childhood he studied a wide range of physical sciences, including chemistry and astronomy, geography, and branches of the humanities. He knew English, German, French, and Latin. He also studied theology and the arts. George's father adored Baroque music and instilled the same appreciation in his children.

But many considered George lacking the aptitude to lead Great Britain well. Tutors described George as a willing student but "lethargic" and "incapable of concentration." He had an agreeable disposition but acted petulant and churlish when angry. Some accounts claim he had the writing level of a child even as a young adult. Whether due to an ineffective education or poor aptitude, George did not engage in intellectual pursuits. His view of royal government was to uphold the House of Hanover, so he preferred to involve himself in administrative affairs no matter how inconsequential. Here he did show interest and enthusiasm.[1]

One oft-repeated story goes that George could not read until he was ten years old. Cambridge University's renowned historian of the eighteenth century, J. H. Plumb (1911–2001), characterized the king as "an unbalanced man of low intelligence." He was "very stupid, really stupid. Had he been born in different circumstances it is unlikely he could have earned a living except as an unskilled manual laborer."[2]

John Brooke, an archivist for the Royal Commission on Historical Manuscripts, responded to this unflattering characterization with a 1972 biography of George that detailed his love of literature and art and his patronage of the King's Library at the Royal Academy. He also patronized the natural philosopher Sir William Herschel, the discoverer of Uranus. Even as a child George was not an imbecile; stories of him being a late reader are unsubstantiated. He was a student of average ability who suffered more from social isolation and emotional immaturity than stupidity. Regarding George's later bouts of madness, Brooke believes his disorder was not due to feeblemindedness or any mental illness of the sort; it was indicative of a delirium induced by recurrent attacks of a blood disease. His illness may have produced physical manifestations easily mischaracterized as schizophrenia, psychoneurosis, or hysteria, but the king was not a simpleton doomed to insanity.[3]

George's reign began far earlier than he expected, but he managed his first years as king competently by hewing closely to his moral beliefs (many said he hewed too closely). His father, heir to the throne, died just as the young prince entered adolescence, making him next in line to be king. Following the death of his grandfather, George II, George III was crowned in 1760 at twenty-two. A year later, he married the German

princess Charlotte of Mecklenburg-Strelitz. The two had a happy marriage, and the queen bore him fifteen children: nine sons and six daughters. They shared a love of music but otherwise had few interests; the
couple went to sleep each night at ten o'clock and maintained, the rumors
go, the dullest court in Europe. His piety inspired boredom. The king
was a thoroughly devout Anglican. He infused his politics and family
life with religion, and pressured family members to uphold the same
principles. Looking scornfully on the deviance of his brothers, he pushed
for the Royal Marriages Act of 1772, which required crown approval
for anyone marrying into the royal family. His children also could not
marry until the age of twenty-five, in the hope of preventing rash
decisions.[4]

As a father, George III ran a loving but obedient household. He
demanded strict discipline and meted out severe punishment to his children. Princesses had to stand when talking to him and exit the room
walking backwards, as if they were foreign envoys. Queen Charlotte
domineered the girls, secluding and isolating them from the world and
eligible marriage partners. The princes responded to such strictness by
seeking secret marriages or carrying on long affairs. The future George
IV wed the Catholic widow Maria Smyth in an illegal ceremony; his
father annulled the marriage on discovering their union. Another prince,
Augustus, married nonroyals twice, while Prince William fathered ten
illegitimate children with his mistress. The princesses, however, had no
chance of escape, trapped in the unimaginable tedium of the court due
to their parents' rejection of all marriage offers. Thirty-year-old Princess
Charlotte only managed to marry King Frederick of Württemberg in
1797. Princess Elisabeth was thirty-eight when she wrote in 1808, "We
go on vegetating as we have done for the last twenty years of our lives."[5]

Unlike other historical figures known for mental instability, George
III was mentally healthy throughout his youth. He did not suffer total
debilitation from madness until well into his fifties. George was beloved
by his people as an extremely popular monarch during a time of tre-
mendous international challenges. He was an active king during the

American Revolution and the Napoleonic Wars. George also enjoyed the favor of his subjects and was known for his generous support of the Royal Academy and charitable contributions, which came from his personal income. The king had unimpeachable piety. As a testimony to his devoutness, he is one of the few British kings who is not known to have ever taken a mistress.

George's first health crisis occurred in 1765. At the time, its character remained unknown. The symptoms were like later attacks. First an eruption on the face appeared, followed by a cough and fever, then a mental disturbance. He suffered severe pain in the abdomen, legs, and back. The king also experienced tachycardia, anxiety, and insomnia. The illness occurred during passage of the Stamp Act. Nineteenth-century American historian George Bancroft, who also served as U.S. Secretary of the Navy and was patriotic to the core, interpreted these symptoms as proof that George III was already irreparably stricken with madness. How unwell he was is unknown, but he recovered completely after a few weeks.[6]

The king's 1765 episode was a state secret and quickly forgotten once he recovered. George enjoyed uninterrupted good health until the summer of 1788. He could walk twelve miles on his way from Windsor to London, more than the Prince of Wales could do. But the tranquility did not last. He relapsed in June 1788, as testified by detailed and independent medical records. He had recurrent instances of severe abdominal pain and obstructive jaundice, which Sir George Baker, the king's physician, diagnosed as "biliary Concretions in the Gall Duct." The king acted excitable in July and August. Then colic reoccurred in October, followed by aches and pains, muscular weakness, and stiffness. Diagnosed as rheumatism and gout, the symptoms severely affected his legs. George's condition then worsened with colic, constipation, a racing pulse, heavy sweating, cramps, lameness, and hoarseness.

He suffered from intractable insomnia, incessant talking, excitement, and confusion, all diagnosed as "delirium" caused by severe bodily disease.

By October 1788, the king started showing signs of mental trouble, albeit in harmless episodes. His physicians tried cures, but medicine was rudimentary in the late eighteenth century and knowledge of mental illnesses practically nonexistent. Mental disorders fell under the umbrella category of "madness" and were treated with therapies that were often ineffective at best and destructive at worst. Treatments included placing poultices of Spanish flies over the sovereign's body in order to produce painful blisters to draw out evil "humors," an application of the ancient Greek notion that the body was made up of black and yellow bile, phlegm, and blood that needed to be kept in proper proportion.

On October 16, after having walking four hours in the rain, George remained at St. James's Place without changing his clothes. Stomach spasms struck the follow day. He remained still for days, which the whole household found terrifying. The king then came into the Equerries' room. There he found Generals Bude and Goldsworth. He opened his waistcoat and displayed two sizable spots on his chest. The two recommended the king take care not to catch a cold or the spots could rupture. George rejected this advice with ill humor. He rode outside and came home very wet. The spots disappeared, but a slight fever followed. Then, derangement struck.[7]

Endless talking was the primary feature of George's illness. Speech came thick and fast, sometimes for hours at a time. He made strange proclamations, two that stood out in particular. First, acts of Parliament could dissolve marriages. Second, his Hanoverian dominion had been restored, and he was to go to Hanover shortly. George may have come from a line of German royals, but he was born in Great Britain and had never visited Hanover. Yet no matter how strangely the king babbled, he retained his prudishness, never speaking any course language or impropriety, even in the depths of delirium. "The highest panegyric," notes

Colonel Digby, who remained in vigil with the king for hours in his room, "that could be formed of his character would not equal what in those moments showed itself; that, with his heart and mind entirely open, not one wrong idea appeared; that all was benevolence, charity, rectitude, love of country, and anxiety for its welfare."[8]

The period of his docility ended when he turned violent. By the end of 1788, his symptoms were unmanageable, and his doctors could find no relief. In early November, the king and his son, George IV, fell into a conflict, which resulted in the king grabbing his son and trying to smash his head against the wall. An observer commented that the king was "foaming at the mouth" and his eyes were so bloodshot, they had the appearance of currant jelly. "The look of his eyes, the tone of his voice, every gesture and his whole deportment represented a person in a most furious passion of anger."[9]

Other accounts by his physician and attendants describe the king as growing so agitated during a meal that he "lost control, grabbed his son the Prince of Wales, and threw him against a wall . . . He often spoke till he was exhausted, and, the moment he could recover his breath, began again, while the foam ran out of his mouth." The king was restrained, placed in a straitjacket, and strapped into an iron chair, where he spent much time while undergoing violent mood swings. Toward the end of his first attack he begged the royal staff to end his life.[10]

On November 6, the Prince of Wales, the Duke of York, physicians, and equerries were reclining on sofas and chairs close to the king's apartment when, to their astonishment, George appeared among them. He was as surprised to find himself among them as they were. The king asked what they were doing there, as he did not recognize the princes in the dim lighting of the apartment. None of them had the heart to approach the sick king. Even his physician, George Baker, declined to lead George back to his bedchamber. The king suddenly recognized Baker, grabbed him, and pushed him up against the wall, telling him that his complaint was a mistake, and nothing more nor less than an old woman's nervousness.

Colonel Digby, the queen's chamberlain, stepped in. He told George that he must go to bed, took him by the arm, and tried to lead him towards his apartment. "I will not go," cried George. "Who are you?" the befuddled king asked. "I am Colonel Digby, sir. Your Majesty has been very good to me often, and now I am going to be very good to you, for you must come to bed. It is necessary for your life." Taken by surprise, the king allowed himself to be taken to his bedchamber as passively as if he had been a child.

George's poor health, and the mysterious nature of his madness, became gradually known to the public. The British in general mourned, as the king was well-loved as a pious royal. George Villiers, a young politician who was close to Princess Amelia, the king's youngest daughter, wrote on November 11 that the stock market had fallen 2 percent. Other nobles were alarmed. "You may easily believe," wrote Lord Sydney on November 13, "that the hurry and ferment are great at present. People in general, of all ranks, seem to be truly sensible of the calamitous effects to be dreaded from an unfavourable termination of His Majesty's disorder."[11]

On November 28, a cabinet council met to discuss recommendations from the king's physicians that George be removed from Windsor to recover in the open air at Kew Palace, the king's favorite royal residence. But he so disliked leaving Windsor that aids realized forcing him out was their only choice. It was not until his physicians swore that the convalescence was necessary that the cabinet adopted the advice. When George finally saw his lodgings at Kew, he burst into tears.[12]

The king's physician was Dr. Francis Willis, a clergyman of the Church of England who received medical training at Oxford. With his dual training in the needs of the body and the soul, Willis prescribed for the physical and the spiritual wants of patients, particularly mental illnesses. Earlier in his career he created an establishment specifically for the treatment of the mentally ill. For almost sixty years, he never had fewer than thirty patients under his care, and he treated over eight hundred mental patients at the asylum at Greatford in Lincolnshire in his lengthy career. Fellow physicians all agreed that he could aid George in his present incapacity. Willis joined the corps of physicians at the palace on December 6, 1788.[13]

Willis and others believed George's madness was the result of over-anxiety in public affairs and overly strenuous exercise, which had caused a "fever on the brain." As George had not suffered from such an attack before, and as nine out of ten patients so afflicted recovered, the physician corps had hopes for the king's full restoration. They believed his malady would be cured in as little as six to eight weeks. Two years was the longest-known duration of any such illness.[14]

Each fresh examination of the king's condition provoked opposing diagnoses from physicians. Some began to rally against his physician for his lenient attitude toward George. Dr. Willis was criticized for permitting the king to read Shakespeare's tragedy of King Lear, a drama in which an elderly monarch's family schemes to marginalize and depose him, ultimately ruining a pitiable king. The offending play was "the most improper in the English language to be put into his hands." He was also criticized for affording George interviews with the queen and young princesses, allowing the royals to see their sovereign in a terrible condition.[15] Prime Minister Pitt was blamed for giving the royal patient a razor and scissors.

By December, George was "under an entire alienation of mind" and considered "mad." The king refused food, became too restless to lie down, tore off bandages covering his septic, suppurating blisters, and threw off his bedclothes. Willis responded to the king's behavior like he would with any of his hundreds of former mental patients and strapped him into a straitjacket. A band across his torso and legs bound him to the bedposts. On Christmas Day, George dubbed his pillow Prince Octavius, who was to "be new born this day." He believed London was under floodwaters and issued orders to those who had long ago died.[16]

During this period, political fault lines were opening in England. Moderate Whigs and Tories supported Tory statesman William Pitt the Younger, while Charles James Fox led the more radical Whig opposition.

Due to squabbling factionalism, George's mental health became a matter of political opportunism. In 1788–89, his mental state was so unstable that the parties fought over whether the Prince of Wales, his son, should be regent, ruling in place of the monarch too incapacitated to lead. Committees of Parliament asked the king's physicians if he could continue as head of state. In January 1789, it became unavoidable that the Prince of Wales's regency be named. A bill passed the House of Commons and was sent to the House of Lords, when George unexpectedly recovered.

George surprised all by his rapid return to health and lucidity. At the end of February 1789, Prime Minister William Pitt claimed that George appeared to be "free from all disorder, that his manner was unusually composed and dignified, and that when he spoke of his illness it was as a thing that had passed, and which had left no other impression on his mind than gratitude to Heaven for his recovery, as well as to those who had stood by him in his calamity." There was no sign whatsoever of mental illness. In March, though "emaciated and enfeebled," George was declared cured and regained his royal authority.[17]

Afterwards the king sent for his old friends. He thanked them for the "affectionate fidelity with which they had adhered to him when so many others had deserted him." On March 10, 1789, an announcement was made to Parliament of George's complete restoration to health. He returned to London to an illuminated St. Paul's Cathedral. The public was ecstatic. At the end of June, the king left Windsor to spend the summer at the seaside town of Weymouth in Dorset, 120 miles southwest from London. During the journey, popular acclaim greeted him. He attended a church service there, and the congregation, unable to restrain itself, burst out into "God Save the King" instead of the appointed psalm.[18]

George resumed political leadership. He suppressed the 1798 Irish rebellion and then unified the British and Irish parliaments through the Acts of Union, which created the United Kingdom of Great Britain and Ireland. There are historians who believe George acted to reestablish the monarchical authority over Parliament that existed before the Glorious

Revolution of 1688, which deposed King James II, who tried to build a centralized autocratic state. But his actions suggest he instead backed his governments instead of dictating to them. He did want to restore the monarch's power to choose his ministers, but once chosen they had freedom to govern as they saw fit.[19]

Further attacks of madness came in 1804 and 1806, but the general impression of these episodes was that they were only temporary. Parliament accepted these explanations and did not suspend any royal functions. Physicians did not examine him, and the public had no idea of the progression of George's madness. It is understandable that they ignored warning signs, as George continued to exercise his prerogatives during these periods. On March 9, 1804, George received fifteen bills and signed them.[20]

Researchers have tried to find the source of George's madness since the end of his reign. He was diagnosed with mania, bipolar disorder, schizophrenia, and countless other forms of mental illness, biological and psychological in origin. In George's lifetime, doctors did their best to diagnose his madness. Dr. Willis testified to a parliamentary committee in December 1810 on the question of whether George was mad or delirious. The doctor though George suffered from delirium, which was less harmful than insanity: "I consider the King's derangement more nearly allied to delirium. In delirium, the mind is actively employed upon past impressions . . . which rapidly pass in succession. In insanity, there may be little or no disturbance, apparently, in the general constitution; the mind is occupied upon some fixed assumed idea and the individual is acting, always, upon that false impression . . . also, the mind is awake to objects which are present. His Majesty's illness, uniformly, partakes more of the delirium than of insanity."[21]

Theories on George's madness remained unfixed until the twentieth century, when most researchers named the culprit porphyria, a blood disease. In 1966, doctors Ida Macalpine and her son Richard Hunter published the landmark paper "The 'Insanity' of King George III: A Classic Case of Porphyria." They claimed that George suffered from acute porphyria, an inherited blood disorder that causes hallucinations, paranoia, confusion, insomnia, and restlessness. The diagnosis was plausible because George's cousins also suffered from this disease. His extended family were royals across Europe, a testimony to the inbreeding of the continent's aristocratic class. The porphyria diagnosis spread and entered popular consciousness. It was the basis of Alan Bennett's long-running play *The Madness of King George*.[22]

Macalpine and Hunter described five attacks of the illness, which began in 1765 and continued until George's death. Although they claimed that George specifically suffered from intermittent acute porphyria, the researchers could not find anyone among George's descendants who suffered from this illness. Their study concluded that George's condition was not a mental one. It may have been the first description of a rare metabolic disorder never completely understood.[23]

The two published "Porphyria in the Royal Houses of Stuart, Hanover, and Prussia" in 1967, claiming that George did not suffer from porphyria alone; he was joined by a multitude of European royals, all of whose conditions originated from Mary, Queen of Scots, two hundred years prior. The *British Medical Journal* thought the research to be so important that it published a supplement in the same journal issue (backed in royal purple) entitled "Porphyria, A Royal Malady." Macalpine and Hunter claimed that James VI of Scotland, who became James I of England, had *porphyria variegata*. He had repeated bouts of abdominal colic and nausea, vomiting and diarrhea, an irregular pulse, and spasms in his limbs. Once an attack had begun, uncontrollable weeping also occurred.

Geoffrey Dean, a physician who practiced medicine for sixty years, challenged the porphyria thesis in a series of articles in the *British Medical Journal* and the *Scientific American*. The British royal family was unafflicted with porphyria, he wrote, because in acute porphyria, the urine is a normal color when passed but darkens when left standing. Medical accounts claim George III's urine was dark when passed. Additionally, the condition was unlikely to have passed directly down the royal family from Mary, Queen of Scots, to George IV through nine generations.[24]

In 2003, Professor Martin Warren put forward an alternative theory that the same medicine which George's physicians prescribed to cure his insanity may have accelerated it. A British museum worker discovered an envelope in a vault that held a lock of King George's hair. Subjected to analysis, the hair was found to contain over three hundred times the toxic level of arsenic. The source of the toxin could have come from any number of products used at the time, such as skin cream or wig powder. But no amount of those substances had that level of arsenic, even before its poisonous properties were known.[25] The answer to this mystery came from the Royal Pharmaceutical Society. George's physicians gave him a "medicine" called antimony that contained dangerous levels of arsenic. Physicians had the good intentions of prescribing him cures, but they unwittingly poisoned him. George consumed a 120-milligram dose of antimony and arsenic every six hours for the rest of his life. Likely, the poisons triggered porphyria attacks. Trying to help the monarch avoid madness that had ended the careers of so many other monarchs, his doctors may have only accelerated it.[26]

More recent studies also dispute the porphyria diagnosis. In 2010, *History of Psychiatry* published an article disputing that porphyria was the cause of George's symptoms. The authors claimed that earlier research dismissed or downplayed medical evidence of the king's condition that did not align with the theory. Macalpine and Hunter were highly selective in their interpretation and reporting of George's signs and symptoms; therefore, more recent researchers believe the porphyria diagnosis cannot be sustained. There was also little evidence of George's discolored urine. Even machine learning algorithms have suggested new theories of the king's madness. A 2017 study analyzed sixty years of George's letters to detect signs of his failing mental health. Researchers used machine learning to "read" letters produced throughout his reign and notice patterns and changes over time.[27]

The researchers taught the computer to identity twenty-nine written features to distinguish between the mentally healthy and those who suffer from disorders. Writing features included the complexity of the sentences, the richness of vocabulary, and the variety of words. To establish a clear basis of comparison between George's mentally well and mentally ill periods, this criterion was then matched against letters written during the king's infamous 1788–89 period of mental derangement and texts written during a period of mental tranquility. They selected letters based on political importance; George did write regularly to members of his family, but researchers only selected letters addressed to leading politicians of the time. The majority of these contained requests to his ministers about political issues to make the data set homogenous. The results point toward his suffering from acute mania, a hyperactive condition that resembles the manic phase of bipolar disorder.[28]

Peter Garrard, professor of neurology at St. George's University of London and coauthor of the study, said the king's usage of English made clear the periods in which he suffered mental illness. "King George wrote very differently when unwell, compared to when he was healthy. In the manic periods we could see that he used less-rich vocabulary and fewer adverbs. He repeated words less often, and there was a lower degree of redundancy, or wordiness." While King George led the British Empire during a period of significant challenges both foreign and domestic, the king's language did not change in wartime and peacetime, suggesting that the differences were due to mental illness, not work-related stress.

George ruled at a time of significant upheaval and social reform for Great Britain. Catholics could not vote or hold political office—a contested policy which the fiercely devout Anglican king upheld. The Industrial Revolution was in full force, and mechanization caused drastic changes to traditional employment. In the 1760s, radical journalist and parliamentarian John Wilkes severely criticized George in the press for his speech that endorsed the Paris Peace Treaty of 1763. He spread libelous innuendo about the king's mother having relations with Prime Minister John Stuart, leading to his arrest. All the while, tensions between Catholics and Protestants simmered in the background, and finally boiled over at the same time as the American Revolution. The year 1780 saw the worst riots in London's history as over one thousand died in the anti-Catholic Gordon Riots, in which Protestants rioted and looted in response to what they thought was the threat of Catholic incursion into British civil society. Attempts to assassinate George occurred with increasing frequency. Certain aggressors were mentally ill, such as a knife-wielding assailant in 1786, who did not injure the king. Others were zealots, such as the millenarian James Hadfield, who believed in the imminent Second Coming of Christ and thought it could be advanced by attempting to kill the king. In 1800, he fired at the king as he entered the box at the Theatre Royal. George remained calm. He told the queen and the princesses to keep back. The audience cheered their sovereign and broke into "God Save the King."[29]

By 1810, George was still on the throne but no longer made decisions. The king suffered progressive blindness from cataracts and required a secretary to record his correspondence. He teetered between wellness and madness, but external events threatened his fragile sanity. The king had recently lost his youngest daughter, Princess Amelia, and had long crying spells and melancholy. The Regency era began when the future George IV began ruling in his place. George III spent longer periods in spells of madness, until he no longer recovered from them and was confined to Windsor Castle.

Hope for the king's recovery persisted to the very end of his reign. At the end of May 1811, there were rumors that he was better. On the night of May 20, excitement swept the Royal Borough of Windsor after it was officially reported that royal physicians would allow the king to appear in public. The next day, his saddled horse was ready. A Windsor inhabitant recalled the scene: "We crowded to the Park and the Castle Yard. The favourite horse was there. The venerable man, blind but steady, was soon in the saddle, as I had often seen him—a hobby-groom at his side with a leading-rein. He rode through the Little Park to the Great Park. The bells rang. The troops fired a *feu de joie*. The King returned to Castle within the hour."

Sadly, he was never seen again outside those walls.[30] George's health irrevocably declined. The final eight years of his long life were, except for rare intervals, passed in mental and visual darkness. He occupied a large and convenient suite of apartments on the ground floor, fronting the North Terrace within the walls at Windsor Castle. But until the very end, he never forgot that he was king, even in the depths of his madness.

Attacks continued in fits and spurts. He had a neurological breakdown and often could not move on his own. George eventually lost his sight and hearing and began suffering regular seizures. He had in-depth discussions with phantom courts and reviewed troop movements while no one was around. He even spoke with his deceased daughter about her funeral. In his final years, those close to George allowed few visitors, in order to prevent reports of his condition, conversation, or habits. He could not understand the news of his wife's death in 1818. In the last year of his life, he had a streak of speaking nonsense that lasted close to sixty hours.[31]

George died on January 29, 1820, at the age of eighty-one. The tolling bell of St. Paul's Cathedral rang soon after, announcing it to London. The king had reigned more than sixty years. At the time, his reign was longer than any other English sovereign's, and he is now surpassed only by his granddaughter, Victoria, and Queen Elizabeth II.[32]

George's madness had positive effects for his nation and world civilization. The king was a lover and patron of the arts, because of—not in spite of—his battles with mental health. For example, he found solace in music while suffering the effects of his illness. Macalpine, chronicling George's 1788 recovery, writes that George amused himself by "walking, reading Shakespeare and Pope, practicing on the flute, brushing up his

Latin, arranging his gardens and hothouses, and entertaining the Queen and the princesses." While the king was weak and dysfunctional during his final years, during times of tranquility and contentment he played the flute or harpsichord. He particularly liked to play his favorite, Handel.[33] The Duke of York, who cared for George after the Queen's death in 1818, reported that after visiting the king in 1819, he was "amusing himself with playing upon the harpsichord and singing with as strong and firm a voice as ever [he] heard him."[34]

Biographers less sympathetic to George III believe the king, even before his descent into complete madness, was feebleminded and in danger of mental collapse. He depended on others for advice, such as the Earl of Bute and his successors. J. H. Plumb wrote, "The tragedy of George III lay in his temperament. His stupidity and obstinacy might have been forgiven . . . if only they had been exercised on the trivialities of politics."[35] But ever since Macalpine argued that George was not mentally ill but suffered from porphyria, revisionist historians have reexamined the king's character. Stanley Ayling, a historian of George, Edmund Burke, John Wesley, and other prominent eighteenth-century figures, wrote in his 1972 biography that the king, while not an intellectual, was also not dull. He called George "a royal John Bull" who was loved and respected by the English people.[36]

His hobbies and interests were those of a man with intellectual taste. In 1762, the king paid twenty thousand pounds for the art collection of Joseph Smith, English consul in Venice, to decorate Buckingham House (later Palace). Among the works were Johannes Vermeer's baroque masterpiece, *Lady at the Virginals with a Gentleman*. George was also a voracious reader and bibliophile. He made literary references even at the onset of his malady. In 1788, he asked for *King Lear* and noted, "I am like poor Lear, but thank God I have no Regan, no Goneril, only three Cordelias," referencing Shakespeares's trio of fictional daughters, the latter being loyal to her father.[37]

His library at the time of his death held 65,000 books and 450 manuscripts. George gave serious researchers access to his works, which became the nucleus of the British national library. John Adams described the library as such: "The books were in perfect order, elegant in their editions, paper, binding, etc., but gaudy and extravagant in nothing. They were chosen with perfect taste and judgment; every book that a king ought to have always at hand, and as far as I could examine and could be supposed of judging, none other."[38]

For 150 years, George III was believed a demented and bumbling imbecile of a monarch. But posthumous diagnoses and new examinations of his artistic interests and support for the arts paint a different picture. He was a courageous but despondent figure who loved his wife, high culture, family, subjects, and humanity in general.

George was not a tyrant nor a feebleminded weakling. He was a heroic figure who fought a brave but losing battle with his own crumbling sanity.

CHAPTER SIX

# King Ludwig II of Bavaria

## 1845–1886

It was midnight in the Bavarian Alps. A dark figure raced through the foothills on a gilded sleigh. Its high curving prow ended in a pair of *putti* holding up a lantern. Four magnificent white horses drew the sleigh. It crossed a snow-covered landscape that glittered in the moonlight as the firs of the forest sagged under the weight of ice and snow. The figure was clad in blue velvet. Outriders donning powdered wigs and elaborate livery lit the path with torches and cleared the roads. Although forbidden to look through their windows at the figure, peasants still stared in wonder.

The rider was the reclusive *Maerchenkoenig* (or "Fairy-tale King"). Others called him the "Swan King." He was Ludwig II of Bavaria, and his nocturnal behavior was legendary among Alpine villagers. He woke up each evening at seven o'clock, lunched at midnight, ate his supper in the early morning, and went on strange adventures in the interim. Ludwig sometimes spent the entire night riding around the Court Riding School in Munich. At the halfway stage he would dismount and have a picnic, even in the foulest weather. Once he stopped in the middle of a blizzard, telling his servants that they were in fact at an ocean resort

97

beneath the shining sun. Other times he dressed as French king Louis XIV, wore the state crown, and carried a scepter. The party then continued until reaching whatever goal existed in his imagination.

Toward the end of his reign, the Swan King spent more time traveling at night through the countryside between his fairy-tale castles and hunting lodges. Sometimes he walked around the shores of Lake Starnberg with a group of lackeys trailing behind. Other times he commanded his sleigh to travel at high speeds in total darkness. One equerry, Richard Hornig, who served the king for eighteen years, sometimes dismounted and adjusted the king's ermine rug with freezing fingers. Only a strong dose of spirits kept him upright in the saddle. As for the king, he could, and did, do this all night.[1]

Ludwig reigned from 1864 until his death in 1886. He was called the Swan King for his fascination with the bird. As a child, he never tired of hearing his mother tell stories from Greek mythology about the swan's creation by the hand of Zeus. He drew pictures of swans and, years later, sealed his letters with a swan and a cross. He adored the times that his family spent at Castle Hohenschwangau, meaning "High Country of the Swan." There were an abundance of swan images painted on the castle walls and vases shaped like them. But the real meaning of Ludwig's sobriquet comes from his obsession with medieval tales. He never tired of hearing about the Swan Knight, a rescuer who came in a swan-drawn boat to defend a damsel. Richard Wagner, a later focus of Ludwig's obsession, adapted the tale in his Romantic opera *Lohengrin*. The Swan King spent his life consuming and patronizing art, poetry, architecture, and compositions. Most famously, he commissioned massive fairy-tale castles that came to personify Bavaria's rustic beauty but drained the coffers of his kingdom, triggering political opposition. As his reign went on, Ludwig rarely showed himself in public. He became known to Bavaria as a hermit king, a royal recluse like those found in the Germanic legends which Ludwig so loved.

A mad ruler like Ludwig could have come at no other time in history. He was a transitional figure who reigned in the nineteenth century, long after the end of the medieval and Renaissance periods but before the full entrenchment of the modern era. He came from a lengthy line of monarchs and was invested with great wealth purely by his accident of birth. But his power as king was heavily circumscribed due to Chancellor Otto von Bismarck's project of uniting the thirty-nine independent German states under the leadership of Prussia, which controlled the newly formed German Empire in 1871. Ludwig had no foreign policy or military power. He functioned as a ceremonial figurehead during peacetime. He was far less powerful than royals of the Middle Ages and could not rule by fiat as they did, yet Ludwig had far more wealth and was far more adored by his subjects than the vestigial, impotent European royals of the twentieth and twenty-first centuries.

Ludwig came from the House of Wittelsbach, a Bavarian dynasty that had reigned since the eleventh century, producing a number of kings, dukes, counts, and Holy Roman emperors. His family's independent political power dried up once Bavaria became subordinate to the central German state. The king responded by turning to a life of increasingly abnormal seclusion. He used his family's fortune to construct fairy-tale-like castles that delighted his imagination but also served as hideaways. The castles included Berg, Hohenschwangau Castle, and Linderhof. His masterpiece was Neuschwanstein, the most beautiful royal dwelling in Europe, with the possible exceptions of Louis XIV's Versailles or Peter the Great's Winter Palace in St. Petersburg. Ludwig withdrew into a dreamworld of his own making and often watched a Richard Wagner opera as the only member of the audience. Ludwig's eccentric behavior alarmed his family, and his building of castles caused near bankruptcy of the Bavarian state. In response, the king's ministers accused him of insanity and deposed him. He was committed to the custody of Berg Castle, nestled on the shores of Lake Starnberg in Upper Bavaria. Only three days after losing the throne, Ludwig took a stroll with his physician. They went missing and were found in the lake not long after. They had drowned in only four feet of water. Did Ludwig die by suicide? Regicide? A political conspiracy? Answers have still not been found. The king's end was as odd as his life.

Ludwig was born in 1845 at Nymphenburg Palace, the summer residence of the House of Wittelsbach. He was the elder son of Bavarian crown prince Maximillian II and Princess Marie of Prussia. Maximillian was a popular king and took an active role in Bavarian politics. He fought to maintain Bavaria's independence while more powerful German states grew in power and threatened to swallow up their neighbors. Maximilian had the businesslike attitude of a nationalist politician concerned with the preservation of the constitutional privileges of Bavaria. He also supported maintaining his kingdom's distinction through artistic patronage. Maximilian financed studies of Bavarian peasant art, costumes, customs, and dialects to promote his own culture as standing apart from the Pan-Germanism supported by Prussia. The House of Wittelsbach had never prided itself on conquest or ruling large domains; it always looked toward patronage of fine art and architecture rather than power or military victory.

As a child, Ludwig explored the valleys and forests around Hohenschwangau Castle, yet another Wittelsbach palace, this one built by his father. The mountainous landscape of Bavaria was the backdrop of his lonely, austere life. The young prince had few in whom he could confide: partly because of his royal upbringing that included many tutors but few playmates, and partly because of his quiet nature. Ludwig showed the tendency to escape into his own imagination as a child. The tendency was so strong that he sometimes appeared to be in waking dreams. His tutor, Ignaz von Döllinger, found him one day alone, buried in a large sofa, unable to read due to eye trouble. "Your Highness should have something read to you, it would serve to pass the tedious hours," he said. Young Ludwig replied, "Oh! They are not tedious to me. I think of lots of things and am quite happy." As Ludwig grew older, he fell in love with the poems and dramas of Romantic author Friedrich von Schiller (1759–1805), who collaborated with Goethe. His romantic and idealistic style suited Ludwig. With Schiller's writing Ludwig could remove himself from the challenging world of warfare and politics, and retreat to an idealized spiritual world of beauty and simplicity.[2]

When Ludwig was ten, Maximilian arranged for him to begin the training he would need to one day assume his royal duties. His education began to shape him to be king. His day began at 5:30 a.m. and continued for the next twelve hours with lessons in history, music, German, French, Latin, English, arithmetic, theology, literature, and equestrian arts. Ludwig became proficient in music, conversant in French, and learned rudimentary English. He loved literature, had a remarkably good memory, and could quote whole passages on a whim. But he could not focus and coordinate his knowledge. His mind was like a private museum, well stocked with exotic items but poorly catalogued and a mystery to those who entered.[3] The young king had little experience in politics or many other practical subjects. Ludwig had not completed any university study and had little worldly experience. Before ascending the throne, Ludwig thus had little opportunity to gain necessary experience in the ways of Maximilian's court.[4]

At the age of sixteen, however, Ludwig met a figure who altered the course of his life. On February 2, 1861, he viewed Richard Wagner's opera *Lohengrin* for the first time. For Ludwig, this was the physical manifestation of all his dreams. Wagner's compositions and publications were the next step in his youthful worship of Germanic knights and poets. He had devoured legends of Parsifal and Lohengrin, characters from literature on King Arthur and his company. Now the composer gave sound and form to the ancient folklore he loved.[5]

Among Ludwig's first acts as king was to order court secretary Franz Seraph von Pfistermeister to bring Wagner to Munich as an artist-in-residence. Wagner happily accepted the invitation. In May 1864, he stood for the first time in front of his new benefactor. He was a worn-out composer in his fifties who had spent years fleeing creditors and struggling with massive debt. It was the king, however, who was awestruck. He worshipped Wagner's earlier works and had heard that the composer was laboring away at a musical drama based on the *The Ring of the Nibelung*, an epic poem written in 1200 considered to be the German equivalent of *The Iliad*. When Ludwig told him that his Nibelung work would not only be completed but also performed in the manner he intended, Wagner bent low, took the king's hand, and remained in the posture without speaking awhile. Ludwig said that he "drew him to my heart with a feeling that I was taking a silent oath to be faithful to him til the end of time."[6]

On the same evening, Richard Wagner wrote to a friend about the life-altering encounter:

> You know the young King had me call on him. Today I was led before him. He is unfortunately so noble and brilliant, so magnificent and soulful that I fear his life must vanish like a fleeting stream in this coarse world . . . My luck is so great that I am crushed by it; if he can only live; he is such an unheard-of wonder![7]

The close partnership between Ludwig and Richard Wagner was fruitful for both. Wagner had been on the brink of financial ruin for years and carried on numerous affairs that destroyed friendships and his own marriage; he was now released from all financial concerns and finally able to create *The Ring of the Nibelung*, which would become a sixteen-hour series of four operas, his magnum opus. Inspired by Norse sagas, the cycle depicted the entire creation and destruction of the world. It was clearly ambitious. Ludwig II also planned to establish a German music school in Munich and envisioned a large new opera house to meet the technical challenges required by Wagner's operas. Munich would be a center of musical education and creation, like Vienna in the eighteenth century. The plan failed, however, due to opposition from the government, his own family, and Munich citizens. Countercurrents grew because of the prohibitive costs of the planned building and the character of the "revolutionary" Wagner.[8] Moreover, rumors have long persisted of a romantic relationship between the composer and the king, as letters between them suggest. Ludwig referred to Wagner as "the star that shines upon my life," and spoke of his ardent love for him. Wagner was expelled from Munich after only a year due to the "improprieties" of an indiscreet affair with Cosima von Bülow, the wife of a local conductor, who gave birth to their illegitimate daughter. He nevertheless stayed a lifelong Ludwig beneficiary.[9]

Rumors have swirled around Ludwig's love life for over a century. The king never married and did not have known mistresses. According to his diary, private letters, and speculation from contemporaries about his close friendships with men, he had strong homosexual desires. Whether or not Ludwig acted on these desires remains speculation. Older accounts of Ludwig's life speculate on his attraction to a Russian princess and his desire to build a castle in the Greco-Muscovite or Russo-Byzantine style. As a lover of opera, Ludwig may have also been interested in two opera stars who captivated him (more by their art than anything else): Josephine Vogel and Josephine Schefsky. One rumor depicts him attracted to a peasant girl in a real-life instance of the folk trope of royalty falling in love with peasantry.[10]

In 1867, Ludwig became engaged to his first cousin, Sophie Charlotte, daughter of Duke Maximilian of Bavaria. She was the sister of his much-beloved cousin, Elizabeth of Austria. A delay in the marriage occurred; excuses were offered. Among the rumored reasons for breaking the engagement—beyond that of his lack of interest in women—was that he had heard Elizabeth was in love with someone else, and he canceled the marriage due to jealousy. Another rumor states that he tarried so long in final preparations that Elizabeth's father asked Ludwig to name a day for the wedding or break off the engagement. Ludwig, feeling himself under compulsion, refused the marriage altogether. This and other increasingly eccentric forms of behavior frightened his cousin.

Despite his odd behavior, Ludwig upheld his kingly duties in the early years of his reign. He carefully considered the advice of ministers and government officials, often coming to long, thoughtful decisions on his own. The greatest challenge for Ludwig was the issue of Bavarian independence that had vexed his father and grandfather: how to uphold a strong monarchy, yet fight against the forces of absolute monarchy in matters which the government tended. The king looked to the example of the Republic of Switzerland for reform. But whatever democratic, populist sympathies he held, Ludwig's strongest inspirations were the most iron-fisted absolute monarchs in European history: French kings Louis XIV and XV. His strongest passions appeared to be for a deceased woman from the same court, the self-indulgent Marie Antoinette, the last queen of France whose excesses of wealth helped provoke the French Revolution at the end of the eighteenth century.[11]

After German unification and the neutering of Ludwig's political powers, he no longer paid heed to any disapproval of his spending the Wittelsbach fortune on his own artistic interests. He spent centuries of family wealth to transform Bavaria from a rustic land to a state of grandeur, on par with France at the height of its prerevolutionary splendor. The costs of his palaces Neuschwanstein, Linderhof, and Herrenchiemsee (all located south of Munich at the foot of the Bavarian Alps) totaled over thirty million marks by 1886. This sum neared the amount that Bavaria paid to Prussia in war indemnity after the Seven Weeks' War of 1866. The construction of Linderhof, the smallest of the three, began in 1869, and it was the only one which Ludwig lived to see completed. Then came Neuschwanstein, the most fairlytale-like of all his buildings. From 1878 to 1885, the magnificent Herrenchiemsee Castle was constructed on Herrenworth Island in Lake Chiemsee. At the same time, Ludwig commissioned special plays by the court dramatist Carl von Hegel about Louis XIV, Louis XV,

Marie Antoinette, and other figures of this period with whom he was so consumed.

Herrenchiemsee symbolized the king's irrevocable withdrawal into a fantasy world. Ludwig bought the island of Herrenworth in 1873 to realize his dreams of becoming Louis XIV incarnate. He would build on Herrenworth an exact copy of Versailles. The two centuries that separated Ludwig from Louis were to be bridged and time itself subdued. The real Versailles was a symbol of gaudy excess, but it at least served as the court of France at the height of its Enlightenment-era power. Ludwig's castle on Herrenworth, by contrast, was the daydream of a king, what Werner Richter, biographer of Ludwig, describes as a "gigantic toy house entirely isolated from the active world by a gloomy lake and . . . the forbidding walls of the Alps."[12]

To Ludwig's credit, he only reproduced the middle section of Versailles; even the Swan King could not lavish enough funds on his project to build a full-scale reproduction. But Herrenchiemsee Castle still had the same enormous facade and perspective of huge park terraces as the original. There were espaliers of green shrubs; carefully tended, giant old trees; cascades and fountains. Upon entering the vestibule, there was the structural vista on both sides of the marble staircase. State rooms included the "Hall of Guards," the "Salon de l'Oeil de Boeuf," the "Parade Bedroom," the "Salle du Conseil" and the incredible "Galerie des Glaces," with its seventeen enormous windows facing seventeen enormous mirrors that reflected each other infinitely. There were seventy private rooms on both sides—including a bedroom with a circular staircase leading into the marble bathroom, another mirror gallery, and a red dining room in which the dining table rose through the floor so as to have the servants remain invisible.

Venturing farther into Herrenchiemsee, the grandeur goes from mesmerizing to suffocating. All the colors of Versailles are present: wine red and old gold, peacock green and plush blue. All the emblems of Versailles are present too: the whirls, plumes, and spirals, trophies and ornaments. Sadly, even symbols of victory in homage to Louis XIV are present, including paintings of battles, sieges, and historic encounters in which Ludwig never took part, along with busts of Louis's generals. Ludwig did not merely imitate the glory of Louis; he outright stole it. The Mirror Gallery is 220 feet long; the interior choked by ornaments. The needlework on the royal bedspread alone kept close to thirty seamstresses busy for seven years. The gulf between the castle's grandeur and Ludwig's nonexistent powers as king was yawning.

Herrenchiemsee was the largest—and, most would say, gaudiest—of all of Ludwig's castles. It was a fantastic and enormously costly effort for a completely purposeless structure. No important war counsels or diplomatic negotiations would ever take place there. Ludwig would never host balls for all of Bavaria's upper-crust society. It was the self-centered wish fulfillment of a king who completely misunderstood his importance in the world. The castle served as a statement that the king had no limits, but he also had no aims. He was waging a battle with emptiness and won victory by default because he had no enemies.[13]

Because Ludwig substituted castle construction for involvement in Bavarian society and politics, he carried on the construction with an exacting passion usually reserved for military campaigns or land negotiations. Ludwig's mental precision, which lasted to the end of his life, astounded Court Secretary Ludwig von Bürkel. Because castle construction was the only domain where he maintained command, he drove contractors to superhuman speed. Bismarck may have had his artillery divisions and cavalry corps, but Ludwig had his masons, carpenters, and sculptors. However, even Ludwig's powers were not unlimited. In order not to have to admit limitations to his power, he overlooked the less expensive substitutes for Versailles's original materials that went into his constructions. Gypsum concoctions covered walls instead of marble. His pillars were of polished sandstone instead of lapis lazuli.

Ludwig walked through the massive halls of flowers, half-tones of light, ornaments, and endlessly reflecting mirrors. He kept a yearly program that included a ten-day period in September during which the Mirror Gallery of Herrenchiemsee was illuminated with 2,500 tall candles in whose yellow light he promenaded all by himself. This was an imitation of Versailles's Galerie des Glaces, which had a satisfactory explanation: it was meant to amplify the brilliance of French court society at the height of its opulence. Ludwig's festival, in contrast, was a sad parody in which the grand spectacle of candlelight, reflected by thousands of glass prisms in an ocean of illumination, was only to satisfy him.

Ludwig adopted yet another strange habit around 1880. He dined alone, yet ordered the table set for distinguished but deceased guests: Marie Antoinette and other long-dead inhabitants of Versailles. Along with these "guests," Ludwig, to the confusion and horror of his servants, enjoyed long conversations with the phantoms and interrupted his soliloquies with laughter, giving merry toasts. When not dining, he hallucinated sounds in adjoining rooms and demanded to know their source. Servants pacified him, pretending one of them had accidentally made a noise while performing his duties and apologizing for the error. His veneration for the French court was so great that he would respectfully tip his hat at the statue of Louis XIV in Linderhof. As for the statue of Marie Antoinette on the terrace at Linderhof, he stroked her cheeks.[14]

Most interactions that the Swan King had with other humans were with servants, with whom he became increasingly tyrannical. He brought down wrath at their smallest offense. The king would box their ears, kick them, or empty washbasins over them. The servants followed an elaborate set of court rules. If they met Ludwig in a corridor or anteroom, they were to bow low and never make eye contact. A valet of his named Mayr broke this rule and had to wear a black mask in the king's presence for over a year, so as not to show his "criminal countenance." Those in the royal presence were also forbidden to clear their throats, cough, sneeze, or speak in the Bavarian dialect. Ludwig ordered flogging for the offenders, but the orders were rarely carried out for the sake of the dutiful servants who put up with his mental illness (had Ludwig actually been a medieval king, when checks on a monarchy's power were weak or nonexistent, many could have died at these commands). While in lucid states, however, Ludwig detested capital punishment and commuted most death sentences that passed to him for signing.[15]

Ludwig was eccentric and reclusive by nature, but even the most damning testimonies of his personality do not portray him as a tyrant. He made every attempt to avoid public exposure while in Munich (probably fearing assassination) but was kind and even munificent while among the deeply conservative Bavarian peasant population. Secure in their affection, Ludwig displayed a kingly mixture of dignity and ease while among them. He lavished gifts on peasant families who sheltered him by their firesides during his nocturnal sleigh rides. The castle staff also received generous gifts. Each year in the Christmas season he filled Hohenschwangau with jewelry, books, pictures, and artistic objects to present as gifts. One cavalryman, whose birthday fell during his service at the castle, was astonished to be presented an enormous cake, two bottles of wine, cigars, and other luxury items by Ludwig. The king's reputation for such generous acts spread among the peasant population. He became adored in the Bavarian countryside as few kings before him had.[16]

Ludwig was long believed to have gone mad due to a self-destructive lifestyle. Many thought the king contracted syphilis, leading to his collapsing mental state and even his deteriorating physical state. But Ludwig's social problems began long before he could have hypothetically contracted that degenerative disease. Even as a child, the prospect of ruling had never held major interest for the absentminded dreamer. As he grew older, Ludwig retreated into his castles and abandoned any semblance of normal human behavior. More contemporary biographies portray Ludwig as less deranged than lonely, self-absorbed, and strange in manner. Scarred by a distant mother, a fiercely strict father, and a demanding but completely impractical education, Ludwig was ill-prepared for political leadership, particularly in the high-stakes period of

German unification of the 1870s. He found himself outfoxed by his ministers and other German politicos.

Furthermore, charges of Ludwig's most eccentric behavior come mostly from servants who were not neutral parties. Most were paid to testify against him by agents working for the regime of Minister-President Johann von Lutz, an ambitious politician who eroded the powers of the Bavarian constitutional monarchy and was a key figure in Ludwig's overthrow. Their testimonies were used to build a case of insanity against Ludwig and arrange for his deposition. Other servants saw nothing strange in the king's behavior. Alfonso Welcker served as the king's valet for many years. He declared, "I could observe no signs of the alleged mental illness of the King. Nor could I perceive any abnormal changes."[17] Fritz Schegler, another servant, testified:

> In the last days of his life, I was often assigned to the King's personal service, and I can only say that he was a good and just master. Although he sometimes scolded and stormed, when someone had done something wrong, his anger usually blew over quickly. I myself never heard about or saw any crazy orders being given, such as scratching at doors for admittance, lying down and having to crawl on the floor, wearing masks and so on. My fellow servant Mayr, who later told so many bad things of the King, often talked to me about the King. If the things he declared had really happened, he would surely have told me about them sooner. On the contrary! I was often surprised of how calm and composed the King was in the last days of his life, when he had to recognize the vastness of the betrayal.[18]

Ludwig was clearly eccentric, an attribute present in other members of the Wittelsbach family. This quality, however, is not coterminous with insanity. Moreover, he had moments of respite in which he approached normal human conduct. Even in the final period before his deposition, when Ludwig bunkered deeper into his fantasies than any other time and held dinnertime conversations with deceased royals (when he wasn't bounding on midnight sleigh rides through the Alps), the king could maintain perfectly lucid conversations with servants and outriders, writing clear letters to defend his regency.[19]

The Bavarian government commission's board of physicians that declared Ludwig insane relied on questionable testimonies of compromised servants and never personally examined him. The only trained psychiatrist to do so (if the primitive field of mental health in the 1880s can be called "psychiatry") was Dr. Franz Karl, a specialist trained in mental disorders. He posed as an ordinary physician and spent hours with the king. Karl declared Ludwig to be perfectly normal and in full command of his senses.[20] It appears that Ludwig, who always remained competent enough to work under pressure, suffered more from degrees of eccentricity than complete mental illness.

The strongest argument against Ludwig's madness was the king's cognizance of his own bizarre behavior. A true madman, he said, would not be aware of his own condition. Before his death in 1886 he reportedly spoke with writer Lew Vanderpoole to answer charges of madness against him. Ludwig's statement is his closing speech on the topic:

> It has often been maliciously hinted and even openly declared that I am a fool. Maybe I am, but I doubt it . . . A real madman is, as a rule, the only person who doesn't recognize his madness . . . If I were a poet, I might be able to reap praise by putting these things to verse. But the talent of expression was not given to me, and so I must bear being laughed at, scorned at, and slandered. I am called a fool. Will God call me a fool when I am summoned before him?[21]

The conclusion of the physicians' board employed by the Bavarian government determined Ludwig's illness to originate from inherited insanity. Physicians have criticized the diagnosis due to a lack of a personal examination of the king ever since it was announced, but in recent decades they have also put forward alternative theories. Ninety years after Ludwig's death, Dr. Christoph Biermann published an article in the medical journal *Deutsches Arzteblatt* suggesting the "postmortem findings point without any doubt to an organic brain disease," which was, in fact, syphilis. At the time of Ludwig's death, syphilis was known as a disease of the nervous system and treated with mercury and potassium. There was no mention of syphilis in Ludwig's autopsy; however, this could be due to the disdain with which the Victorian era treated the sexually transmitted disease.

Ludwig biographer Greg King writes that if he did have syphilis, he most likely contracted it before his thirtieth birthday through homosexual activity, in which, many rumors suggested, he began to engage after breaking his engagement with Sophie in 1867. The disease may have remained dormant for years but then appeared decades later, manifesting itself in his bizarre behavior, rapid mood swings, and, in the end, paralysis. The theory accounts for Ludwig's paranoia and withdrawal from society. He would have felt shame for contracting a disease so disdained in the traditional culture of Catholic Bavaria, particularly among peasants whom he so loved. The secrecy of his final years, King argues, could even have been an attempt by the Wittelsbach family to protect their throne and guard the memory of Ludwig.[22]

The castles of Ludwig's dreams came to life, and the Bavarian countryside was transformed from a collection of Alpine villages to an enchanted landscape conjured out of another world. Government and family opposition to the king continued to grow in intensity. From 1885, foreign banks threatened to seize Ludwig's property for his debts. In early 1886, Ludwig had an annual income of 5.5 million marks but had already added liabilities amounting to 13 million marks. By the time of his death, the total amount of his debt—that is, money owed to the State of Bavaria by Ludwig (or, more accurately, by his family)—had increased to 21 million marks.

In June 1886, the crisis between Ludwig and the government intensified to the point that members of the House of Wittelsbach awaited the summons of the family counsel. They discussed by what means Ludwig II could be convinced to return to affairs of the state and curtail expenses for his buildings. The family fortune built over a period of eight hundred years risked annihilation in the course of one generation. At the same time, a group of politicians, led by Minister-President Lutz, decided to remove Ludwig by declaring the king mad through a medical report provided by a doctor. The king would be dethroned and his uncle, Prince Luitpold of Bavaria, would be appointed ruler.

The king had only a few supporters, and he lacked both defenders in high positions and the energy to counter the plotting. Resigned to his political fate, Ludwig loathed any diagnosis of insanity. Such public defamation was said to have made him consider suicide. To his servant Weber he remarked, "It is not the worst that they want to rob me of my throne. But it will be the death of me that they want to have me declared insane and buried alive." Supporters suggested he escape across the Austrian border, but Ludwig declined. He feared it could cause bloodshed. The deposition finally came. At midnight on June 1, 1886, a pretense was made to get the king out of his bedchamber and seize him. A chamber lackey named Mayr was instructed to inform Ludwig that a key to the south tower of the castle which was lost had been recovered. Mayr handed the key to Ludwig, who started through the dining room to the south tower. Passing through the servants' room, he was surrounded by a group of men who subdued him. Led back to his bedroom, his psychiatrist, Dr. Bernhard von Gudden, appeared.

"Your Majesty," he said, "This is the most unfortunate task of my life. Four specialists for mental diseases have given their opinions on Your Majesty and after their pronouncement, Prince Luitpold has taken over the Regency. I have been ordered to escort His Majesty to Berg Castle this same evening." "How can you declare me to be mentally ill?"

Ludwig asked. "You have never before examined me!" Gudden replied, "Your Majesty, that was not necessary. Our records contain a wealth of information and give overwhelming evidence." Ludwig asked how long the proposed treatment would take. "At least one year," Gudden replied. The king, resigned to his fate, remarked, "Well, it will probably go faster; it can always be done as with the Sultan!" (He was insinuating that he might fall victim to a political murder as Ottoman sultan Ibrahim I had.) "How easy it is to get a person out of the way!"[23]

Finally deposed, forty-year-old Ludwig didn't have long to live. Three days later, Gudden accompanied the king on a stroll on the grounds of Berg Castle. Two attendants joined them. Gudden spoke optimistically to the other doctors, saying that his royal patient might recover. In the evening, Ludwig asked Gudden to join him on another walk along the shore of Lake Starnberg. The doctor told the aids not to join them. They left at 6:30 p.m., never to be seen alive again.

By eight o'clock that evening, a growing worry had spread among the castle staff. Three guards on patrol claimed they had not seen or heard anything unusual. The chief of police assigned to Berg ordered a search of the gardens surrounding the castle. There was no sign of Gudden or the king. An hour later, police, orderlies, and doctors joined in a search for the missing men. Rain and wind covered the estate. A group of men walked slowly on the shoreline with their torches and lanterns piercing the darkness. Half a mile from the castle, a guard spotted the king's rolled umbrella, laid on a park bench. He then discovered the king's overcoat and suit jacket, turned inside out, suggesting quick removal. The men raced down a path to the lake. Bushes and small trees obscured their view. Broken branches showed someone had been pushed into the foliage. They reached the shoreline. The guard stepped into the water. In the reeds he saw two hats floating. They were Gudden's silk top hat and the king's bowler.

Dr. Müller, Gudden's assistant, feared the worst. He ran to a nearby fisherman's hut, awoke Jacob Lidl, and told him to row along the shoreline to look for the two missing men. Other castle staff joined him in the boat. One spotted a dark object floating among the reeds, ten feet from the shore. It was a man's body, facedown, arms stretched outward. The men turned him over and saw it was Ludwig. His body was cold. His eyes stared vacantly. He had drowned in water that was only four feet deep. They quickly found the second corpse, also floating facedown in the lake. It was Gudden. Both men had been dead for a while, as rigor mortis had set in. Müller worked frantically to revive them, giving Ludwig mouth-to-mouth resuscitation. At midnight he finally gave up and pronounced the king dead. There were no visible injuries to the king. On his face he had a "dark, domineering, almost tyrannical expression."[24]

The Bavarian government issued an official statement on the king's death, declaring murder–suicide. The report claimed that Ludwig had raced into the lake to commit suicide. Gudden tried to stop him, so the king murdered him. He then waded into deeper waters to drown himself. The official autopsy, however, conflicts with this ruling. Water wasn't found in his lungs, which is inconsistent with drowning. Ludwig was a strong swimmer in his younger days and could have easily managed shallow water. Left blank in the autopsy was the cause of death. Rumors claimed he had been a victim of an assassination plot and drowned or died from chilly water exposure trying to escape. No conclusive evidence exists.[25]

News of Ludwig's death shocked Bavaria. Empress Elizabeth of Austria heard the news while visiting her family at Possenhofen Castle, on the western shore of Lake Starnberg in Bavaria. The empress cried to her mother, "The King was no madman, only an eccentric living in a world of dreams! They might have treated him more gently and spared him such a terrible end."[26] Church bells tolled and capital buildings were draped in black. Thousands of Bavarians flooded into Munich to pay final respects. Crammed into the cathedral to view the king lying in state, more than a few fainted from heatstroke. Although Ludwig was reclusive, many Bavarians thought his deposition was unjust and his "suicide" a conspiracy and final insult to their anointed sovereign.[27]

Ludwig's state funeral occurred on June 19, six days after his death. It was the largest state occasion ever held in Munich. The procession included representatives of the city's religious orders, officials of the court staff in full dress uniform, crown princes, a German field marshal, Bavarian noblemen, foreign ambassadors, and deputations from various Bavarian towns. To honor the king's love of folk myths, eight white horses draped in black palls drew the king's hearse through the city. The hearse was a large vehicle, draped in black, covered with wreaths of garlanded flowers. At the center was a gilded base that hoisted up a replica of the Wittelsbach crown. A crossbearer and two pages with lighted tapers followed the hearse, followed by a squadron soldier. The whole procession lasted two hours.[28]

Ludwig was a tragic and helpless figure, reclusive and mysterious, a prisoner in his own kingdom, mistreated by his court and family.[29] One of the saddest anecdotes of his lonely life was told by Ludwig von Bürkel, the last of his court secretaries with whom he came in contact. Bürkel relates a story of when he came to bring the king an invitation to an event in Munich. The king refused, explaining how he could no longer bear to be present in large crowds, to smile and extend greetings a thousand times, or to ask questions of people who meant nothing to him and receive answers that did not interest him. Then he leaned closer to his secretary, and he softly yet sadly explained the true depths of his permanent isolation: "Sometimes, when I have read myself to exhaustion and everything is quiet, I have an irresistible urge to hear a human voice. Then I call one of my domestic servants or outriders and ask him to tell me about his home and his family. Otherwise I would completely forget the art of speech."[30]

If his artistic patronage could be separated from his careless stewardship of Bavaria's finances, the most charitable interpretation of Ludwig's life is that he should be remembered as one of history's greatest patrons of the arts. Ludwig's name might stand among the great families of the Italian Renaissance, such as the Medicis or the Sforzas. This charitable view is, however, debatable. He did not possess creative powers of his own and was fortunate to find the right artist in Wagner. His tastes were described as basic in character. As king, he was marred by mental illness, a self-centered egotism, an uneven temperament, and the tendency to follow his own desires rather than control them. But Ludwig's mental powers were also stronger than his critics admit. Despite his introversion, the king had an extraordinary memory. Ludwig could recite pages from Voltaire and Victor Hugo. When he wanted to be, he was strongly charismatic, compelling and arresting. His personality could be magnetic and winsome when the need arose. Stories abound of his generosity and kindness.

In the beginning of his reign, Ludwig looked to increase the educational level of Bavarians. He commissioned schools and colleges, including the Academy of Fine Art and the Institute of Technology in Munich. The king was among the first to support Henry Dunant's Relief Action of the Red Cross, an idea that quickly spread across the German Reich. His legacy among music lovers is uncontested; Richard Wagner's voluminous compositions would never have existed to the degree they do without the royal support of Ludwig. Ludwig is still admired today by those who consider the king an aesthete who looked for the good and the beautiful. [31]

Not long after his death, Ludwig's life—which was already the stuff of myth—passed into legend. Novels about his eccentricities appeared even in his lifetime. He first appeared in fiction in 1875 in a work by Joseph Emruwe called *The Royal Castles: A Poetic Dream*. The narrator takes a dream tour of the Bavarian royal domiciles, guided by the spirit of the House of Wittelsbach. Ludwig also appears to the slumbering narrator. After his mysterious death, paraphernalia of the Swan King spread and multiplied. Postcards of Bavaria featured maidens kissing his statue. Kitschy items also appeared: beer mugs and brooches with his portrait; painted busts and statuettes. A cult even developed around the Swan King. The queen mother, who outlived Ludwig by two years, had a wooden cross placed in the lake where Ludwig drowned. On the bank, she built a simple chapel. Later, a sturdier cross donated by members of the Ludwig II society replaced hers. A group of Ludwig admirers gather by the shore every year. To this day, they pray and place a wreath on the cross.[32]

Today, Ludwig is considered mad for his irresponsible spending on vanity projects. Yet, if we look at modern Bavaria through the eyes of Germany's tourism board, Ludwig's contribution is impressive. Every year millions of visitors come to Bavaria's castles, palaces, and residences. They are the biggest tourism magnets in the region. If Ludwig's goal was to transformed Bavaria from a rustic, rural kingdom to the Versailles of the Alps, then he succeeded wildly. Bavaria's role in shaping the cultural landscape of Germany surpasses its population or landmass. In those terms, Ludwig's contribution to German history was far better than Bismarck's legacy.

CHAPTER SEVEN

# PRESIDENT IDI AMIN OF UGANDA

## 1925–2003

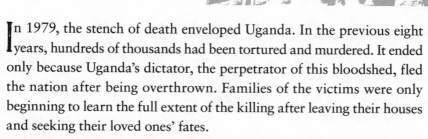

In 1979, the stench of death enveloped Uganda. In the previous eight years, hundreds of thousands had been tortured and murdered. It ended only because Uganda's dictator, the perpetrator of this bloodshed, fled the nation after being overthrown. Families of the victims were only beginning to learn the full extent of the killing after leaving their houses and seeking their loved ones' fates.

Nevertheless, everyone knew where the dictator housed his torture cells and execution chambers. Thousands died at this site: an L-shaped slaughterhouse called the State Research Bureau. In a fitting symbol of the inextricable connection between Idi Amin's charming, gregarious public persona and the weapons of political terror that he kept close at hand, the State Research Bureau sat beneath the lavish residence of the Ugandan dictator. Many believed the police headquarters were connected to the presidential lodge by an underground tunnel.

Idi Amin was president of Uganda from 1971 to 1979. His rule of terror was akin to Hitler's dictatorship, although it was far less publicized. He killed an estimated 300,000 Ugandans, close to 4 percent of the population of the small African nation of 12 million residents. The murdered were from all social classes and backgrounds, but they were primarily farmers, students, clerks, and shopkeepers. There were also prominent men and women among the victims: Supreme Court judges, diplomats, educators, clergymen, cabinet ministers, bankers, surgeons, hospital directors, and business executives.[1] Sometimes armed groups executed them; sometimes they were forced to bludgeon each other to death.

*Washington Post* journalists Tony Avirgan and Martha Honey visited the headquarters of the secret police days after the dictator, Idi Amin, absconded. As the journalists approached, they saw a dozen corpses piled near a bloodstained drain gutter. A cloud of flies hung overhead. One of the victims was a twelve-year-old boy. Forced to lie down in the floor drain before death so their blood would not pool up and stain the ground of the torture chamber, the prisoners were shot, hacked, or bludgeoned with sledgehammers. Victims carried the recently murdered to the pile at the side of the building. They then climbed into the gutter to die.[2]

They discovered the compound had a labyrinthine network of dungeons and prison cells. There were prisoners found alive. They were living skeletons, having been deprived of food for weeks. Officials said they had been forced to subsist on human flesh. Signs of human suffering were everywhere. Pools of blood covered the floor. Blood was smeared on the walls. There were corpses piled against the walls in various stages of decay. Most were mutilated; all showed signs of torture. Relatives searching for loved ones refused to ignite lanterns for fear the fumes from decaying bodies would trigger an explosion. In one cell, relatives searched through a pile of corpses. More than a few of the dead were stripped from the waist down, suggesting torturers mutilated their sexual organs—one of Amin's favorite methods of humiliation. Others searched in the parking lot of the State Research Bureau through the files of inmates, which were scattered on the ground. They desperately sought clues about the last known whereabouts of the missing. In the files were identity cards of Ugandans killed by bureau agents, the most feared and notorious among Amin's death squads.

One diplomat who lived near the compound claimed that Amin ended his reign as he began it, with a wave of killings and purges of incriminating information. An endless staccato of gunshots echoed from the prison. Trucks moved back and forth. Blue smoke poured from the compound's chimney as Amin's men burned mountains of documents. One file that escaped incineration exposed an informant network in which eight bureau agents paid $70,000 a week to buy information from Ugandans. Not that the evidence was damning; the corpses were condemnatory enough. And Amin's brutality had been so brazen for so long that many believed nothing worse could remain hidden.[3]

Amin had no qualms about using horrifying violence, and he did so from at least the beginning of his presidency. A rumor spread that in January 1972, he murdered over five hundred troops at Mutakula Prison. The dictator used the opportunity as an initiation of sorts for his three-year-old son, Moses, into the art of political murder. To seal the initiation, the boy was led to a tied-down army officer so that the child could strike his neck with a *panga*, an African variant of the machete. The blows were severe enough to cause massive bleeding but not enough to issue the coup de grâce. It was whispered among the victim's tribesmen that he took two hours to die.

Such stories, whether true or not, were believable in Amin's Uganda. His methods of torture and execution were as creative as they were barbaric. The widespread fear of brutal retribution made the Ugandan police never challenge the dictator. Fear was the mortar of Amin's rule and murder the bricks. Neighbors did not speak to each other openly for fear the other was an informant.

The pseudonymous David Gywn described in detail the omnipresent terror of Amin's Uganda. Gywn spent twenty years as a technical advisor in the African nation and authored the 1977 book *Idi Amin: Death Light of Africa.*

> Life became increasingly lonely. It had to be. You kept away
> from your friends so as not to involve them. Your mere

acquaintances had abandoned you long since. In any event, there was nothing that either category could do. This was not war-time. There was no sense of common purpose among a coherent group against an open enemy. There could not be. The fear and the bribery of informers had split the groups wide open. The man with whom you had worked for twenty years might remember the guinea fowl you had eaten together one cool evening following a hot day after elephant. But his daughter would not, and she was the girlfriend of a man in the State Research Department. . . . It was not a companionable period, though there were many who, at risk to themselves, tried to make it so: Americans, British, Germans, Ugandans.[4]

Amin masterfully pitted Ugandans against one another, pulling on every loose thread in the nation's loosely woven social tapestry. He pitted tribes against tribes, districts against districts, religious sects against sects. He favored the Nubian ethnic group, which formed his goon squad in the State Research Department. Even members of his personal mercenary group distrusted one another, as individuals were frequently purged. Each group feared it could be turned on at any moment. The only solution was continual vigilance and constantly proving one's loyalty.

Idi Amin's story would be inspirational if he were not so cruel. He rose from humble tribal beginnings in a remote part of Britain's African colonial holdings to become leader of the newly independent Uganda. He was a consummate showman and could wow crowds, foreign leaders, and the international press with his charm. Neither educated in British boarding schools in Africa nor thoroughly inculcated in English manners and speech (unlike the typical African economic and social elite), Amin was considered an authentic son of Africa. After he gained power in 1971, a period of short-lived international enthusiasm for Amin followed, along with foreign financial and military support.

Amin crafted an image as a progressive champion of marginalized groups. He called himself a defender of women's rights and placed women in high-profile government positions. But he began to express his creeping authoritarianism and despotism as a twisted form of paternalism toward Ugandan females. He outlawed miniskirts in 1972 and called fashion-minded women "immoral" and subjected them to public shaming and assault. Women policed each other due to fear of speaking up against Amin's policies.[5] As he settled into his reign, Amin did other things to shatter early optimism about reform possibilities in Uganda. In his first year alone, his regime murdered ten thousand. Many more were to be imprisoned and tortured. To him, this was a necessary cleansing to purify the nation. "In any country, there must be people who have to die," he said. "They are the sacrifices any nation has to make to achieve law and order."[6]

Idi Amin was born at the end of one of the most transformative periods in his homeland's history. Africa was the site of intense colonial competition among the great powers of Europe at the end of the nineteenth century. In this era, known as the Scramble for Africa, 90 percent of the continent fell under formal European control. Britain, Germany, France, Italy, Portugal, Spain, and Belgium controlled trade, extracted resources, sent missionaries to convert native populations, and set up colonial imperial governments. After World War II, African nationalists rallied for independence. European leaders relented, as their war debts had stripped them of resources to keep their colonies. Franklin Roosevelt and Winston Churchill signed the Atlantic Charter, which stipulated respect for all peoples to choose their form of government. Decolonization happened rapidly, and independence movements swept across Africa in the 1960s and '70s.

Born in 1924 or 1925 in the British Protectorate of Uganda, Amin began his military career in 1946. He joined the King's African Rifles

(KAR), a multi-battalion British colonial regiment formed from various East African British colonial possessions. Details of his service record are hard to come by due to his deliberate falsification. Amin claimed that he fought with KAR in Burma during World War II, and he wore honorary medals in the early part of his reign. The claims are false; no records mention his service in any World War II theatre. He quietly put away the honors in 1971 and made no mention of such war service again.[7]

Ugandan military records show that Amin began his career as a cook. His original recruitment owes to British officers posted to the Fourth Battalion of the KAR in Uganda. He was, Gwyn claims, the sort of soldier preferred by the British army. He was physically vigorous, poorly educated, and subservient. British officers believed Ugandans like Amin lacked the ability to question orders and would accept discipline at once. They considered Amin a "splendid chap." He was an excellent athlete, a boxer, and a rugby player. At six-and-a-half feet tall, he towered over his comrades. One official praised his vitality but cautioned that he was "virtually bone from the neck up, and needs things explained in words of one letter."[8]

Amin's commanders also praised his cutthroat manner—sadism, more like it—as efficient. They applauded his method of disarming the Karamajong, a group of eight tribes who dwelled in the semidesert of northeast Uganda. The tribesmen were nomadic cattle owners who raided each other periodically to grow their herds and prove their mettle in battle to qualify for manhood and marriage. They walked around unclothed until Amin's troops appeared in 1971 and told them to "get dressed or get shot." Amin then ended the raids by disarming the Karamajong with the following method. He would bring them before a safari table, place a man's penis on the table, hold up a *panga*, and threaten to sever the organ unless he produced his spear and shield to lay down arms. The method worked. Amin's commanding officers commended him for translating colonial policy in terms any tribesman could understand.

Some British officers worried these methods crossed the line from African tribal realpolitik into sadism, but as Uganda accelerated toward independence, a native soldier like Amin could not be marginalized, no matter how much his sadistic tendencies troubled them. He showed signs of leadership despite worrying character flaws. Amin was a part of the Ugandan society favored in the pre-independence army. The British traditionally recruited from Muslim Nubians, of which Amin was a member. While poorly educated, he had more schooling than his compatriots, who had resisted attempts to enroll them in the national education system. He continued to receive promotions.[9]

But some superiors reprimanded him for his brutality in putting down tribal revolts and exceeding his orders. In one instance, which occurred shortly before Ugandan independence, there was trouble on Uganda's northeastern border, where the Turkana tribe of northwestern Kenya lived. They, like the Karamajong, were nomadic cattle pastoralists and were pushed west from Kenya toward Uganda due to population shifts. They occasionally spilled over the border. Raids against the Karamajong for cattle began. The Turkana drove down into valleys that cut across the high slopes falling from Uganda to Kenya. By 1961, the Turkana had accumulated firearms and ammunition and could mount armed raids on the Karamajong.

Amin was sent to Kenya with a company of native troops to aid them. A few weeks later, the Kenyan government protested that his company had tortured and killed many Turkana to disarm them. British army officers merely shrugged at the report. They considered the Turkana to have received justice for their raids. Other troubling reports about Amin were ignored. He had been earlier charged with failure to seek treatment for venereal disease, presumed to be syphilis. This could explain his later mental deterioration and erratic behavior. None of it mattered. He was one of a limited number of Ugandans promoted to the rank of officer before his nation achieved independence in 1962, holding the highest rank of any African in the Ugandan army at the time of its independence. He was considered an exemplary soldier, and there were few bad marks in his record book.[10]

Amin's twisted career path from cook to officer to supreme commander to president was only possible due to circumstances in Uganda. Its history as a nation-state began in the 1890s, when Britain combined preexistent African states into one country. The largest among these was Buganda, still the dominant state when Uganda gained independence in 1962. Mutesa II, the king of Buganda, served as Uganda's first president and continued the colonial tradition of Bugandan preeminence. Prime Minister Milton Obote, who became president in 1966, took power by suspending the constitution and announcing himself president, thereby deposing Mutesa. Obote, who was not a Bugandan, sought to create a new Uganda unbound by old tribal loyalties. He fought against centrifugal forces that pulled Ugandans away from their national identity and back to tribe, clan, and family. Many rejected his reforms. Riots followed in Buganda after Mutesa's deposition, but they were put down by Idi Amin, now one of the army's chief officers.[11]

Amin was on excellent terms with Obote, who approved his promotion to major in 1963. Amin received special training in Britain and Israel, learning, among other skills, to become a paratrooper. In 1964, he was promoted to colonel and appointed deputy commander of Uganda's army and air force.[12] But Obote came to fear the growing power of Amin, who built up support in the army by recruiting from the Kakwa and other ethnic groups that inhabited his homeland in the West Nile district. He demoted Amin from his post of commander of the armed forces to commander of the army in 1970. The rift between the two became impassible after Amin learned Obote intended to have him arrested for embezzling military funds. He plotted to seize power.

While Obote was abroad attending a summit meeting in Singapore, Amin overthrew the government in a military coup on January 25, 1971. Soldiers took the airport, major roadways, and the rest of Kampala within days. In a press conference on January 26, Amin claimed only one soldier had been wounded in the coup. This marked the beginning of his lies and use of torture. He jailed a former brigadier named Hussein and a battalion commander, Lieutenant Colonel Oyok, at Luzira Prison in Kampala. They were brought into the prison courtyard, beaten with rifle butts, and kicked until they bled to death from internal injuries.[13]

Over the first six months of 1971, the rate of killing in Uganda, either on a tribal basis or at random, increased exponentially. The first killings in Amin's regime were mostly among enemy tribal groups. Milton Obote's people, the Lango, were among those who suffered the earliest. They were considered to be a potential hotbed of sedition and arrested and beaten at the military police prison in Kampala's western suburbs. Observers noticed early in Amin's regime that every Friday night there was a mass execution in the Karuma Falls area on the Nile. Prisoners were lined up, shot, and thrown into the river. The river was a useful depository for the bodies as it ran swiftly, carrying away the deceased . . . at first. Along stretches where the current was less swift, however, the corpses began to pile up. There were too many bodies bumping against the papyrus-lined banks for the river to accommodate. As the dead clogged the river, Ugandans who lived downstream could no longer use the Nile for drawing drinking water and washing their clothes. Many also lost their primary source of food; they could no longer fish for the Nile perch, a massive fish that often weighed over two hundred pounds. They had consumed too much human flesh.[14]

As his reign went on, Amin piled up honorary titles for himself. In 1971, he named himself "His Excellency President for Life, Field Marshal Al Hadji Doctor Idi Amin, VC, DSO, MC, Lord of All the Beasts of the Earth and Fishes of the Sea." After Great Britain cut diplomatic ties in 1976, Amin included in his title "Conqueror of the British Empire in Africa in General and Uganda in Particular," which he kept even after going into exile in 1979.[15]

Despite the omnipresent threat of violence, Amin still worked to woo Ugandans with a charm offensive. He traveled throughout the country in his first year as dictator and promised to make the economy grow. In a move to shore up support from working-class ethnic Africans, he expelled Uganda's financially prosperous Asian community, which he blamed for stealing jobs. The expulsion order came in one fell swoop on August 5, 1972, when Amin announced all Ugandan Asians who held British passports would need to leave the nation within ninety days. Among the forty thousand who fell under this order were third-generation descendants of workers brought by the British from the Indian subcontinent. Many who left were only allowed to take what they could carry.[16]

The foreign media were fascinated by his buffoonish antics and gaudy excesses. To them, he was a caricature of incompetent African dictatorship. Amin even claimed the throne of Scotland, fashioning himself as a William Wallace of the Nile, defying the British at every turn. He relentlessly mocked Queen Elizabeth and requested a pair of her twenty-five-year-old knickers to commemorate her Silver Jubilee. Shoving Uganda's status as a former colony back in Britain's face, he offered them a cargo ship full of bananas in "gratitude" of the "good days of colonial administration." The media relentlessly documented his playboy lifestyle. He loved motorsports and collected foreign race cars. He kept five wives and openly flaunted them.[17]

Despite his public life of luxury and the open secret of his using torture against enemies, Amin had his supporters and sympathizers. In 2016, investigative journalist Kim Wall visited Uganda and spoke with former servants of Amin. One, Mukasa, who was in his seventies, recalled the stagnant economy of his home and how Amin had brought a small measure of progress. He brought roads, jobs, and technological novelties, such as the nation's first cancer radiotherapy machine. "He did so many good things and so many bad things," said Mukasa. "Idi Amin is dead. We should treat him fairly." Others remembered his histrionics and loved the braggadocio he brought to the executive office. Amin once challenged Tanzania's president, Julius Nyerere, to a boxing match, even promising to tie one hand behind his back to provide Nyerere a "sporting chance."

And not everyone thought Amin was solely responsible for his regime's brutal actions. Yes, he carried primary responsibility, but he was also an actor on an international stage. His audience was the Western media. "Idi Amin represented what Africans were able to do," explained Professor Katono Nzarwa, head of Kampala's Makerere University's history department and a specialist in Anglo-American media representations of Amin. "And newspapers make rulers and kings."[18] But while Amin was able to weaponize Western fascination with African rulers and their unconventional uses of democratic institutions for their own purposes, shifting focus away from his murderous program, he deeply reinforced stereotypes of postcolonial African rulers. He was a monstrous figure who reinforced long-held clichés of the European colonial era, such as the belief that inhabitants of the Dark Continent could not rule according to the standards of the modern world. For more than a few, Amin was proof that Africa was not ready for or even capable of independence. "In Western Europe you have more than 200–300 years of democratic experiments, right?" Nzarwa said to Kim Wall in 2016. "And in Africa, we have fifty years. But you expect those with fifty years of experience to behave like we have 300 years. Is it really fair?"[19]

Africa's young nations churned in the crucible of democracy, but Amin made the fires burn hotter than anyone else. He refashioned Ugandan institutions in military terms. The government was renamed "the Command Post." Military tribunals superseded the rule of law. Underground prisons sprang up across the country. In the early months of his reign, he dispatched enemies by shooting them, a clean form of execution. When the death toll mounted and the need for privacy dissolved, mercenaries abandoned firearms in exchange for *panga* blades. They were cheaper than firearms and more suitable for inexperienced troops who could not keep a gun clean or shoot straight.[20]

Amin murdered competent government officials who would not rubber-stamp his agenda. On January 9, 1973, the president's office reported eighty-five missing. Among them was Joseph Mubiru, a graduate of an American university and former Bank of Uganda governor. He was one of the brightest minds in African finance. Anyone could have guessed his fate after he had a minor disagreement with Amin the previous year. Months earlier, the government had said Mubiru would not be kept as bank governor. He then wrote to *The People*, a government-controlled newspaper, to dispute the government's statement. The dustup was minor, but it had displeased Amin. He later threatened to detain Mubiru "under cold water." All knew what this meant. "Under cold water" was a torture method in which detainees stood for hours under a cold shower. Amin's public sanction of torture was one of the first times that he let his gentle-giant facade slip.[21]

Amin ruled without intermediaries and created a direct link between himself and the people, a cult of personality of his own choosing. He used state radio to openly discuss social issues once decided in private government chambers under the purview of experts. The public believed they were seeing the decision-making process for consumer prices, the cleanliness of city streets, and taxation. The disadvantage of his method of direct rule was the impossibly of hiding his erratic personality. In public appearances, he quickly shifted from clownish to mercurial to volcanic. His deep feelings of inadequacy and desire to shake his fist at Uganda's former colonial masters were apparent.

Throughout his reign, he continued to insult Great Britain and the United States, aligning himself with their opponents. Uganda became part of the anti-Western bloc of Middle Eastern and North African nations led by similarly flamboyant rulers. He formed ties with Libya and Palestine and undermined Uganda's connections with Israel. Amin was directly involved in the 1976 hijacking of a French airliner, in which Palestinian terrorists took an Airbus A300 and its passengers hostage and diverted it to Uganda's main airport in Entebbe. He knew of the plan from the beginning and personally welcomed the hijackers. Israel Defense Forces rescued the hostages, but four were killed in the operation. The victims included Dora Bloch, a seventy-three-year-old who was dragged from a hospital and killed on Amin's orders.

By 1976, Amin had declared himself "President for Life," but his absolute rule did not last as he hoped. Tanzania, to the south of Uganda, had never recognized Amin's dictatorship. By 1978, the tensions between the nations grew to the point of a full-scale war. Britain increased its Tanzanian aid budget to enable President Julius Nyerere to launch a military attack and oust Amin. The Tanzanian army, backed by anti-Amin Ugandan troops, invaded. It faced a Ugandan army that had doubled in size since the beginning of Amin's reign but was also considerably weaker. Amin ordered imprisonments and executions for experienced officers suspected of seditious behavior, leaving behind an army of loyal but incompetent troops. The Tanzanian army reached Kampala in April 1979. They were too late. Amin had already fled.[22]

His reign lasted less than a decade but was remarkably durable, considering the number of attempted assassinations he survived. David Gwyn credited three factors for Amin's ability to outfox conspirators. First, he had a strong survival instinct, "a kind of tingling in the big muscles of the thigh and stomach that warn you when you are in danger and when it is time to move." As a soldier on Uganda's dangerous frontier, he had cultivated that instinct well. Second, there was a lack of resources or will to depose him. Other than a September 1972 invasion attempt by Tanzania, no foreign power tried to kill him. They believed Amin to be a threat contained to Uganda. Locals themselves did not have the resources to hire a skilled assassin or arrange the necessary weapons and military abilities necessary for such a task. Ugandans, of course, wanted to kill him, but Amin's schedule was too erratic for any long-term planning. Third, Amin had thousands of informants on his payroll. He rewarded those loyal to him with luxury goods flown in from England and terrorized them with the threat of execution for even supposed disloyalty. The combination of loyalty and fear kept his informants close. They worried that the moment he stepped down, other Ugandans would kill them in a spate of vigilante justice.[23]

Amin was a showman, a self-promoter, a tyrant, a buffoon, and a megalomaniac. But was his behavior an act to court the world stage and play into low expectations of African leaders (while the real, calculating mastermind plotted to secure his regime), or was the fool on stage one and the same as the leader of Uganda? Was he truly mad, and if so, what sort of madness did he suffer?

There are theories for Amin's madness. The most straightforward explanation is syphilis, a common diagnosis for mad rulers, from Caligula to Ludwig. The disease can trigger erratic behavior and a Messiah complex for those with megalomaniacal tendencies. He was known to have left the sexual disease untreated while serving with the King's African Rifles, leading some physicians to believe he suffered from debilitating syphilis. However, this diagnosis is unlikely, because he lived for decades in exile in Saudi Arabia in reportedly good health.

Psychopathy is also a fitting diagnosis to explain Amin's use of murder. He made murder a legitimate tool of government, as commonplace as tax collection and voter registration, used against criminals and political prisoners alike. Proponents of this diagnosis argue that only the disordered brain of a psychopath could use murder so casually and callously. Yet he was not so unhinged that he did not know what he was doing or that it was wrong. Amin knew it was wrong and simply didn't care. He also showed signs of hypomania, a mood state of perpetual disinhibition and mood elevation. The sufferer appears normal in various periods but then explodes with total irrationality. The irrational periods grow longer, and the normal periods shrink. One doctor familiar with Amin noted that "unfortunately, in this case, it means that he is just short of being certifiable."[24]

Such observations complicate defining Amin's insanity. He sits among the Hitlers, Stalins, and Saddam Husseins, often described as mad yet certainly able to perform the duties of their offices, even if they did transform their offices into execution chambers. His madness appeared to grow with his political powers. Former British foreign secretary David Owen, who served during Amin's reign, said his madness struck at the heart of darkness in any individual:

The very question reflects a wish of those who live within democracies to underplay the latent evil within society, and to forget or ignore the brutalizing effect on personality that stems from living within, let alone presiding over, a Communist or Fascist dictatorship, or an ethnically divided country such as Rhodesia or the former Yugoslavia. The longer a leader lasts in office in these regimes, the more their power stems not from popular consent but from imposition. National minorities within a divided country can give their leaders ethnic electoral support, but such leaders are vulnerable to coups or assassination. They tend to lead ever more secretive lives, become out of touch with the people they lead and the reality of the world around them, and develop paranoiac tendencies. In addition, such leaders almost always become corrupt.[25]

The international community slowly became aware of the horror in Uganda, but Amin did not hide from the press; he directly addressed the criticism. Rather than diplomatically rebut the claims, he insulted victims. Amin approved of the Holocaust and the killing of six million Jews. He again insulted Tanzanian president Julius Nyerere, labeling him a coward, an old woman, and a prostitute. Then, in an about-face, he announced his love for Nyerere and said he "would have married him if he had been a woman." Zambian president Kenneth Kaunda was an "imperialist puppet and bootlicker"; Henry Kissinger a "murderer and a spy."[26] Amin forced Kampala's white residents to carry him on a throne and kneel before him in humiliation as photographers snapped away. He ejected U.S. Marines who guarded the American embassy in the capital and Peace Corps volunteers.

His brutish policies terrorized Ugandans and international watchdogs. Harold Wilson, leader of the British Labour Party, called him "mentally unbalanced." Amin's contempt for elite global opinion nevertheless earned him the admiration of radicals, anti-establishment figures, and leaders of rogue states. African nationalists cheered him on. Muammar Gaddafi courted him, as did the Soviet Union. His supporters included Yosef Ben-Jochannan, an American professor of African Studies whose research is riddled with historical errors and whose academic credentials have been falsified. When trying to defend Amin's record, Ben-Jochannan largely ignored his actual deeds and pivoted to an anti-Semitic tirade and criticism of cartoonists' depictions of Amin as having exaggerated African features.

Other foreign observers correctly feared the danger that Amin posed. He was more than a madman and shrewdly dangerous. Christopher Munnion, a *Daily Telegraph* reporter who was detained at the Makindye military barracks, reported that four of his cellmates were bludgeoned to death with sledgehammers. He said of Amin: "Capricious, impulsive, violent and aggressive he certainly is, but to dismiss him as just plain crazy is to underestimate his shrewdness, his ruthless cunning and his capacity to consolidate power with calculated terror."[27]

Idi Amin killed for political, financial, and personal reasons. He first massacred Obote supporters, then thousands of members of the Acholi and Lango ethnic groups. Army officers from these groups were the first to disappear, then rank-and-file soldiers, then civilians. Ugandans themselves thought little of these murders at first; they were merely "mopping-up operations" that followed any coup. But as those close to the victims spoke out against Amin, they were labeled treasonous and themselves targeted. Violence begat violence as these dissenters were executed. The first political killings snowballed into an ongoing program of torture, mutilation, and murder.

As independence swept Africa, Amin embarrassed the entire continent by his terrible abuse of power. He embodied the Ugandan proverb, "One frog spoils a water hole." He was, as Gwyn saw, as dangerous to the peace and security of Africa as Hitler was to 1930s Europe. The difference was that opponents defeated Amin before he achieved any-thing close to Hitler's death toll. He still inflicted huge damage, how-ever. Ugandans died, their nation's reputation was shattered, and other African nations were implicated by association. Amin offered decades of propaganda fodder to the apartheid states of South Africa and Rho-desia, the final holdouts against black independence. He embodied the worst fears of those who thought Africa a primitive region unable to govern itself, distorting the image of the entire continent. David Gwyn wrote, "No African face can now avoid the overprint of Amin; millions of non-Africans carry with them the suspicion that there, underneath, no matter how civilized the exterior, the black skin hides the same brutality. This is what racism is all about; this is why Amin is Africa's problem." He turned Uganda from a rapidly modernizing hub of devel-opment in postcolonial Africa to a squabbling collection of tribes, clans, and extended families, hunkered down into whatever confines of security they could find. Perhaps only the shared hatred of Amin kept Uganda from completely reverting to tribalism.[28]

His politics of division opened old wounds in Ugandan society. In the 1960s, those who were middle-class, university-educated, and main-tained weak tribal links with their hometowns were driven into the refuge of their families, abandoning Uganda's burgeoning cosmopolitan culture as it crumbled. It was a victory for traditionalists but augured poorly for the future of the nation. The fear of death hung over the atom-izing culture of Uganda. The defensive perimeters of family, clan, and tribe once again were the only security for scared individuals retreating from the cities.[29]

What did it feel like to live in Uganda at the height of his reign of terror? Survivors said it was numbing. A cloud of anxiety hung over everyone and fogged their senses. One could not follow a set pattern and stay home if Amin's thugs were after you, for they would find you. If marked for death, you had to stay constantly on the move. If you had the means, you changed cars. Moving locations brought peace briefly, but then it was time to move on. Even in stable times, you subconsciously always eyed the rearview mirror. If a car followed you—or if you imagined it—you changed routes and prayed that you were not caught in a dead end. If your name came up on one of Amin's radio broadcast tirades, then the situation was truly dangerous. In those situations, you left your house and stayed at the residence of friends. Then you drove home to breakfast at dawn and found a servant who said that soldiers had come the previous night. That servant might have been paid off with a year's wages, but the treachery was for nothing. His money was confiscated by troops if he tried to cross the border and escape Uganda.[30]

You wanted to be within sight and sound of others, but not close enough to involve them; it was not the easiest combination. And this was before Amin had gathered his full head of killing steam. Later it became much more difficult. Hear the agonized confession of a church pastor in 1977: "We passed by on the other side—we had to. We saw them being shot down in the open street. If we had even shown that we had seen, they would have shot us too. They did not want witnesses."[31]

After his exile, Amin kept a low profile in Saudi Arabia. He no longer had a bully pulpit to hurl insults at other world leaders and display gaudy demonstrations of power. He nevertheless enjoyed an easy life in the Red Sea port town of Jeddah, living in a large villa with nearly half of his thirty or so children. Amin prayed at a local mosque, went to a nearby health club to receive massages, and shopped for his own groceries at a supermarket. He strolled around the city in the customary white robe of Saudi Arabia, receiving greetings from locals as "Mr. President."[32]

"The Butcher of Uganda" died peacefully in 2003, afforded all the comforts denied to his victims. He was seventy-eight, surrounded by excellent doctors, living on a stipend supplied by the government of Saudi Arabia. Amin's home village mourned him as a misunderstood hero who rose far above his humble tribal upbringing. All accounts say he died without regrets.

CHAPTER EIGHT

# PRESIDENT SAPARMURAT NIYAZOV OF TURKMENISTAN

## 1940–2006

In 2007, two residents of Turkmenistan's capital were riding in a car together, discussing the devastation wrought by their former president, an erratic and self-absorbed man. The previous year, their president for life, Saparmurat Niyazov, had died. He created a personality cult that was so destructive it made simple orientation to the rest of the world almost impossible. Before he died, he left behind a whole slew of chrono-myns named after himself, his mother, and patriotic items associated with his nation. As a result, they were trying to figure out the nation's new names for the months of the year.

"January is now Turkmenbashi," said Gulnara, an educated woman. "February is Bay´derk—the flag. March is Nowruz. April is Gurban-soltan Eje—his mother. June is Oguz—our hero. But May is . . . what is May?"

"May is Sanjar," said Mamed, a man who was having similar difficulty remembering the new months.

"No, that's November."

"Are you sure?"

"I know September is Ruhnama [the president's book of ethics]," Gulnara said.

"August is Alp Arslan," Mamed said. "He was sultan."

"You forgot July," Gulnara said.

"I don't remember July. What is it?"

Gulnara shook her head. She concentrated and said, "Then there's October."

Mamed said, "Garas,syzlyk."

"Independence," Gulnara said.

They were similarly confused on the new names for the days of the week, though Gulnara began confidently. "Monday is Bashgün—Main Day. Tuesday is Yashgün, Young Day. Wednesday is Hoshgün."

"Tuesday is Hoshgün," Mamed said. "Wednesday is Yashgün."

"I don't think so," Gulnara said.

Their confusion was amusing but not confidence-inspiring for the direction that Turkmenistan was now headed. Earlier in the decade, a government decree said that all ministries, schools, colleges, the police, the army, and all citizens had to demonstrate a knowledge of these changes and use them.[1] In most of the world, confusion about the days of the week and months of the year is uncommon. But the Turkmens had lived for decades under an uncommon ruler. Saparmurat Niyazov, the leader of the tiny Central Asian nation of Turkmenistan from 1985 until his death in 2006, did such eccentric acts throughout his reign to create a cult of personality. He led Turkmenistan while it was a Soviet republic, from 1985 until the USSR's dissolution in the early nineties. When he became the first president of the newly independent nation in 1990, Niyazov sought to keep the flame of Soviet propaganda burning. He spent the next fifteen years becoming the Stalin of the Caspian, replacing enormous pictures of the Soviet premier with himself and plastering his visage on every available public building, commemorative memorial, statue, fountain, and even bottles of vodka. The nation was his cathedral and his image the votive candle.

Niyazov launched this personal branding campaign in the beginning of his presidency with the goal of uniting the fragile desert nation of five million. Turkmenistan lacked a strong unifying identity because it was still an infant nation. Until the nineteenth century it had few cities, and its residents were mostly seminomadic, living in conditions that would have been recognizable to Genghis Khan six hundred years earlier. Inhabitants lived in yurts, tents made of animal hides that could be disassembled and transported on the backs of their camels and horses. They led massive herds of sheep and goats on migrations to fresh pastures throughout the year. They maintained this lifestyle until Russia expanded into Central Asia in the nineteenth century and forcibly settled them into towns. The Soviets ruled from 1918 until 1991, building block apartments, factories, and schools that taught Russian. After the fall of the Soviet Union in 1991, Turkmenistan had independence, but it risked falling into civil war or despotism as its neighbors had. Niyazov, who had served as the area's chosen governor for the Communist Party in the eighties, shepherded the nation through this dangerous transitional period as president. He worked to swap Communism as the national ideology with "Turkmenism."

But he did more than promote Turkmenism and lead Turkmenistan; he *became* Turkmenistan, and Turkmenistan became him. From the time he took office as president until his sudden death in 2006, Niyazov made it his primary order of business to promote himself. Turkmenistan abounds with the most magnificent dedications, honorariums, and memorials to the country's first leader, each memorial commissioned by Niyazov himself. After his appointment to president for life by Parliament in 1999, Niyazov freely gave massive amounts of municipal resources toward his own public praise. President Niyazov gave himself the title of Akbar Turkmenbashi, or "Great Leader of All Turkmen," in 1993. Renamed after him or his family members were days, weeks, and months on the calendar. Multiple streets and schools became Turkmenbashi; the name of Turkmenistan's largest port city, Krasnovodsk, was changed to Turkmenbashi.

Scientists even named a meteorite after him. Space, time, and religion all became an *instrumentum regni* (instrument of monarchy).

Niyazov, like other megalomaniacs, projected his personal likes and dislikes onto public policy. Makeup on female newscasters was not allowed because it made the president uncomfortable; he believed Turkmen women to be pretty without it. He outlawed the use of gold caps in dental work—a common dental treatment in Central Asia—in favor of his exhortation that Turkmen chew on bones to strengthen their teeth, thus eliminating the need for gold caps. He banned dogs from the capital city for their "unappealing odor."

The autocratic madman mostly escaped international scrutiny because he ruled one of the least-known nations in the world. Other than being the natural gas hub of the Caspian Sea and a major energy exporter for Russia, Turkmenistan was little known except for the strange reputation of its president. While academics have studied and journalists have ridiculed Niyazov's strange feats, few have asked *why* he behaved in such a bizarre manner. The challenges faced by Turkmenistan after the fall of the Soviet Union, after all, were common to those of its neighbors Uzbekistan, Kazakhstan, and Tajikistan—rampant unemployment, hyperinflation, the crumbling of the administration system, the withdrawal of Soviet financial support that propped up their economies, corruption across the government spectrum, and heavy-handed rule by presidents for life. Observers have argued that Niyazov's bizarre antics owe to the peculiar backwardness of Turkmen culture. Why did Turkmenistan alone produce a ruler who considered himself virtually deified, on the level of an Old Kingdom Egyptian pharaoh? It was argued that Turkmenistan would collapse soon after Niyazov's death.[2] But in 2006 the transfer of power to Deputy Prime Minister and Minister of Health Gurbanguly Berdimuhamedow went smoothly. Niyazov's cult of personality has diminished and been replaced with the new president's milder cult of personality. However, the question of why Niyazov rose in Turkmenistan and not elsewhere continues to linger.[3]

Perhaps Niyazov's rise has to do with his unique approach to nation building. He crafted an idea of citizenship in which one's first loyalty was not to the state, as in the United States or Western Europe, but to the leader. This client–patron form of government resembled other young nations in Africa and Southeast Asia coming out of colonialism in the twentieth century, where there was no established history of sovereign statehood. Nobody young or old had a conception of what an independent Turkmenistan was when it appeared in 1991. This was a challenge for Niyazov, but also an incredible opportunity. He could create a fictional past for Turkmenistan in which it was the great power of the Middle Ages, master of the steppe and ruler of the Silk Road, besting rivals like China and Persia in battle. The purpose of creating this fictionalized history was not merely a creative writing exercise; it was a necessary step to overcome Turkmenistan's factionalized society in which tribal roots still mattered. A fictional past that could create national cohesion was preferable to a splintered reality that would create civil war.

The problems Niyazov faced as a leader were Turkmenistan's weak national identity, a long history of domination by stronger neighbors, an economy highly dependent on energy exports for economic development, and the 1990s ideological vacuum between the Cold War and the War on Terror. Through it all, a personality like Niyazov's could strangely dominate. He made the nation drunk on his mix of paternalism, fierce patriotism, and paranoia of outsiders, crafting a myth of national unity that Turkmens understood, but that outsiders found utterly bizarre.[4]

Niyazov's reign is a textbook example of a cult of personality. This concept was first formulated by Max Weber, a nineteenth-century political theorist and sociologist who studied power politics across history. In a cult of personality, an individual uses the tools of government communication, mass media, and official celebrations and demonstrations to create an idealized, quasi-religious image of a leader. Niyazov was imbued with Weber's notion of charisma, "a certain quality by which [a person] is set apart from ordinary men and treated as endowed with supernatural, superhuman, or at least specifically exceptional powers or qualities."[5] Thus the unifying concept that rallies together a nation is a man, not a pledge of allegiance, a flag, a collective memory of winning great battles, or a constitution. But while a cult of personality can function well in the lifetime of a leader, problems arise when he dies. The goal of a cult of personality is to take the leader's charisma, extract it from the individual, and transmute it into institutions, statues, acts of collective memory, and even holy books in order to make him immortal. Niyazov followed all these steps perfectly.

He was a charismatic authority. This is a different form of authority than Weber's other two types of authority: traditional and legal. A traditional authority is a regime tied to a long history of governing, such as a king in a well-established dynasty. The ruler has legitimacy because most think it has always been that way. Traditional and premodern societies often followed this method; the inertia of government prevented most challenges to a traditional monarch. Legal authority is inseparable from legal legitimacy and bureaucracy found in modern republics. Constitutional safeguards and multiple layers of courts secure a ruler's reign. Citizens may not like the leader, but they respect the governing system. Since Turkmenistan had no traditional form of independent government, and its legal system sprang up *ex nihilo* after the fall of Communism, with the constitution and legal system weak and very susceptible to tampering, Niyazov chose to rule as a charismatic authority with gusto.

The president went beyond displaying large photos in the public squares of Ashgabat. He looked to displace the understanding of time by having days and months renamed after himself, his family, and his fantasy-based understanding of Turkmenistan's history. Along with the new months named after the president and his late mother that were mentioned earlier, his father received a village named after him, although he was a Soviet soldier who died in World War II shortly after Niyazov's birth.[6]

New holidays were added to the Turkmen calendar as part of this national building effort. The goal was to accumulate centuries' worth of civic unity and national esprit de corps within a decade. France had two hundred years to institute such national celebrations as Bastille Day and Armistice Day, commemorating the French Revolution and the end of World War I, respectively. Turkmenistan dug deep into its back bench of national memory to fill out its calendar. New national holidays included the commemoration of the 1880 Battle of Göktepe (January 12), in which the Russian army killed twenty thousand Turkmens as part of its conquest of Turkestan; Turkmenbashi's birthday (February 19); the Day of Mourning (October 6) to recognize victims of the 1948 earthquake in Ashgabat; and Neutrality Day (December 12), the anniversary of the United Nations' recognizing the neutrality of Turkmenistan and a day to commemorate the nation's commitment to peace.

Other holidays exalted Turkmen cultural identity, including Turkmen Stallion's Day to acknowledge the Turkmen legacy of warfare and pillaging across the Eurasian steppe. Then there is Turkmen Melon Day (the second Sunday in August) to recognize the melons that are grown in abundance there; Niyazov justified this holiday by stating that "the bygone glory of melon . . . is inseparably linked to the fate of the Turkmen People." There is also Carpet Day, Harvest, and the festival "A Drop of Water; a Grain of Gold" in April. These holidays reframe carpets and horses as being not just typical products of the country but expressions of natural genius. A carpet appears on the state flag and a horse on the state seal.[7]

Beyond new holidays, the greatest tool in Turkmenbashi's arsenal for sculpting a new national Turkmen ideology was architecture. His ambitions for monuments, statues, commemorative plaques, and enormous structures that filled the flat desert space of Turkmenistan emerged from his desire to turn the Platonic ideal of Turkmenness into a physical structure that could be understood by its viewers to improve their visual literacy and shape their understanding of the universe. Ashgabat has the most white-marble-clad buildings in the world, at least 543 in 2013, totaling an area of 4.5 million square meters. Like his fellow Central Asian leader of a post-Soviet government, Nursultan Nazarbaev, president of Kazakhstan, Niyazov reorganized the old Soviet-era squares of his capitals and replaced images of Lenin and Stalin with himself. Ashgabat became choked with statues of Niyazov. They featured him in all poses: saluting, smiling, waving, walking, and sitting, as if the monuments were a stop-motion film of his life, cast in twenty-four-karat gold. The promotion of Niyazov was so aggressive that the lingering statues of Lenin appeared humble in comparison. One diminutive monument featured the first Soviet premier as a bronze, life-size figure (small for the city's standards); its message—"Leninism Is the Way to Free the Peoples of the East"—appeared understated in comparison to Niyazov's grand proclamations that it was the Turkmen people who moved the very levers of history.[8]

Ashgabat was a perfect city to redesign. It sprang up around a Russian military outpost in 1881, the year after the conquest of Turkmenistan. The city developed during the following decades but was leveled by a terrible earthquake in 1948 that killed thousands, among them Niyazov's mother. Today the city features the same indistinct architecture found in any post-Soviet city: endless rows of rectangular apartments, large boulevards for tramway systems, and open spaces in the metropolitan center for public marches. Ashgabat is surrounded by both mountains and a flat desert. But out of this empty land came otherworldly structures. The six-hundred-foot-tall Constitution Monument looks like a cross between a giant's broom and an astronomical antenna array in the American Southwest. The Serdar Health Path is an endless walkway of stairs and tracks that winds into the bare hills south of Ashgabat. Extending over five miles, it is a central feature of Turkmenistan's Health Week. Niyazov forced his cabinet to walk the entire path in 2000. They struggled to finish, but he rooted for them to make it up the steep walkway, even though he had been flown in via helicopter.[9] In all these projects he was the master architect, working to reform the city into the Turkmenistan of his dreams.

Niyazov's effort to reclaim the old glory of Turkmenistan has limited basis in historical fact. In the Middle Ages, the land now known as Turkmenistan was home to Silk Road trading centers such as Merv, once among the wealthiest and largest cities on earth. In the tenth century, the oasis trading city had a population of half a million (London and Paris barely had thirty thousand inhabitants at the time). UNESCO World Heritage sites dot Turkmenistan, with ruins dating back to the first millennium BC. Niyazov boasted of these sites but reluctantly acknowledged that Turkmen architecture had fallen into decay in the last few centuries and neglected its contribution to world civilization. As such, he said, every town and village should aim to display its unique characteristics. And Ashgabat should become a world city like Berlin, Paris, or Istanbul.[10]

But whatever his architectural ambitions for Ashgabat, they could never match up to the grandeur of the city's street names and public squares. The main thoroughfare became Turkmenbashi Avenue. Marx Square became Independence Square. Other sites renamed Turkmenbashi were Ashgabat's airport and a number of schools, streets, universities, factories, communal farms, public buildings, and the state farm, which breeds special horses. Turkmenistan's attempts to break from the spirit of its tsarist and Soviet pasts were more fictional than real. The ideological reasons for nationalistic buildings and renaming of streets was no different than the Soviet or Imperial Russia periods; only the ideological project changed, from fierce socialism to fiercer nationalism.[11]

The result of these projects in Ashgabat was not a cosmopolitan wonder combining the modern sleekness of Dubai with the old-world charm of Florence. It was Disneyland of a mythical past clogged with expensive but tacky eyesores, such as the Oguzkhan Presidential Palace, the Palace of Culture (where Niyazov's quotations were inlaid in gold at the entrance of the building), and the Monument to Independence (a column surrounded by fountains featuring a crescent with five stars on top), which was faced by a statue of Niyazov surrounded by historical rulers from past Central Asian empires, such as the Seljuks and the Sanjars. Greatest of all was the gigantic marble Arch of Neutrality hoisting up the golden statue of Niyazov with his arms raised and rotating according to the sun, directing it as if he were Helios, Greek god of the sun.[12]

As a former secretary of the Communist Party in Turkmenistan, Niyazov carried over the artistic stylings of Soviet-era propaganda into the nation's independence. Posters of him had the same large, striking image as an illustration of Brezhnev from the 1970s. In this way he betrayed a conservative mindset—the Turkmen Communist Party under his leadership was among the most resistant to reform in the entire Soviet Union and borrowed much of its visual language. There were Eastern touches to his propaganda, however. Sometimes, Niyazov is depicted holding his hands prostrate before him in Islamic prayer, the mosques of Turkmenistan filling the background. Other times smiling, scarfed women with an armful of cotton smile at the viewer, a perfect likeness to a Soviet-era female factory worker enjoying the riches of Communism's productivity.

Like other aspects of public life in Turkmenistan, religion was subordinated to Niyazov's rule. Although the nation is constitutionally a democratic, secular state, Sunni Islam was the de facto religion, so Niyazov faced the challenge of accommodating the free expression of the faithful while not allowing radical religious belief to infringe on the rights of others. After World War I, revolutionary figures like Mustafa Kemal Ataturk of Turkey radically subordinated Islam and made secularism the law of the land. Religious reactionaries, such as the Taliban in Afghanistan next door, destroyed spheres of life not under the purview of Islam. Niyazov struck his own idiosyncratic balance by becoming the nation's "imam-in-chief." He declared in 1994 that the Council of Religious Affairs would be housed in the presidency. Its board members—a governmental official, two Muslim religious leaders, and the head of the Russian Orthodox Church—would be personally appointed by him to handle religious affairs within the republic.[13]

As his reign continued into the twenty-first century, Niyazov banned various forms of art, entertainment, and consumer goods under the guise of protecting Turkmenness. Then, in the same way Communists attacked symbols of capitalism, he forbade forms of Russianness in his own version of ethnic cleansing. He outlawed circuses, ballet, and opera in 2001 for being too foreign. He prevented men from wearing their hair and beards long in 2004. He also shut down the last Russian-language radio channel in 2004, to place greater emphasis on the country's Turkmen language. Other times he appeared to be applying his personal preferences to matters of state law. Following his decision to quit smoking in 1997 after his heart surgery, Niyazov outlawed smoking in all public places and among all government employees; chewing tobacco quickly followed suit.[14]

The president was clearly a megalomaniac, but he remained too isolated for many personal accounts to offer a larger picture of the madness he suffered. Niyazov was obsessively clean. According to a neighbor of his who lived in Moscow among other Turkmen dissidents, his Russian wife forced him to smoke outside. "After he shook your hand, he had to wash his own hands. This was strange—first because shaking hands is not a Turkmen custom, and second, because in the East water is so scarce, it's sacred. Normal people don't care if they have dirty hands." He also obsessed over his image. One artist had responsibility for airbrushing official portraits of Niyazov. Pockmarks, scabs, and burst capillaries were all removed. His hair was darkened and full; crumpled suits, ironed. His shadow was removed from group photographs. Fitting for a president who always faced the sun.[15]

His magnum opus was the Ruhnama, part revisionist history, part political treatise, part autobiography, part moral instructional manual, all packaged in the guise of a medieval hero epic—complete with stories and poems. He intended it to be a foundational work of Turkmenistan's culture that would guide the young nation to its destiny of greatness and be an eternal source of inspiration for the Turkmen people.

Oddly enough, the genesis for this Turkmen nationalist bible was an academic project born at the end of the Soviet period. Khudaiberdy Orazov, the former leader of the Central Bank of Turkmenistan, claimed that the original idea came before Turkmenistan's independence, during a convention of government officials, when the dean of the department of history at Turkmen State University said his department had been collecting ethnographic and historical information about Turkmenistan for two decades. Such material would have been difficult to promote in the Soviet period. The Soviet ideology always deemphasized ethnic groups to promote a state historical methodology, in which society marches inexorably through the stages of feudalism, capitalism, and Communism. But with independence looming on the horizon, the possibility of producing a comprehensive critical history of the Turkmen people was nearing.[16]

The first edition was published in 1994, but it displeased Niyazov. He formed a new committee and replaced the historians with fiction writers and poets. The result still disappointed Niyazov, so he authored the book himself. The book was published in 2001, then translated into English, Russian, and Turkish in 2004. Niyazov clearly believed that although the book was a sacred text for Turkmen, the message would resonate with an international audience. He also believed that the book would cut across class lines. It did do this, although only by force: along with the Hippocratic Oath, doctors swore on the Ruhnama. Truck drivers had to memorize passages in addition to vehicle safety.[17]

The Ruhnama was read in all schools and its memorization was required for graduation from school, to get a state job, and even to obtain a driver's license. School children spent one day a week reading and learning the Ruhnama, which had to be prominently displayed in all bookstores and government offices. The purpose of the book was to supply moral guidance for all Turkmen, regardless of their educational level. Ultimately, the president decided, the only books necessary for laymen were the Qur'an and the Ruhnama. So, Niyazov ordered the closure of libraries outside of Ashgabat. If only two books mattered, why make more available? So strong was his belief in his writings that in 2006 he said that he had personally interceded with Allah to ensure that anyone who read the Ruhnama three times would automatically enter paradise upon death.

The Ruhnama was adopted as a school subject and by 2006 was a principle subject in all primary, secondary, and university-level curricula. Quotes from it appeared widely in the media. Conferences were held in its name; competitions, school Olympics, and TV programs dwelled on it. Soviet-style rooms once dedicated to Lenin reappeared in the form of "Saparmurat Turkmenbashi Rooms." There students learned the history and customs of their nation and took part in patriotically themed musical and literacy events. Portraits of Niyazov were displayed, along with the flag, the Turkmen oath, the seal, and the anthem.[18]

The Ruhnama lacks a central theme and rambles from history to moral philosophy to pronouncements of God's justice that sound like they are from a holy book. But there are also strange passages of self-improvement advice that would not be out of place in books by self-help gurus such as Deepak Chopra or Tony Robbins. One passage exhorts readers to keep a smiling face. "A smile can make a friend for you out of an enemy," it instructs. "When death stares you in the face, smile at it and it may leave you untouched." Smiling was a manner of discourse: "Talk to each other with smiles." It is a way of delaying aging: "'There will never be any wrinkles on a smiling face,' as the saying goes." Smiling was even the source of a treasured memory for Niyazov. "I often remember my mother. Her smile . . . is visible to me in the dark of night, even if I have my eyes shut."[19] But whether he is propounding on Turkmen history or how his people should smile, the Ruhnama always returns to how Turkmen, men and women, should behave, because "the spiritual perspective of the individual must be shaped by national values."[20] He explained his intention by quoting the thirteenth-century Anatolian mystic Rumi (whom he described as Turkmen) about alternate perceptions of the same thing:

A new spiritual approach is required to encompass the whole Turkmen nation and history. . . . Ruhnama is the veil of the Turkmen people's face and soul. It is the Turkmen's first and basic reference book. It is the total of the Turkmen mind, customs and traditions, intentions, doings, and ideals. It will be our legacy to the future after drawing lessons from the past.[21]

Rafis Abazov, author of the *Historical Dictionary of Turkmenistan*, claims that the style of the Ruhnama in some degrees replicates a popular Central Asian genre of traditional exhortations that were prepared by the wise rulers. It also resembles ancient Turkic epics like the *Book of Gorgut Ata* (fifth to sixth century) and the *Oguznama* (eleventh to thirteenth century), which recount the deeds of ancient heroes on the Central Asian steppe.[22] The Ruhnama is divided into five sections on the history and morals of the Turkmen people. The first page claims that the Turkmen nation originated five thousand years ago and descended directly from Noah. The text is above all a mythological account of Turkmen history. Niyazov embellishes the story with complete fabrications:

This book, written with the help of inspiration sent to my heart by the God who created this wonderful universe and who is able to do whatever he wills, is Turkmen Ruhnama. Allah has exposed the Turkmen nation to great and difficult problems since the creation of humankind. My people has successfully passed through these hard times. The Turkmen people, whose history goes back 5,000 years to the period of Oguz Khan, contributed to the universal values which emerged in the lands between the Eastern Mediterranean and India, and indeed, cannot be underestimated. In its own lands, the Turkmen people founded more than 70 states, including the Anew, Altyndepe, Margus, Parfiya, Seljuks, and Könergenq states. The Turkmen people has a great history which goes back to the Prophet Noah. Prophet Noah gave the Turkmen lands to his son Yafes and his descendants.[23]

The narrative quickly falls apart as non sequiturs follow, such as a list of good manners that includes the admonition to wear clean, decent clothing. Then Niyazov writes about meeting an elderly man as a student in Leningrad. The man described the death of his father in World War II, and Niyazov relates this feeling of despair to the loss of his mother. The moral teachings, garbled history, and personal stories continue for page after page until he notes, "If the spirit of the Turkmen is the universe . . . then Ruhnama must be the center of this universe." The text then stumbles forward.

The narrative is often undercut by Niyazov's genealogy, which links him to nonexistent, legendary figures. A centerpiece of the Ruhnama is Oguz Khan, a mythological khan of the Turkic peoples who first started appearing in narratives in the fourteenth century. The story goes that he could talk as soon has he was born, drank horse milk instead of his mother's milk, and grew into adulthood in forty days. He then slayed a dragon that was besieging Turkic lands. The khan went on a conquering spree, subduing the four corners of the earth. Turkmenbashi clearly loved Oguz (he appears on the 100 manat, the Turkic currency), but to claim a fictional character as an ancestor is like a British prime minister producing a family tree with King Arthur at the top. Other legendary Turkmen figures make cameos in the Ruhnama:

> My guiding souls, my father and my mother, said: "Allah selected the four heroes of the Turkmens—Oguz Khan, Gorkut Ata, Gorogly, and Magtymguly—as the inheritors of the prophets. Today, Allah the Great has designated you as their inheritor. Son, devote your life to maintaining the unity of the Turkmen nation and to sustaining the golden life for them."[24]

With his new family tree in hand, Niyazov presented himself as the end result of centuries of heroic Turkmen; he often mentioned these heroes in his long rambling speeches and tied himself into this mythological genealogy of great figures who displayed virtues of self-denial, sacrifice, courage, and discipline. To Niyazov, he was like Moses, leading his people to a promised land filled with abundance, where they would live in luxury, subdue their enemies, and enjoy the blessings of God. But these blessings would only come if "stability" were preserved and his people obeyed the edicts of the Ruhnama, essentially the Ten Commandments of the Turkmenistan president.[25]

The history of the Turkmen people under Russian and Soviet rule gets little mention in the Ruhnama. The Russian rulers are mentioned only as an obstacle to overcome, as they were foreign rulers to the Turkmen people and robbed them of their past glories. This is, in fact, the purpose of the Ruhnama, to merge a nonexistent golden age of conquest, independence, and cultural flourishing with the present. To tie these periods together, Niyazov talks of the timeless qualities of Turkmens. They are specially endowed with kindness, integrity, humility, courage, respect for others and for one's family. The men are brave and self-sacrificing, the women beautiful, humble, and gentle.[26]

The book sustains a commanding, sacral tone from beginning to end, which explains Niyazov's decree that the book was second only to the Qur'an in degree of holiness. Religious leaders, whether Muslim or Christian, were told to incorporate the Ruhnama into their public places of worship. During Niyazov's reign, mosques were required to display the book as prominently as the Qur'an. Orthodox churches required two copies at each site. Some imams considered a politician's manifesto being equated with the eternal word of God to be blasphemous. Their mosques were bulldozed.[27] But even Niyazov had his limits. He knew that he could not insult or debase Islam by equating his book with the Qur'an. He notes in the Ruhnama that the book is not religious in nature and that the Qur'an should be consulted first for guidance and to strengthen the people's values, empowering them in this "Golden Age of Turkmens."[28]

Niyazov connected his personal tragedies to those of the nation. In discussing political persecution in the 1930s Stalinist purges, he mentioned the exiling of his shopkeeper grandfather in 1932. The deaths of his mother and three brothers in the 1948 Ashgabat earthquake were stepping-stones on his path to the presidency. Since he lacked a natural family, all Turkmens were now his family, and his life experience thus connected him inextricably with all of Turkmenistan.

> The reason for intimate connection between my fate and the fate of my homeland is the similarity between them. When, after leaving my family and brothers, I was left feeling isolated and bereft, the homeland was afflicted in the same way. . . . The homeland reminds me of a woman who has been slapped and abandoned in the street.[29]

Throughout the Ruhnama, Niyazov conflated his own life story with that of the nation. He equates good moments for the nation with his own: "The date of the establishment of the Republic of Turkmenistan has been written in golden letters in history. That date was the worthiest, most defining, and happiest moment of my life." He also says that his autocratic form of direct power, in which one and only one ruler should lead, is supported by the wisdom of Central Asian tribal government going all the way back to the time of Genghis Khan: "Two persons shall never be your rulers at the same time. If there is one khan it means order, but two khans means disorder. Old, wise people said, 'A sheath cannot handle two swords.'"[30]

Turkmenistan suffers from the resource curse of abundant natural gas and little else. Only some of the wealth generated by this fossil fuel (an estimated $3 billion in exports in 2006, the year Niyazov died) found its way to the public. While natural gas and electricity were free, and gasoline so cheap that fifty cents was enough to fill up a car, the largest part of the export wealth remained with the government and went toward lavish state projects. Close to 60 percent of the population lived below the poverty line, and residents of Ashgabat hunted through the garbage to make a living. They lacked access to work, education, training, pensions, and food.

Tom Mayne, an activist with the anti-corruption advocacy group Global Witness, said Turkmenistan's resource wealth helped only Niyazov and his cronies and impoverished everyone else. "If you look around at the country, you see all these fabulous marble buildings, opulent palaces, mosques," he said. "You kind of get a suggestion of where the money is going. Under Niyazov, it didn't seem to be going to the people."[31]

Close to half of the population lived in poverty during Soviet occupation. Most roads were unpaved. Only 30 percent of households owned a telephone. Unimaginably, things got worse after Turkmenistan gained independence. A quarter of adults were unemployed. Public education attendance was cut from ten years to nine years. Universities completely lost their international credentials. To prevent brain drain, visas became virtually impossible to obtain. The government issued a maximum monthly wage on public sector jobs. A bank teller, for example, earned a maximum of thirty-six dollars a month.[32]

As his people became poorer, Niyazov became richer. He sold natural gas reserves to Russia, the Ukraine, and Iran at reduced prices and deposited much of the earnings in his foreign accounts, earning an estimated $3 billion. An estimated 75 percent of government revenue flowed into shadowy reserve funds that were largely controlled by the president. Hardly any money went back into the nation unless toward public works that directly honored the leader. Public services were scarcer than their meager Soviet-era levels. He replaced health care professionals with soldiers in all but a few hospitals to save on health care costs. He canceled pensions for the elderly and demanded they pay back two years' worth of earlier pensions. This move reportedly led to elderly Turkmen deaths.

Niyazov died in 2006 from a sudden heart attack (he was unhealthy and a heavy drinker). Because he named no successor, foreign analysts feared that the nation, built on a vainglorious ruler who made himself the node out of which all power flowed, would quickly collapse. Surprisingly, succession went smoothly. The state security council declared Deputy Prime Minister Gurbanguly Berdimuhamedow the new president. He restored Soviet festivities; repealed the ban on ballet, opera, cinema, and circus shows; and removed certain statues and monuments of Niyazov. The Ruhnama's importance partly diminished, but it remained a compulsory subject to gain access to university.[33] Niyazov's portraits may no longer hang on the walls of public offices, but the rest has remained largely untouched.[34]

Despite his death in 2006, the president's visage and voice appeared for years on Turkmenbashi TV. The president's image was required to appear on the faces of all watches and clocks. Turkmenbashi vodka also bore his image. One of the most well-known public displays, along with the golden statue, is a thirty-foot-tall replica of the Ruhnama that opens daily and broadcasts a recorded passage from the book.

Niyazov believed that his actions served his people. In a 2004 interview with the television show *60 Minutes*, he was asked about his public cult of personality. He answered that the public displays were a show of humility and contrition on his part; not for his good, but for the good of an average worker. He said, "If I was a worker and my president gave me all the things they have here in Turkmenistan, I would not only paint his picture, I would have his picture on my shoulder, or on my clothing. I'm personally against seeing my pictures and statues in the streets, but it's what the people want."

Those that could speak freely disagreed. The *New York Times* analyzed the eccentricities of his rule and asked Turkmen in exile about their former ruler's self-aggrandizement. Shrali Nurmuradov, a poet who fled to Sweden, responded sharply, calling the renaming of the months a sign of madness. "You know, there is a cult," he said, "but there is no personality. We cannot refer to him as a personality. It's imbecility, and it's progressing. There is a saying in our country: 'There is a limit to wisdom, but there is no limit to foolishness.'"[35]

## CHAPTER NINE

# Supreme Leader Kim Jong-il of North Korea

## 1941–2011

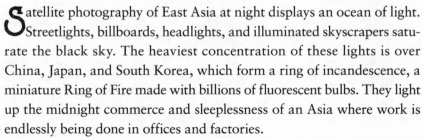

$S$atellite photography of East Asia at night displays an ocean of light. Streetlights, billboards, headlights, and illuminated skyscrapers saturate the black sky. The heaviest concentration of these lights is over China, Japan, and South Korea, which form a ring of incandescence, a miniature Ring of Fire made with billions of fluorescent bulbs. They light up the midnight commerce and sleeplessness of an Asia where work is endlessly being done in offices and factories.

In the middle of that nocturnal glow is a mysterious black hole. It is the Democratic People's Republic of North Korea, an area the size of Pennsylvania with twenty-three million inhabitants. Every single person sits in the dark, save for high-ranking officials in the capital of Pyongyang. One compound, however, always stays powered. It even boasts of luxuries. Surrounded by an electric fence (and security checkpoints), it has gardens, man-made lakes, underground tunnels, and even a private underground train station. This structure is the presidential palace of North Korea's despot. It was once home of Kim Jong-il, the Dear Leader.

His lights stayed on, but his nation went dark in the early 1990s. It was dependent on fuel from the Soviet Union, which subsidized equally poor Communist regimes in Asia, Africa, and Latin America throughout the Cold War. When the Soviet Union collapsed, the flow of oil stopped, and so did the supply of skilled technicians to keep the nation's electricity running. Power grids fell apart. Machines with instructions written in Cyrillic script rusted. Poor residents ripped apart power lines to get bits of copper to sell for scrap. Lights began to go out across the country. As darkness enveloped cities and towns, Koreans retreated into their homes. Even streets in Pyongyang were darkened.[1]

Outsiders who ventured into North Korea found it remote and alien. It was not primitive like the developing parts of Africa, which were building modern infrastructure for the first time, with sleek gas stations next to squat villager huts. North Korea carried the misery of a once-thriving civilization hit by a terrible catastrophe that threw its people into a dark age. Chernobyl is a better comparison for the nation than Kenya. Barbara Demick, former bureau chief for the *Los Angeles Times* in Seoul, described the endless power lines dangling overhead alongside every major North Korean road. The skeletal wires were archeological remains of the electricity that once flowed through the country.

North Koreans who are middle-aged and older remember when they looked down upon South Koreans for their backwardness. Communism had clearly bested capitalism. As the South eventually caught up and surpassed them, they could not blame themselves, their leadership, or their ideology. Failure had to come from outside. The United States was the go-to scapegoat. The U.S. had fought on South Korea's behalf in the Korean War and enforced sanctions against the North in the 1990s for Kim Jong-il's development of nuclear weapons. Residents still blame the United States for the sanctions that leave them in total darkness.[2]

Any journalist who visits North Korea tours the accomplishments of Kim Jong-il and his father, Kim Il-sung. Two men always chaperone them. Rote praises of their Dear Leader pepper most statements. Those who have escaped to South Korea have vastly different accounts of their experiences. Demick spoke to a former kindergarten teacher from a mining town. She had watched her five- and six-year-old pupils die of starvation. As they withered away from malnourishment, she taught them how blessed they were to be born in North Korea. Kim Il-sung was revered as if he were God, and Kim Jong-il as if he were Christ.[3]

In the students' mathematics courses, a simple math problem was turned into an indoctrination lesson on the Korean War. Here is a sample from a North Korean textbook:

> During the Fatherland Liberation War [North Korea's official name for the Korean War] the brave uncles of Korean People's Army killed 265 American Imperial bastards in the first battle. In the second battle they killed 70 more bastards than they had in the first battle. How many bastards did they kill in the second battle? How many bastards did they kill altogether?[4]

North Korea has a dark tranquility. There are deep greens from rice paddies in the summer, but for the rest of the year the color fades into yellow and brown. Unlike South Korea, the nation is full of open spaces and devoid of noise. Few cars run on the highway. Oxen drive plows, as they have been doing on the Korean peninsula since time immemorial. Only cement block and limestone houses show that it is the twenty-first century. City dwellers and those high-ranking enough in the Communist party live in "pigeon coops," which are one-room units in squat apartments. In the countryside, villagers live in single-story white and grey buildings called harmonicas, which are rows of one-room homes, stuck together like little boxes that make up harmonica chambers. The only color found is in propaganda posters with images of the Great Leader and Dear Leader. Rays of yellow and orange radiate out from him, as if he were the sun. Propaganda signs have such slogans as the following: "Long Live Kim Il-sung Kim Jong-il, Sun of the 21st Century," "Let's

Live Our Own Way," and "We Will Do as the Party Tells Us. We Have Nothing To Envy in the World."[5]

The Democratic People's Republic of Korea (DPRK) functions as a dictatorship under the absolute rule of the Korean Workers' Party (KWP). The first dictator was Kim Il-sung, who led North Korea from its founding until his death in 1994. His title was president, but that office was abolished after his death; the position was "retired" due to the elder Kim's flawless execution of his duties. Kim Jong-il was born to Kim Il-sung and Kim Jong-uk in the village of Vyatskoye in 1941, according to Soviet records. The biography approved by the North Korean state claims he was born in a secret military camp on Paektu Mountain in Korea one year later. It also claims a prophecy preceded Kim Jong-il's birth. At the moment of his birth, a double rainbow appeared in the sky, and a new star took its place in the heavens.

Kim Il-sung and Kim Jong-il built their personality cults around the idea of *Juche*, a national ideology of self-reliance. The ideology conveniently grew in strength, as North Korea increasingly found itself on the wrong side of the Cold War, Communist ideology receded, and global capitalism grew. North Korea is one of the last Communist holdouts still fighting the Cold War, keeping the tenets of a dead religion. North Korea is Communism distilled in its near purest form, the geopolitical equivalent of the Japanese soldier in World War II who hunkered down in the Philippines until the 1970s, unaware the war was over. As initially defined by Kim-Il sung, *Juche* is a quasi-mystical concept in which the people's collective will obtains a corporeal form as a supreme leader who executes the needs of the state and society. If a leader's actions are strange or inscrutable (such as living in obscene luxury while his people starve), it is merely *Juche* working out its mysterious ways for the betterment of society. Opposing a leader or the rules and regulations established to secure his reign is opposing the collective will of the people.[6]

The state directs all formal economic activity. Private enterprise is unofficial and illegal. The only labor unions allowed are government controlled, ensuring that the state has total control over the means of production. Not that there are many means to produce. Rusted, broken factories are in need of Soviet-era parts no longer manufactured. Trade and aid have never recovered to the levels of the 1980s. After the DPRK defaulted on its foreign debt, no other international financial institution offered it loans. Any efforts at building a sustainable economy are hampered by investment of the nation's few resources into the military budget, which sucked up one-quarter of the gross domestic product *before* the economy tanked and never recovered in the 1990s. The total percentage of military spending as a total of the overall economy now is much higher. North Korea has never been self-sufficient in food production, so it relies on international aid to supplement local farming. Terrible agricultural policies have hobbled output, even in good growing years.[7]

The droughts and floods of the nineties caused failed harvests and severe famine. It was estimated that anywhere from hundreds of thousands to two million died from starvation. The government, realizing it could never supply enough food through the state distribution system, allowed farmers to set up markets to make up for the broken supply chain. Everything is rationed in North Korea—energy, food, and clothing.[8]

Kim Il-sung died in 1994. The Communist Party ground the nation to a halt to celebrate his funeral. His family sat on the funeral dais. Kim Jong-il was stone-faced at the ceremony, remaining silently in the background as he had done during his father's reign. In terms of governing, however, he was no background player. In the fifteen years before his death, Kim Il-sung publicly led the nation, while Kim Jong-il ran the day-to-day affairs of the government. The son labored hard. He prepared comprehensive reports on the condition of the military and the economy. It is unknown if these reports were based on hard empirical data or the rosy projections that officials fed to him. It did not matter. Soviet and Chinese aid smoothed out most of the Communist regime's economic problems. Both father and son were sheltered from the starvation conditions of the peasants.

Kim Jong-il ended any potential challenges to his authority on assuming power in 1994. Rival politicians, descendants of landlords, and Christian clergymen faced arrest and execution. Any North Korean could be arrested: someone caught reading newspapers or writing anti-party words in their diary, for example; or a man who, after a few drinks, was heard insulting Kim Jong-il for his diminutive height. All of these infractions and many others fell under the rubric of anti-state crimes. Disappearances in the night happened often.[9] Whatever he lacked in economic training, Kim Jong-il made up for with the autocrat's skill of eliminating any nascent political opposition by keeping competitors out of power and promoting loyalists and sycophants. By the time he took his father's place as North Korea's dictator, he had already moved relatives, friends, and associates into key positions. Kim Kyong-hui, his sister, was an industrial manager, while her husband was a close advisor. All top government and military posts went to extended family.[10]

The near-collapse of his nation made Kim Jong-il more opportunistic and dovish. In June 2000, he met with South Korean president Kim Dae-jung in Pyongyang, the first summit meeting between the leaders of North and South Korea since the Korean War. Dae-jung initiated the summit as part of his Sunshine Policy, to "actively push reconciliation and cooperation between South and North," as Kim explained. This meeting was his first international diplomatic meeting. In sharp contrast to his later years, he spent the early years of his leadership working quietly and never appearing in public. He was gracious and courteous towards his southern counterpart. Following the summit, the two leaders issued a joint declaration calling for "Korea's reunification at the earliest possible date based on the three principles—independence, peaceful unification and great national unity [in] a federal state of the nation."[11]

As North Korea worked furiously on its nuclear weapons program, playing the arms race game that was popular in the Cold War, the rest of the world passed it by. Russia did not care to prop up a client state that could not pay its creditors an estimated $10 billion. Instead, Russia opened trade agreements with South Korea, whose economy roared ahead of its northern neighbor in the 1980s. Kias and Hyundais filled Russian streets. Russia opened diplomatic relations with South Korea in 1990, as did China two years later. Both nations stopped supporting the hermit state. Russia charged it prevailing world prices for imports instead of the Soviet era "friendship prices" for Communist allies. China once supplied 75 percent of North Korea's fuel and over 60 percent of food imports on little more than good faith. Now it required an up-front payment.

North Korea began an economic free fall. Without hard currency, fuel, manufacturing imports, or electricity, little could be produced. Agricultural output collapsed as farmers abandoned their tractors and mechanized harvesters for medieval forms of farming, relying on animal and human sources of power. Crop quality fell without the benefit of fertilizers; insects devoured crops due to the lack of pesticides. The twenty-three million residents had always had to work hard to eke out enough harvest in the rocky, mountainous nation, even with the benefit of machinery. Now they had to bring in the harvest by hand. As they ran out of food, the hungry farmers lacked the energy to plant enough crops to live. North Korea, like any industrialized nation, was dependent on machines. Deprived of them, the nation fell apart.[12]

Up until the end of Kim Jong-il's reign, North Korea was the last nation on earth where collective farms grew staples. The theories of Marx lingered in the hermit kingdom (so dubbed for walling itself off from the rest of the world) even after they had failed everywhere else in the twentieth century. At harvest time, the state confiscated everything and returned a small remittance to farmers. Growers found ways around these collections. They cultivated "kitchen gardens" next to their houses or hidden plots of land on mountain slopes away from the eyes of government agents. They even found ways to hide harvested grain from their known plots. During the famines of the 1990s, what little was salvaged had to be stashed away by farmers. In the countryside, many roofs collapsed from the weight of grain hidden in the eaves.

It was obvious that North Koreans took care of their private gardens and neglected the collective fields. Foreign observers saw gardens chock-full of well-tended vegetables, with massive pumpkins and towering bean poles. The collective fields, in contrast, had jagged rows of drooping corn. It was the result of the bare minimum labor performed by "volunteers" fulfilling their duty to the state.[13]

As Kim Jong-il consolidated power, North Korea suffered one of the greatest natural disasters in its history. On June 26, 1995, torrential downpours flooded the nation. Up to eighteen inches of rain fell in one day, continuing at three to five times the normal level until mid-August. Floods washed away homes and swept away entire fields. Over five million people were displaced and two million tons of grain were lost. The total cost of the flood damage was $15 billion, an enormous part of the nation's GDP. Food was severely rationed. In the north, residents ate 1,000 calories a day, only one-half of their daily recommended allowance. Rains struck again the next year, followed by a severe drought in 1997. Over a million people died from starvation during this period, around 6 percent of the nation's population. North Korea appealed to the capitalist United States for aid, which it provided.[14]

The only functioning part of the state is its legal system (mostly police and prison guards). The nation's legal system is not based on a system of justice, however, but on subservience to the state.

North Korea's constitution does supply a semblance of legal rights, such as the right to petition the government. But this "right" is another form of control. When an anonymous complaint is given to the government, the Ministries of State Security and Public Safety attempt to identify the author using forensic techniques such as handwriting analysis. Once caught, the suspect is investigated and punished according to the nature of his complaint. Most punishments result in imprisonment or death. The legal system assigns the death penalty for all activities "in collusion with imperialists" aimed at "suppressing the national liberation struggle." Death sentences have been handed out for the vague crimes of ideological divergence, opposing socialism, and counterrevolutionary crimes. Executions reportedly occur at public meetings attended by workers, students, and schoolchildren. Border guards have orders of shoot to kill for defectors.[15]

With a spike in complaints about North Korea's handling of the famine, arrests increased. The government detained up to 200,000 for political reasons (the families of "offenders" were also detained if the crime was considered severe enough) in remote camps, referred to euphemistically as "education centers." A defector who was an official in the Ministry of Public Security described two types of detention areas. One consisted of closed camps where prisoners never escaped or left. Others were "rehabilitation centers." There were a dozen such camps and thirty more forced labor and education camps. Visitors could not communicate with detainees. A 1997 report from the South Korean Ministry of National Unification claimed a sizable percentage of the hundreds of thousands of prisoners starved to death in the camps. Located in mining areas or on remote mountains, the camps had no electricity or heating. Those who tried to escape were executed.[16]

No state pries into the private lives of its people more intensely than North Korea. The state has a vast, multitier network of informers who incriminate coworkers, friends, and family members. If word of a low-level conspiracy reaches higher officials, whole communities can be slapped with intensive security checks. Incriminatory evidence includes "reactionary material," foreign broadcasts, or even rumors of intentionally or unintentionally defacing Kim family photographs. Spotless pictures of the two Kims had to be displayed in homes. Local party officials often conducted unannounced inspections of homes to see the condition of the photos. A softer punishment for failure to have them displayed in spotless condition was writing self-criticisms for one year.

Since the beginning, North Korea has divided society into three classes: "core," "wavering," and "hostile." Within each category are subcategories and endless gradients of suspected loyalty to the state that result in security ratings. Ratings determine access to education, employment, quality of residence, health care, and high-end stores (at least by

North Korean standards). They also determine leniency in cases of legal infractions. A "core" will get off lightly with an unclean picture of the North Korean leader, while a prison camp awaits someone "hostile." Since the end of Kim Jong-il's reign, the system has relaxed. Children of the religiously observant, for example, are no longer denied entrance into universities. Points for loyalty, however, are not easily earned. According to estimates, half of the population is "wavering" or "hostile."[17]

In North Korea, there are multiple types of prisons and confinement. One who commits minor offenses, such as shirking "patriotic" duty or skipping work, is sent to a *jibkyulso*, a detention center managed by the People's Safety Agency, a police unit with little power. More serious offenders go to a *rodong danryeondae*, a labor camp, which typically means one to two months of hard labor, such as paving roads or clearing avalanche debris from roadsides. The worst offenders go to prisons, the *kwanliso*— which translates as "control and management places." These massive labor camps stretch for miles in the northernmost mountains of the nation. They are modeled after Russia's Siberian prison camps and gulags. According to Western intelligence agencies, they can house up to 200,000.[18]

Everyone knows of the camps and fears them. All have seen a friend or loved one disappear. Defectors from North Korea describe how one disappears. Individuals tied to political crimes are taken from their homes in the dead of night by state security officials without trial. The government is also known to kidnap foreigners abroad suspected of plotting against North Korea. South Koreans, Japanese, and other foreign nationals have been taken to these camps.[19]

North Korean prison camps are barbaric, like Hitler's concentration camps or Stalin's gulags. The DPRK State Security Agency oversees the camps through forced labor and routine beatings, torture, and public executions. A former prison guard who defected reported that fellow guards routinely raped female prisoners. According to the NGO Human Rights Without Frontiers, authorities ordered the newborns from these rapes killed. According to another account of a defector, inmates spent sixteen to seventeen hours a day performing grueling labor; they were routinely beaten and tortured. One cruel method involved water being forced into their stomachs and pumped out by guards jumping on a board on the victim's abdomen. The army also evaluated chemical and biological weapons on inmates.

Echoing the Nazi idea of *Sippenhaft*, entire families can be held responsible for the crimes committed by one of their members; they are imprisoned together and "reeducated through labor." Sometimes they fell trees or tend crops. When food runs scarce, they continue to work in starvation conditions. The sick receive no medical attention. They wear leg-irons, metal collars, and shackles. Execution is swift if they commit small infractions or the workers are too burdensome for the guards. In one prison, according to defector sources and international NGOs, clothing was only issued once every three years. There are "punishment cells" that are too low to allow standing upright and too small for lying down flat. Rule breakers can spend weeks there.

Conditions were always terrible at these camps, but they fell to the level of Auschwitz during the famine in the mid-1990s. A former inmate who later defected to South Korea claimed to the South Korean press that food rations were reduced to 2.6 ounces daily. A fifth of the prisoners in the camp quickly starved. When the camp authorities learned an international human rights group would soon be visiting, they forced inmates to take shelter in nearby mountains after they destroyed evidence of the camp housing. The camp overflowed with those punished for contacting South Korea to try to defect. Others were defectors to China, whom the government returned. Anti-government groups rounded out the camps' populations.

North Koreans in jail for religious beliefs were regarded as insane, as authorities claimed, quoting Marx, that "all religions are opiates." In one instance, a severely kicked victim lay on the ground for days. The crime? Praying for a beaten child.[20]

The adoration of Kim Jong-il and his father Kim Il-sung surpassed political fealty and entered the realm of a state religion, like Roman-style emperor worship. As loyalty to the state was inseparable from loyalty to the current Dear Leader, the two were mutually reinforcing. According to the state ideology, one could not end without the other collapsing.

Kim Jong-il repeatedly wrote on the need for such indoctrination. He blamed the Soviet collapse on the abandonment of inculcating citizens in the Communist value system, compounded by foreign influences that undermined traditional cultures and weakened the people's resolve. North Korean mass media, schools, and neighborhood associations all worked together as an efficient countermeasure to these threats with relentless indoctrination. Ideological education had a clear precedence over academic education in the nation's schools.[21]

North Koreans were not only taught state doctrine; they were also forced to take part in it through involvement in stage performances, rallies, and mass marches involving hundreds of thousands. The fiftieth anniversary celebrations of the founding of the DPRK in September 1998 included hours of meticulously choreographed demonstrations of worship of *Juche* and state leadership. Over a million participated in the October 2000 celebrations of the fifty-fifth anniversary of the Workers' Party of Korea.[22]

Starvation was seen on the faces and bodies of North Koreans. Children in remote areas suffered from long-term malnutrition. A UNICEF survey conducted after the flood disasters reported that 16 percent of children under seven suffered from severe malnutrition and 62 percent from stunted growth. A senior UNICEF official said in 1997 that around eight thousand children in North Korea were in immediate danger of dying from severe hunger and disease. An added eight hundred thousand suffered from serious malnutrition. As a result, North Koreans are, on average, six inches shorter than South Koreans.

What proved most deadly for the North Korean people was the ruling dynasty's taking Kim Jong-il's bizarre acts of self-aggrandizement and making them regular practice, obliterating personal rights. Journalist Christopher Hitchens reported from his 2000 trip, "Every minute of every day, as far as regimentation can assure the fact, is spent in absolute subjection and serfdom. Private life has been entirely abolished. One tries to avoid cliché . . . but George Orwell's *1984* was published about the time that Kim Il-sung set up his system, and it really is as if he got hold of an early copy of the novel and used it as a blueprint."[23]

As a result of this hyper-totalitarian system, everyone in the capital city had to be home by curfew time when lights were turned off (although the lack of electricity was more effective than any state ban on venturing outside after sundown). Restrictive trade policies created perpetual starvation. Hitchens reported that even though his native handlers kept him from wandering out too far, he could not help but see people drinking from sewers and picking up individual grains of food from barren fields. Whole towns were ruined and abandoned.

To rally his people around a North Korean identity, Kim Jong-il instituted a system of extreme racism and prejudice toward non-Korean groups. Posters depicted Americans as hook-nosed monsters (a typical anti-Semitic caricature) and the Japanese as barbarians. During the Soviet period, a black Cuban ambassador claimed that he and his family were almost lynched when he showed his family the sights of Pyongyang. Many North Koreans believe they have genetic superiority to South Koreans because South Koreans have married foreigners and become a mongrel race.[24] Such racist rhetoric echoed World War II–era fascist Japan, what B. R. Myers describes as a racially based dictatorship. In 2006, the official paper of the Workers' Party proclaim the following: "Mono-ethnicity is something that our nation and no other on earth can pride itself on . . . There is no suppressing the nation's shame and rage at the talk of 'a multi-ethnic, multi-racial society' . . . which would dilute even the bloodline of our people."[25]

Whatever his sadistic and racist tendencies, Kim Jong-il became more famous in his later years for unintentional buffoonery, due to incredible self-regard mixed with cowardliness. Crippled by a deathly fear of flying, he traveled long distances only by a private armored train and would not go where a train could not. While he was said to be firm and fearless during international negotiations, a psychological profile compiled by

Frederick L. Coolidge and Daniel L. Segal, with help from a South Korean psychiatrist said to be a leading authority on the ruler's behavior, affirms that Kim Jong-il possessed what is called the "big six" diagnoses of personality disorders: he was sadistic, paranoid, antisocial, narcissistic, schizoid, and schizotypal—the last two concern the inability to maintain relationships, whether due to a fear of others or complete indifference. Coincidentally, Saddam Hussein, Joseph Stalin, and Adolf Hitler had those traits. Even among this ilk, Kim Jong-il managed to stand out, measuring extraordinarily high in sadism.[26]

As with other mad rulers, one wonders how a person with such a potentially debilitating condition could run a nation, an endless propaganda campaign, and even a nuclear weapons program with cold logic. Coolidge and Segal answered the lingering question with examples of other famous cases of "murderous schizophrenic persons" who showed control over their followers, namely cult leaders Jim Jones and Charles Manson. They noted that "grandiose delusions may predispose schizophrenic individuals to violence, that such individuals may have a superior or patronizing manner in interpersonal interactions, and that such individuals may display little or no cognitive impairment and have a good prognosis in the areas of occupational functioning and independent living."[27]

As a narcissist, Kim ruthlessly demanded attention on the world stage. He discovered a way to receive it on October 9, 2006, when a massive underground explosion originating from the Korean peninsula rocked seismographs across the world. Scientists concurred that a nuclear detonation had taken place. Several months earlier, the North Korean government had tested intercontinental ballistic missiles, the sort that would deliver a nuclear payload.[28]

An alarmed world feared, among other things, that North Korea's neighbors would develop their own weapons, leading to an East Asian nuclear arms race. Governments around the world, including China, Japan, South Korea, Russia, and the United States, tried to persuade Jong-il to resume talks on weapons disarmament. Others feared North

Korea would sell its weapons to terrorist groups. A baffled world wondered why Kim Jong-il was devoting so many resources to a nuclear program less than ten years after a terrible famine had killed hundreds of thousands in his impoverished nation. He may have been responding to a 2002 speech by U.S. president George W. Bush, who referred to his nation as part of the "axis of evil," along with Iraq and Iran. According to *The Economist*, Kim Jong-il believed that "if you do not want to be invaded by America, as was Iraq, then it is best to get your weapons of mass destruction up and running. Once your own security is assured, you can bargain from a position of strength."[29]

Bush branded North Korea part of the "axis of evil" because U.S. intelligence showed that Kim was accelerating his nuclear weapons program. At the same time, the United States cut off oil shipments and other aid to North Korea. The shipments began in the 1990s after the end of the Cold War to convince North Korea not to develop its weapons. Weapons inspections occurred to confirm the program was not developing. The nuclear program restarted in 2002 at the end of oil shipments. Kim Jong-il no longer allowed international inspections. While the nuclear weapons program only came to fruition in the 2000s, it may have begun as early as the Korean War. The North wanted the strongest deterrent possible against an invasion from the United States or South Korea.[30]

The Kim family has dreamed of nuclear weapons since the United States bombed Japan at the end of World War II. Kim Il-sung desired to make his nation a nuclear power. Government scientists labored away at a Soviet-designed nuclear compound in Yongbyon, tucked away in the mountains north of Pyongyang. Nothing came of the research, but there was no pressing need for the weapons. North Korea was safely under the Soviet defense umbrella. Kim Jong-il led his nation in the early years of independence and put the nuclear program back on the fast track. He thought it was the ticket to international recognition and respect at a time when North Korea's standing was flagging. Rather than rebuild the rusting infrastructure and restart aging factories, the nation invested in its weapons project as a deterrent again the United States, fearing a rehash of the Korean War.

By the early 1990s, a reprocessing plant at Yongbyon began producing enough weapons-grade plutonium for one or two nuclear bombs. "Kim Jong-il didn't care if he bankrupted the rest of the country. He saw the missiles and nuclear weapons as the only way to maintain power," Kim Dok-hong, a high-ranking defector from Pyongyang, said in an interview in Seoul in 2006.[31]

South Korea used its meeting with Kim Jong-il as a pretense to offer more aid to its starving kin. But overtures of peace were quickly set aside. Many doubted that Kim Jong-il ever seriously considered closer ties with the South. Reunification would have been impossible for a leader who was part of a dynasty lacking any sort of belief in democracy. At the same time as its peace summit, North Korea was supplying missiles to other nations and rogue actors. North Korean scientists also continued to develop their nuclear weapons program.

Nuclear weapons gave North Korea a seat at the table with powerful nations. Kim Jong-il negotiated with the United States over his nuclear facilities. In Geneva, American negotiators pushed for inspections at the facility at Yongbyon to reduce the nuclear threat. Kang Sok-ju, leader of the North Korean negotiating team, refused this request. He claimed the program was for producing much-needed electricity. The two sides eventually came to an agreement in 1994 called the Agreed Framework. It specified that inspections would be delayed until the nuclear reactors were delivered—some five years away. Until then, the United States would provide North Korea with fuel oil and "provide formal assurances against the threat or use of nuclear weapons against North Korea." Kim Jong-il approved the agreement against the advice of his military advisors, who worried that pulling the United States closer into their orbit could impede sovereignty. No matter; the Dear Leader's word was final. One American negotiator, Thomas Hubbard, heard of Kim's decision and recalled, "I became convinced that there was a supreme being there, and that probably it is Kim Jong-il."[32]

The Agreed Framework between the two Koreas may have been a response to worsening relations with the United States. However, little progress occurred after signing the Agreed Framework. The light-water reactors and fuel oil promised by the United States were late. Relations did not improve. As Ambassador Charles Kartman, special envoy for the Korean peace talks, said after the conclusion of the talks, "There are reasons why the North Koreans might think we weren't totally sincere."

During the Clinton administration, Kim Jong-il also offered to end production of ballistic missiles if the Clinton administration followed through with the Agreed Framework. But the Clinton administration lost interest in the Agreed Framework for both political and financial reasons. Kim then tested a long-range ballistic missile over the Sea of Japan in 1998. Over the next two years, a series of offers, assurances, and promises were made by U.S. diplomats, all while North Korean officials expected Clinton himself to come and sign an agreement. When this did not happen, Kim allowed missile production to continue. Peace talks between the two Koreas stalled. The Kim dynasty continued to rule North Korea unchallenged. [33]

Kim Jong-il's rule was one of strict order for his subjects and marvelous freedoms for himself. He was an Elvis Presley fanatic, to the point of sporting "the King's" signature bouffant hairstyle and oversized spectacles. The leader was a film buff with a personal library of over twenty thousand films. Among his favorites were Hollywood Westerns, Japanese monster movies, and the *Friday the 13th* series. His love for these imaginative fantasy and horror films enabled him to create an even wilder, more contrived autobiography. The first time he golfed in 1994, Kim claimed, he shot 38-under par, sinking five holes-in-one and beating a professional golfer's average score by at least two dozen strokes. As a lover of theatre, he wrote six operas and directed musical productions.

To round out his abilities as a polymath, he authored more than one thousand books in a thirty-six-month period.

Every town in North Korea, regardless of size, has a movie theatre due to Kim Jong-il's conviction that film is the most powerful propaganda weapon in a dictatorship's arsenal. When he was thirty, he received his first job overseeing the Workers' Party's Bureau of Propaganda and Agitation, which managed the country's film studios. In 1973, he published a book called *On the Art of Cinema*. He argued that "revolutionary art and literature are extremely effective means for inspiring people to work for the tasks of the revolution." He used his growing power to build up the North Korean film industry. The Korean Feature Film Studio expanded to a ten-million-square-foot lot, with some forty films made a year. Most were melodramas that featured the same themes: happiness came from self-sacrifice and suppression of the individual for the good of the country. There was an unofficial *Juche* code in the films. They demonized capitalist excess, particularly depictions of South Korea, where the directors imagined a Seoul street lined with porno stores, strip clubs, and dingy storefronts.[34]

There were those with whom Kim Jong-il's propaganda campaigns were successful. When he died in 2011, Simon Winchester from the London *Times* lamented his passing, because he saw Kim Jong-il and his father as true champions of a pure Korean culture. He argued that North Korea had honorably retained its heritage, while South Korea had abandoned it for globalization: "But seeing how South Korea has turned out—its Korean-ness utterly submerged in neon, hip-hop and every imaginable American influence, a romantic can allow himself a small measure of melancholy: North Korea, for all its faults, is undeniably still Korea, a place uniquely representative of an ancient and rather remarkable Asian culture. And that, in a world otherwise rendered so bland, is perhaps no bad thing."[35] However, North Koreans forced to exist on pine bark and corn husks to survive might have a profoundly different view of whether or not foreign influence always constitutes evil.

Kim Jong-il died as he lived—with his personal achievements being outlandishly fabricated. The North Korean leader either died in a "fit of rage" over problems with a construction project in Huichon or, as his official biography reports, from a heart attack while on an early morning train trip to Pyongyang. His death stopped a fierce snowstorm and reddened the sky above the sacred Mount Paektu. At that same moment, the ice covering a famous lake cracked so quickly and deeply that the sound of its breakage shook the heavens and the earth.

# Conclusion

After Kim Jong-il's death "shook the heavens and the earth," a fatherless nation was also left directionless.

More than five million turned out to pay respects to the fallen Dear Leader after his death, the state media reported. A three-hour funeral procession marched solemnly in the falling snow (called "heaven's tears" by local newscasters). The convoy included military escorts, generals, and every person of any note in civil society. Soldiers wailed, beating their chests, crying out, "Father, Father!" A massive limousine carried a giant portrait of Kim Jong-il. A second limousine carried his casket.

"The great heart of Comrade Kim Jong-il has ceased to beat . . . such an unexpected and early departure from us is the biggest and the most unimaginable loss to our party and the revolution," said Kim Yong-nam, chairman of the presidium. He resolved that the nation would not crumble after Kim's death. North Korea would "transform the sorrow into strength and courage 1,000 times greater under the leadership of comrade Kim Jong-un."[1]

North Korea is a nation built on gigatons of propaganda, but the mourners appeared authentic in their grief of Kim Jong-il's death. Images from the international media showed North Koreans wailing with anguish, kneeling, bowing their heads, and beating the ground with their fists. State media said others were "convulsing with pain."[2]

Thousands shuffled past an enormous painting of Kim Jong-il and his father, pictured standing on Mt. Paektu, the birthplace of the Dear Leader. They slowly laid wreaths at the foot of the painting.

"How could the heavens be so cruel? Please come back, general. We cannot believe you're gone," Hong Son-ok said, her body convulsing, in an interview with North Korea's official television station. "He passed away too suddenly to our profound regret," said an official statement from North Korea's Central News Agency. "The heart of Kim Jong-il stopped beating, but his noble and august name and benevolent image will always be remembered by our army and people."[3]

The power that megalomaniacs like the Kims had over their people appeared supernatural. Subjects worshipped them in ways that resembled the deification of Roman emperors. Control over their subjects was so complete that a premodern observer might ascribe to the rulers malevolent powers. Biographers of ancient mad rulers such as Caligula did exactly that, claiming that temple worship of the rulers could summon dark forces.

The modern mental health field has completely abandoned such metaphysical approaches. It has also eschewed social and cultural dimensions in its understanding of madness. Biology is the lens through which madness is seen. Psychiatry approaches madness as a product partially of environment but mostly of biology. Diagnoses of mental conditions are according to neuroscience, genetics, and epigenetic triggers in a patient's environment. There could be a genetic mutation, increasing the risk of schizophrenia. Or, a lack of Vitamin A due to no sunlight exposure in the winter could trigger seasonal affective disorder. There could be a family history of bipolar disorder.

Madness, however, has meant much more than faulty biology in cultures across time. It carries deep cultural meanings and can say as much about the people who ascribe madness to someone as it does about those who are labeled mad. For example, Old Testament madness is connected to disobedience against Yahweh. King Saul, who disobeyed the Lord, was paranoid the rest of his life. King Nebuchadnezzar, an enemy of Israel, was robbed of his senses after gloating over the glory of his empire.[4] There were no biological reasons given for either of their madness; only God's displeasure.

Even though the ancients often believed in supernatural causes as the source of madness, from the earliest systematic studies of medicine, they also embraced naturalistic theories. While Greco-Romans went to temples of the god Asclepius to seek purification rites and spells from priests to cast out their mental infirmities, Hippocrates and later Galen developed models of mental and physical illness. European and Middle Eastern physicians drew upon that research throughout the Middle Ages and Renaissance until the emergence of modern psychology and psychiatry in the nineteenth century. The medical sciences dropped supernatural causes as a reason for illnesses (except as placebo effects for patients). Drug therapies that eradicated diseases such as smallpox and polio have moved into the realm of mental health. Thorazine was prescribed as an antipsychotic in 1954, followed by the anti-anxiety and anti-depressant medications Valium and Prozac.

These pharmaceuticals have not wiped out mental disorders with the efficacy of the smallpox or rinderpest vaccines. They are, *Madness and Meaning* author Andrew Scull argues, a set of palliative measures that dampen the effects of psychosis and reign in violent tendencies but only function like a Band-Aid; they are not corrective surgery. These medications can bring a set of side effects, including neurological tics and disturbances that resemble signs of Tardive dyskinesia (TD), along with weight gain, impotence, and metabolic disorders.[5]

The elimination of madness at all costs should not be the goal. One theme that has appeared in this book is the connection between genius

and madness. Flashes of greatness often appear alongside eccentric per-
sonalities. Janna Levin, author of the book *How the Universe Got Its
Spots: Diary of a Finite Time in a Finite Space*, looked in particular at
mathematicians who had brushes with insanity in the course of their
professional exploration of infinity—a concept that is by definition
incomprehensible, a mesmerizing expanse beyond one's senses from one
perspective, but an endless, terrifying abyss from another. She writes:

> Insanity, madness, obsession, math, objectivity, truth, science
> and art. These friends always impress me. They're sculptors
> and tailors, not scientists or spies. I've chosen them with the
> peculiar attentiveness of a shell collector stupidly combining
> the overwhelming multitude of broken detritus to hold up one
> shell so beautiful that it finds its way into my pocket, lining
> my clothes with sand. And then another. Not too many, so
> that the sheer number could never diminish the value of one.[6]

Madness does not make a ruler inherently better or worse. Abraham
Lincoln and Winston Churchill suffered depression, which, as discussed
in the introduction, arguably formed part of their greatness. Jimmy
Carter was by all accounts perfectly sane, but few people would argue
Carter was a better president than Lincoln. Moreover, madness does not
seem to strip away one's core character. George III never swore in the
depths of his madness. Madness in a ruler is a quality to be taken into
consideration and often accompanies poor leadership, but it is not syn-
onymous with being a tyrant or a brute. Every mad leader examined in
this book has his apologists. Rural Bavarians adored Ludwig for his
patronage. Anti-Israeli figures loved Idi Amin for supporting the Palestinian hijacking of an airliner flying out of Tel Aviv. Arguably due to Stock-
holm Syndrome, in which hostages form an alliance with their captors,
North Koreans mourned outrageously at the death of Kim Jong-il.

Levin then explores the obsessive-compulsiveness, curiosity, and
eccentricity that marked so many great thinkers:

Some very clever people were obsessive-compulsive. I don't believe insanity is either a requirement or a guarantee for brilliance. But I find the anecdotes so interesting, so much more interesting than the usual hero worship. I'm subjected to my brothers in science . . . I find their weaknesses so much more touching. Newton wasn't obsessive-compulsive to my knowledge, but the tenacity of his mental health has certainly been called into question, particularly in his later years. Newton was a secret alchemist, conducting covert experiments in his college rooms in Cambridge, including very peculiar ones that involved staring at the sun and stabbing himself in the eye with a small dagger.

His mental ailments are usually described as paranoia and depression. Some have even suggested that he was as mad as a hatter, meaning his insanity was induced by mercury and other chemicals he ingested in the course of his alchemy—chemicals that led to the mental disintegration of traditional hat makers . . . Any mental lapses seem to have had little impact on his intense scientific clarity, at least for most of his production. Newton was so right about so many things that it seems ungenerous to dwell on where he was wrong.[7]

Madness and greatness are neatly combined in one person in Newton, but Albert Einstein sat more squarely at the intersection of compulsiveness and genius. Levin, along with writer Maria Popova, describes how the greatest physicist in modern history was pushed into the realm of madness by trying to comprehend a universe that refused to conform to classical physics and kept curving away from his view.[8]

Einstein had created an unwieldy monster that in a way he couldn't tame. He conjured up a theory reliant on mathematics in a curved spacetime that still demands years of its students' attention. Though he managed to use those tools,

compared to his mathematician friends he used them clumsily
. . . His fragility, his defiant brilliance in the face of his own
limitations . . . He ploughed right past his inadequacy. Maybe
this is what he meant when he said "Imagination is more
important than knowledge."

Like a bad plumber he hacked and hammered and slapped
together a mathematical model of curved space, correcting
error after error in his own formulation. Sloshing between
despair, doubt, and conviction. When he finally pulled something together, something that worked, he was overcome with
elation for days. He had trudged through the darkness of his
own confusion and found what he set out to discover; a theory of gravity based on curved spacetime and faithful to his
principle of relativity. It's like Michelangelo revealing the
sculpture he believed hidden within each stone.[9]

Arthur Schopenhauer made an effort to define madness in his 1818
work *The World as Will and Representation*.[10] Madness is not as easily
defined as a physical illness. "Madmen" can have reason too. It is not
their mental processes in the present that are damaged, but their understanding of the past. They suffer from a broken memory, an aspect of
mental illness that mental health professionals are continuing to try to
understand.[11] Schopenhauer wrote:

A clear and complete insight into the nature of madness, a
correct and distinct conception of what constitutes the difference between the sane and the insane, has, as far as I know,
not as yet been found. Neither reason nor understanding can
be denied to madmen, for they talk and understand, and often
draw very accurate conclusions; they also, as a rule, perceive
what is present quite correctly, and apprehend the connection
between cause and effect . . . For the most part, madmen do
not err in the knowledge of what is immediately present; their

raving always relates to what is absent and past, and only through these to their connection with what is present.

Therefore it seems to me that their malady specially concerns the memory; not indeed that memory fails them entirely, for many of them know a great deal by heart, and sometimes recognize persons whom they have not seen for a long time; but rather that the thread of memory is broken, the continuity of its connection destroyed, and no uniformly connected recollection of the past is possible. Particular scenes of the past are known correctly, just like the particular present; but there are gaps in their recollection which they fill up with fictions, and these are either always the same, in which case they become fixed ideas, and the madness that results is called monomania or melancholy; or they are always different, momentary fancies, and then it is called folly, *fatuitas*.[12]

Mad rulers are united by a misunderstanding of the past, but there are other common factors that group them together. Almost all ascended the throne at a young age, making them pawns of family members and court officials. Caligula grew up in a war zone; Charles VI and Ivan the Terrible in family courts in which enemy factions wanted to neutralize them and exploit them, or, failing that, kill them. Charlatans surrounded them. Ibrahim's court advisor Cinci Hoca told the sultan that his selfish whimsies were the whisperings of the divine. Wealthy Romans enthusiastically joined Caligula's cult of worship to obtain lucrative positions as temple priests.

These rulers also grew up isolated from others and suffered psychological damage. Ibrahim lived in the Gilded Cage. Confined to royal palaces, tutored in arcane humanities and royal duties, Ludwig was molded into a Bavarian ruler. Learned men considered this training to be the best upbringing for a royal—a life isolated from commoners, but from most everyone else as well. Modern psychology could point to personality disorders and health problems that spring from a lack of human contact. This royal upbringing protocol had a similar operational logic to royal Egyptian inbreeding practices to keep a pure bloodline—a program that sought to uphold "purity" but resulted in inbreeding and disgusting abnormalities. It had the same result in psychological development as inbreeding did in physical development: gross deformities.

Let us return to the question posed at the beginning of this book. Are modern leaders becoming more insane than those in the past? The answer to this question is equivocal.

One type of insane ruler common in the ancient and medieval periods is almost extinct: the mad monarch. Rulers such as Caligula, Charles VI, and Ibrahim I were tolerated because continuation of a royal dynasty required an unbroken chain of family members on the throne, even if a link were crazed. Most heads of state were hereditary monarchs and part of a royal dynasty. Maintaining this dynasty helped to keep peace in the state by preventing the nobility from challenging its right to rule. Furthermore, these kings and queens were believed to be God's anointed sovereigns, with a divine right to rule. This divine right even extended to the mentally challenged and insane. Most advisors worked around their mad rulers by declaring a regency counsel, as was done in the eras of Charles VI and George III, but keeping the royal dynasty still demanded these rulers hold power at least in name.

Mad kings began to disappear with the abolition of the monarchy in Europe following the French Revolution. France dissolved its monarchy in 1792. With the Napoleonic Wars, the French Empire brought the Revolution to much of Europe, ending serfdom and introducing constitutional limits on monarchs. Royal dynasties lingered in a long twilight, but they eventually lost any meaningful form of power and became easily ignored by once-loyal subjects. Today, dynastic rule is effectively dead as a political force, except for lingering outliers like North Korea. Modern monarchs have few official duties beyond the ceremonial.

Are mad rulers, then, outdated? The answer is no; especially in the cases of autocratic strongmen-turned-megalomaniacs. Until very recently, political scientists thought democracy would mean the end of mad rulers. They believed that after the collapse of the Soviet Union in 1989, a democratic tidal wave would flood the earth. The will of the people would force out crazed dictators, who ran roughshod over their people, through popular uprisings. Anti-Communist protest movements in Poland, East Germany, and throughout the Eastern Bloc suggested that the proliferation of free information through the samizdat (Soviet-era underground press) had ended totalitarian strangleholds on facts. At the time, the facts were on the side of these analysts. In 2005, there were three times as many democracies as there had been in 1974.

At the same time, recent technologies in mass communication allowed megalomaniacs to develop a cult of personality in ways unprecedented in history. In Caligula's era, he could not manage more than building temples for emperor worship. Almost nobody in the Roman Empire had ever seen him in person or really knew what he looked like. Contrast that with Joseph Stalin and Chairman Mao Zedong, whose images were omnipresent on buildings, in schoolrooms, and in public parades. They and their descendants spoke directly to all members of society in radio and television appearances. The propaganda powers of a totalitarian state could invade every living room in the nation.

The twenty-first century has shown us that dictators whose thirst for power has affected their mental faculties are highly adaptable to modern sensibilities. Russian president Vladimir Putin is an excellent example. Although by no means crazy, he has started to nurture a personality cult by letting the twenty years of formal and informal Russian premiership go to his head. Macho displays of his bravery are flaunted in the Russian media. The exploits that he allowed to be captured on camera include shirtless hunting expeditions, hunting whales with a crossbow, scuba diving to research underwater archeological sites, and dropping water on forest fires from the cockpit of a firefighting plane.

Putin is far more tactically clever than Niyazov and Kim Jong-il. He has been far more tempered in demanding worship from citizens but uses a similar strategy to amass power. According to Will Dobson's book, *The Dictator's Learning Curve: Inside the Global Battle for Democracy*, Putin said, "He who does not regret the breakup of the Soviet Union has no heart. He who wants to revive it in its previous form has no head." He realized a highly controlled system made up only of yes-men was a failed state, because it could not gather valuable information; independent intelligence-gathering mechanisms had been destroyed. So, Putin won elections and the popular vote, which makes it more difficult to define him as a dictator. He centralizes power through mostly legal mechanisms and keeps just enough trappings of electoral democracy in Russia to placate international human rights groups. He controls the legislature, but it is also still a functioning legislature.[13]

Late Venezuelan president Hugo Chavez is another example of a bombastic, crazed ruler who adapted himself well to modern times. When he appeared in front of the United Nations several years ago, he immediately genuflected and claimed that he smelled sulfur because "the devil had been there," a reference to the spot where George W. Bush had stood to deliver a speech. He ruthlessly controlled Venezuela by nationalizing industries, packing the court with his cronies, and cracking down heavily on those in the media who opposed him. But he did not seek absolute control. He had an electoral council that allowed quasi-open elections. Chavez required opposition on the ballot to support the illusion that he was a democratically elected leader.

Modern dictators are typically not stupid, even if they are self-absorbed megalomaniacs. They know how to adapt to the modern era. They understand that terrible forms of brutality are better conducted with greater discretion. Rather than sending police to slaughter protestors in front of presidential palaces, there are far more subtle means at these dictators' disposal. They intentionally leave the law vague to give themselves legal cover to quietly suppress opposition. They send bureaucrats to shut down businesses or tax collectors to audit opposition-owned businesses. They shut down critical TV networks and newspapers for minor technicalities or legal infringements. They have mastered the language of the rule of law to perpetuate systems in which they can rule unopposed.

Sometimes they become so comfortable in their positions that the mask occasionally slips, and the mentally unbalanced ruler underneath shows his real face. But the mask quickly goes back on, and they once again cover themselves with the pretense of being modern, enlightened democratic leaders. They know how to conceal their intentions with democracy's trappings. Many stay in office indefinitely, regardless of how mad they truly are.

# Acknowledgments

This book could not have begun without the support of Alex Novak at Regnery History, who has given me the incredible latitude to unconventionally explore explore history on this project and many others.

This project was also assisted by many who generously gave their time to offer critical feedback in the earlier drafts. Special thanks go out to Maureen Rank, Billy Joaquin, Alan Ellis, Carlos Brefe, Wayne Wilson, Linda Cypert, Larry Williams, Erica Kitzman, Jose Pagan, Joaquin Buitrago, John Schall, Beth McGinn, Roberto Gómez, and Paritosh Deshpande. Thanks also to editor Stephen Thompson for connecting ideas in ways I never would have considered.

To fellow authors and podcasters James Early, Buddy Levy, Stephen Guerra, and Bruce Carlson; it was a great pleasure to collaborate on past projects and to also work together on this one. I hope for many more in the future.

To the Legendary Society of Men—upholding the fealty of Paul Sabino's admonition to "stay on the right path."

Finally to Ellie, Sophie, Theo, and Melissa for putting up with my hours buried in the office to put this baby to bed.

# Notes

## Introduction

1. John Gartner, "Mental Health Professionals Declare Trump Is Mentally Ill and Must Be Removed," Change.org, https://www. change.org/p/trump-is-mentally-ill-and-must-be-removed.
2. Adrian Chen, "When a Populist Demagogue Takes Power," *New Yorker*, November 14, 2016.
3. Kim Hjelmgaard, "Brazil's New President Jair Bolsonaro Has Said Many Offensive Things," *USA Today*, October 29, 2018.
4. "In Quotes: Italy's Silvio Berlusconi in His Own Words," BBC, August 2, 2013, https://www.bbc.com/news/ world-europe-15642201.
5. Noah Millman, "Why Are Right-Wing Populists Winning Everywhere?" *The Week*, October 30, 2018.
6. Justin A. Frank, "I Used Applied Psychoanalysis to Assess Trump. The Diagnosis Is Frightening," STAT News, September 25, 2018, https://www.statnews.com/2018/09/25/donald-trump-applied-psychoanalysis-diagnosis/; Justin Frank, *Trump on the Couch* (New York: Penguin Random House, 2018).

7.  Eugene Vodolazkin, "Russian 'Umberto Eco' Demystifies the Holy Fool," *Russia Beyond*, June 6, 2013, https://www.rbth.com/literature/2013/06/06/russian_umberto_eco_demystifies_the_holy_fool_26401.html.

Andrew Scull, *Madness in Civilization: A Cultural History of Insanity, from the Bible to Freud, from the Madhouse to Modern Medicine* (Princeton: Princeton University Press, 2016).

8.  Ryan Howes, "The Definition of Insanity: Perseverance versus Perseveration," *Psychology Today*, July 27, 2009.

9.  Nassir Ghaemi, *A First-Rate Madness: Uncovering the Links Between Leadership and Mental Illness* (New York: Penguin Press, 2011).

# Chapter 1

1.  Anthony A. Barrett, *Caligula: The Corruption of Power* (New Haven: Yale University Press, 1989), 241.

2.  Philo, *Legum allegoriae*, 93.

3.  Ibid., 76.

4.  Suetonius, *Caligula*, xxvii.

5.  Ibid., l.

6.  Vin Massaro and Iain Montgomery, "Gaius—Mad, Bad, III, or All Three?," *Latomus* 37, no. 4 (1978): 894–909; Barbara Sidwell, "Gaius Caligula's Mental Illness," *Classical World* 103, no. 2 (2010): 187.

7.  Suetonius, *Caligula*, 10.2.

8.  Arther Ferrill, *Caligula: Emperor of Rome* (Thames and Hudson, 1991), 2.

9.  Suetonius, *Caligula*, 37; Nero, 30.1; Dio Cassius, 59.2.6.

10. Suetonius, *Caligula*, xxii.

11. M. P. Charlesworth, "The Tradition About Caligula," *Cambridge Historical Journal* 4, no. 2 (1933): 113.

12. Suetonius, *Caligula*, xlv.

13. Ibid., xlvi.

14. J. P. V. D. Balsdon, *The Emperor Gaius (Caligula)* (Oxford: The Clarendon Press, 1934), 165–66.

15. "Was the Roman Emperor Caligula As Crazy As They Say?" The Straight Dope, June 10, 2003, https://www.straightdope.com/columns/read/2102/was-the-roman-emperor-caligula-as-crazy-as-they-say/.

16. Suetonius, *Caligula*, li.
17. Barbara Sidwell, "Gaius Caligula's Mental Illness," *The Classical World* 103, no. 2 (2010): 183–206.
18. H. Willrich, "Caligula," *Klio* 3 (1903): 85–118, 288–317, 397–470.
19. Aloys Winterling, *Caligula: A Biography*, trans. Deborah Lucas Schneider, Glenn W. Most, and Paul Psoinos (Berkeley: University of California Press, 2011).
20. Sidwell, "Gaius Caligula's Mental Illness," 187.
21. Arther Ferrill, *Caligula: Emperor of Rome* (London: Thames and Hudson, 1991), 39.
22. Suetonius, *Caligula*, 50.3.
23. Suetonius, *Caligula*, 23.3; *Philo of Alexandria, De legatione ad Gaium*, trans. E. M. Smallwood (Leiden, 1970).
24. Robert D. Hare, *Psychopathy: Theory, Research and Implications for Society* (New York, 1970), 907.
25. Robert S. Katz, "The Illness of Caligula," *Classical World*, 65 (1972), 223–25.
26. Suetonius, *Caligula*, lii.
27. Ibid., liii.
28. J. Lucas, "Un empereur psychopathe: Contribution a la psychologie du Caligula de Suetonie," in *L'Antiquité Classique* 36 (1967): 159–189; Sidwell, "Gaius Caligula's Mental Illness," 198.
29. Sidwell, "Gaius Caligula's Mental Illness," 192; M. P. Charlesworth, "Gaius and Claudius," in *The Cambridge Ancient History: The Augustan Empire 44 B.C.—A.D. 70.*, vol. 10, eds. S. A. Cook, F. E. Adcock, and M. P. Charlesworth (Cambridge University Press, 1934), 656.
30. Massaro and Montgomery, "Gaius—Mad, Bad, Ill, or All Three?," 905; Sidwell, "Gaius Caligula's Mental Illness," 199.
31. Suetonius, *Caligula*, xxi.
32. Winterling, *Caligula: A Biography*.
33. Ibid., 98–99.
34. Ibid., 141–47.
35. Ibid., 100.
36. Charlesworth, "The Tradition About Caligula," 105–109.
37. Ibid., 112.
38. Charlesworth, "Gaius and Claudius," in *The Cambridge Ancient History*, 660.
39. Sidwell, "Gaius Caligula's Mental Illness," 200–5.

## Chapter 2

1. René de La Croix, *The Lives of the Kings & Queens of France* (Knopf, 1979); Vivian Green, *The Madness of Kings* (The History Press, 2016); John C. G. Röhl, David Hunt, and Martin Warren, *Purple Secret: Genes, "Madness" and the Royal Houses of Europe* (Bantam, 1998).

2. Richard Vaughan, *John the Fearless: The Growth of Burgundian Power* (Boydell Press, 2002), 29; Sarah Alger, *The Politics of Madness: Government in the Reigns of Charles VI and Henry VI*, Honours Thesis (University of Tasmania, 2001), 28.

3. Osvaldo Ferrero, "Un fou sur le trône de France," in *Les dossiers indiscrets de l'histoire*, 1998, quoted in "King Charles VI of France," *Splatter* (blog), January 24, 2011, https://marilynkaydennis. wordpress.com/2011/01/24/king-charles-vi-of-france/.

4. Green, *The Madness of Kings*.

5. Tracy Adams, *The Life and Afterlife of Isabeau of Bavaria* (JHU Press, 2010), 223; "Charles VI of France," New World Encyclopedia, https://www.newworldencyclopedia.org/entry/ Charles_VI_of_France.

6. Rachel Gibbons, "Isabeau of Bavaria, Queen of France (1385–1422): The Creation of an Historical Villainess: The Alexander Prize Essay," *Transactions of the Royal Historical Society* 6 (1996): 57–58.

7. Jean Froissart, *Chronicles of England, France, and Spain and the Adjoining Countries from the Later Part of the Reign of Edward II to the Coronation of Henry IV*, vol. 2 (London: W. Smith, 1842), 533.

8. Froissart, *Chronicles of England, France, and Spain*, 532–36; Alger, *The Politics of Madness*, 14–15.

9. Green, *The Madness of Kings*.

10. Ibid.

11. Alger, *The Politics of Madness*, 24.

12. Froissart, *Chronicles of England, France, and Spain*, xv, 26–48.

13. Ferrero, "Un fou sur le trône de France."

14. Froissart, *Chronicles of England, France, and Spain*, xv, 42.

15. M. L. Bellaguet, ed., *Chroniques Du Religieux de Saint-Denis: Contenant La Regne de Charles VI de 1380 á 1422*, vols. 1–6 (Paris, 1994), 21–2; Alger, *The Politics of Madness*, 14, 27; John Henneman, "Who Were the Marmousets?" *Medieval Prosopography* 5, no. 1, 1984.

16. William Grimshaw, *The History of France, From the Foundation to the Monarchy, to the Death of Louis XVI* (Philadelphia: Towar & Hogan, 1829), 125.
17. Grimshaw, *The History of France*, 124–25.
18. Bellaguet, *Chroniques Du Religieux de Saint-Denis*, 86–88.
19. Enguerrand de Monstrelet, *Chronicles,* vol. 1 (London: Bradbury & Evans Printers, 1840), 4.
20. Green, *Madness of Kings.*
21. Bellaguet, *Chroniques Du Religieux de Saint-Denis*, 405.
22. Jan R. Veenstra, *Magic and Divination at the Courts of Burgundy and France: Text and Context of Laurens Pignon's Contre Les Devineurs (1411)* (Brill, 1998), 68–69.
23. R. C. Famiglietti, *Royal Intrigue: Crisis at the Court of Charles VI, 1392–1420* (New York: Ams Pr Inc, 1987), 4–6.
24. Michael Camille, *Master of Death: The Lifeless Art of Pierre Remiet, Illuminator* (Yale University Press, 1996); Alger, *The Politics of Madness*, 18.
25. Juvenal des Ursins, *Histoire de Charles VI,* ed. Theodore Godelay (Paris: 1614), 220.
26. Adrian van Heck, ed., *Commentaries of Pius II* (Vatican City: 1984).
27. Petteri Pietikäinen, *Madness: A History* (Routledge, 2015), 64.
28. Pietikäinen, *Madness: A History.*
29. E. Perroy, "Feudalism or Principalities in Fifteenth Century France," *Bulletin of the Institute of Historical Research* 20, no. 61 (October 12, 2007): 181–85.
30. Monstrelet, *Chronicles,* vol. 1, 61–81.
31. Richard Cavendish, "The Duke of Orleans Is Ambushed," *History Today* 57, no. 11 (November 2007); Vaughan, *John the Fearless*, 67.
32. R. C. Famiglietti, *The French Monarchy in Crisis, 1392–1415, and the Political Role of the Dauphin,* 1984; Alger, *The Politics of Madness*, 32.
33. L. C. Hector and B. Harvey, trans., *The Westminster Chronicle 1381–1394,* UK ed. (Oxford: New York: Clarendon Press, 1982), 501.
34. Edward Peters, *The Shadow King: Rex Inutilis in Medieval Law and Literature, 751–1327* (Yale University Press, 1970).
35. Grimshaw, *The History of France.*

## Chapter 3

1. Isabel de Madariaga, *Ivan the Terrible: First Tsar of Russia* (New Haven: Yale University Press, 2008).
2. "Ivan IV of Russia," New World Encyclopedia, https://www.newworldencyclopedia.org/entry/Ivan_IV_of_Russia.
3. Madariaga, *Ivan the Terrible*, 43.
4. Ibid., 61–63.
5. Ibid., 142.
6. Ibid., 142–49.
7. Albert Schlichting, "A Brief Account of the Character and Brutal Rule of Vasil'evich, Tyrant of Muscovy," trans. Hugh F. Graham, *Canadian American Slavic Studies* 9, no. 2 (1975): 204–266. Madariaga notes that there is little point in discussing Ivan as a homosexual; events such as these indicate his bisexuality, not terribly surprising for the period. Accounts depicted Russians as addicted to sodomy and attached significance to the wearing of beards specifically as a guard against this vice.
8. Madariaga, *Ivan the Terrible*, 210–11.
9. Ruslan G. Skrynnikov, *Ivan the Terrible*, trans. Hugh F. Graham (Academic International Press, 1981), 114–15.
10. Stephen Graham, *Ivan the Terrible: Life of Ivan IV of Russia* (Hamden, Connecticut: Archon Books, 1968), 215–17.
11. Graham, *Ivan the Terrible*, 220.
12. Robert O. Crummey, *The Formation of Muscovy, 1304–1613* (Routledge, 1987), 170.
13. Kazimierz Waliszewski and Mary Loyd, *Ivan the Terrible* (London: W. Heinemann, 1904), 225.
14. Graham, *Ivan the Terrible*, 261–62.
15. Madariaga, *Ivan the Terrible*, 358–59.
16. Richard Hellie, "Introduction," *Russian History/Histoire Russe* 14 (1987), 3.
17. Madariaga, *Ivan the Terrible*, 63, 143.
18. Ibid, 210, 358–61.
19. Charles J. Halperin, "Ivan IV's Insanity," *Russian History* 34, nos. 1–4 (2007): 208.
20. Halperin, "Ivan IV's Insanity," 212.
21. Ibid, 213–14.
22. Ibid., 217.
23. Waliszewski and Loyd, *Ivan the Terrible*, 380–83.

24. Ibid, 396–97.
25. Sergei Bogatyrev, "Ivan IV (1533–1584)," in Maureen Perrie, ed., *The Cambridge History of Russia Vol. 1: From Early Rus' to 1689* (2006), 245.
26. Waliszewski and Loyd, *Ivan the Terrible*, 398–99.

## Chapter 4

1. Pierre Antoine Noël Bruno Daru, *Histoire de la République de Venise*, vol. 1 (Paris: 1821), 40.
2. Donald Quataert, *The Ottoman Empire, 1700–1922* (Cambridge: Cambridge University Press, 2005).
3. Halil Inalcik, *An Economic History of the Ottoman Empire, Volume 1:1300–1600* (Cambridge: Cambridge University Press, 1997).
4. Melissa and Michael Rank, *The Most Powerful Women in the Middle Ages: Queens, Saints, and Viking Slayers, from Empress Theodora to Elizabeth of Tudor* (Five Minute Books, 2013).
5. Rank, *The Most Powerful Women in the Middle Ages.*
6. Günhan Börekçi, "Ibrahim I," in Gabor Agoston and Bruce Masters, eds., *Encyclopedia of the Ottoman Empire* (New York: Facts on File, 2008).
7. Börekçi, "Ibrahim."
8. Norman M. Penzer, *The Harem: An Account of the Institution As It Existed in the Palace of the Turkish Sultans, with a History of the Grand Seraglio from Its Foundation to the Present Time* (New York: AMS Press Inc, 1937).
9. Edward Shepherd Creasy, *History of the Ottoman Turks: From the Beginning of Their Empire to the Present Time. Chiefly Founded On Von Hammer* (London, 1856), 4.
10. Leslie P. Peirce, *The Imperial Harem: Women and Sovereignty in the Ottoman Empire* (New York: Oxford University Press, 1993).
11. Caroline Finkel, *Osman's Dream: The History of the Ottoman Empire* (Basic Books, 2007), 223.
12. Creasy, *History of the Ottoman Turks*, 5–6.
13. Finkel, *Osman's Dream*, 225; Selcuk Aksin Somel, *The A to Z of the Ottoman Empire* (Rowman & Littlefield, 2010), 124.
14. Tayyib Gökbilgin, "İbrahim," in *İslâm Ansiklopedisi*, 880–85.
15. Finkel, *Osman's Dream*, 227–82.
16. Creasy, *History of the Ottoman Turks*, 11.

17. Patrick Kinross, *The Ottoman Centuries: The Rise and Fall of the Turkish Empire* (New York: Harper Perennial, 1979).
18. Owen Wright, *Demetrius Cantemir* (Ashgate, 2000).
19. Creasy, *History of the Ottoman Turks*, 9–10.
20. Ibid., 11.
21. Colin Imber, *The Ottoman Empire, 1300–1650: The Structure of Power* (Palgrave Macmillan, 2003); Börekçi, "Ibrahim."
22. Mustafa Naima, *Tarih*, vol. 4 (Istanbul, 1863), 195–96.
23. Creasy, *History of the Ottoman Turks*, 6.
24. Ibid, 7.
25. Daru, *Histoire de la République de Venise*, 40.
26. Wright, *Demetrius Cantemir*.
27. Necdet Sakaoğlu, *Bu Mülkün Kadın Sultanları* (Oğlak Yayıncılık, 2008), 353.
28. Kinross, *Ottoman Centuries*; Alan Palmer, *The Decline and Fall of the Ottoman Empire* (New York: M. Evans and Company, Inc., 1993).
29. Abdülkadir Dedeoğlu, *The Ottomans* (Istanbul: Osmanli Yayinevi, 1982); Börekçi, "Ibrahim."
30. Naima, *Tarih*, 303.
31. Leslie P. Peirce, *The Imperial Harem: Women and Sovereignty in the Ottoman Empire* (New York: Oxford University Press, 1993).
32. Creasy, *History of the Ottoman Turks*, 16.
33. Ibid, 18.
34. Kâtib Çelebi, *Fezleke*, vol. 2 (Istanbul: 1869–71), 329.
35. Kinross, *Ottoman Centuries*, 317.
36. Dedeo lu, *The Ottomans*; Börekçi, "Ibrahim."

## Chapter 5

1. Nesta Pain, *George III at Home* (London: Eyre Methuen, 1975); Isaac Ray, *Insanity of King George III : Read Before the Association of Superintendents of Insane Hospitals*, May 22, 1855 (Utica, New York: Asylum, 1855), 3; "George III of Great Britain," Mad Monarchs, http://madmonarchs.guusbeltman.nl/madmonarchs/george3/george3_bio.htm.
2. J. H. Plumb, *Men and Centuries* (Houghton Mifflin: 1963), 37, 45
3. John Brooke, *King George III: A Biography of America's Last Monarch* (New York: McGraw-Hill, 1972).

4.  Jenny Uglow, "The Strangest Family: The Private Lives of George III, Queen Charlotte and the Hanoverians—Review," *The Guardian*, August 28, 2014, https://www.theguardian.com/books/2014/aug/28/strangest-family-private-live-george-third-queen-charlotte-hanoverians-janice-hadlow-review.
5.  Pain, *George III at Home*; "George III of Great Britain," Mad Monarchs.
6.  George Bancroft, *History of the United States, from the Discovery of the American Continent*, vol. VII (Boston: Little, Brown and Co., 1858), 248. Ray, *Insanity of King George III*, 5.
7.  John Heneage Jesse, *Memoirs of the Life and Reign of King George the Third*, vol. III (London, 1888), 39–40.
8.  Willson, *George III, as Man, Monarch and Statesman*, 448.
9.  Ed Crews, "The Poisoning of King George III," *The Colonial Williamsburg Journal* (Spring 2010).
10. Jane Ambrose, "Madness and Music: Handel's Porphyric Patron, George III," *Bach* 27, no. 1 (1996), 59; Ida Macalpine and Richard Hunter, "The Insanity of King George III: A Classic Case of Porphyria," *British Medical Journal* (1966).
11. Heneage Jesse, *Memoirs of the Life and Reign of King George*, 48–50.
12. Ibid., 81.
13. Ray, *Insanity of King George III*, 6–7.
14. Beckles Willson, *George III, as Man, Monarch and Statesman* (London: T. C. & E. C. Jack, 1907), 451.
15. Willson, *George III, as Man, Monarch and Statesman*, 454–55.
16. Christopher Hibbert, *George III: A Personal History* (New York: Basic Books, 1999); "George III of Great Britain," Mad Monarchs.
17. Macalpine and Hunter, "The Insanity of King George III," 66.
18. Willson, *George III, as Man, Monarch and Statesman*, 459–60.
19. Mark Baer, "George III (1738–1820)," Encyclopedia Virginia, September 17, 2014, https://www.encyclopediavirginia.org/george_iii_1738-1820.
20. Ray, *Insanity of King George III*, 22.
21. Macalpine and Hunter, "The Insanity of King George III," 67.
22. Ida Macalpine and Richard Hunter, *George III and the Mad Business* (London: Allen Lane, 1969).
23. Macalpine and Hunter, "The Insanity of King George III," 65–71.

24. Geoffrey Dean, *The Turnstone: A Doctor's Story* (Liverpool: Liverpool University Press, 2002), 128–29.
25. "King George III: Mad or Misunderstood?" BBC News, July 13, 2004, http://news.bbc.co.uk/2/hi/health/3889903.stm.
26. Timothy M. Cox et al., "King George III and Porphyria: An Elemental Hypothesis and Investigation," *Lancet* 366, no. 9482 (July 23, 2005): 332–35.
27. Sarah Pruitt, "Letters May Prove George III 'Madness' Theory," History.com, March 24, 2017, https://www.history.com/news/letters-may-prove-george-iii-was-mad.
28. Vassiliki Rentoumi et al., "The Acute Mania of King George III: A Computational Linguistic Analysis," *PLOS ONE* 12, no. 3 (March 22, 2017).
29. "King George III of Great Britain," Mad Monarchs.
30. Willson, *George III, as Man, Monarch and Statesman*, 555.
31. Ray, *Insanity of King George III*, 29–30.
32. Willson, *George III, as Man, Monarch and* Statesman, 556.
33. Macalpine and Hunter, *George III and the Mad Business*.
34. Ambrose, "Madness and Music," 57.
35. John H. Plumb, *The First Four Georges* (London: B. T. Batsford, Ltd., 1961), 121.
36. Ambrose, "Madness and Music," 60.
37. Stanley Edward Ayling, *George the Third* (Collins, 1972), 197.
38. Brooke, *King George III*, 305.

## Chapter 6

1.  Christopher McIntosh, *The Swan King: Ludwig II of Bavaria* (London: Robin Clark, 1986), 168–71.
2.  Gertrude Norman, *A Brief History of Bavaria* (Heinrich Jaffe, 1906), 100.
3.  McIntosh, *The Swan King*, 21–22.
4.  Julius Desing, *King Ludwig II: His Life, His End* (Lechbruck, Germany: Verlag Kienberger, 1976), 5–7.
5.  Norman, *A Brief History of Bavaria*, 101.
6.  Greg King, *The Mad King: The Life and Times of Ludwig II of Bavaria* (Secaucus, New Jersey: Carol Pub. Group, 1996), 78.
7.  Desing, *King Ludwig II*, 9.
8.  Ibid, 10.

9.  Editors of Encyclopedia Britannica, "Louis II: King of Bavaria," *Encyclopedia Britannica*, last updated January 14, 2020, https://www.britannica.com/biography/Louis-II-king-of-Bavaria.
10. McIntosh, *The Swan King*, 153–57.
11. Norman, *A Brief History of Bavaria*, 100–106.
12. Werner Richter, *The Mad Monarch: The Life and Times of King Ludwig II of Bavaria* (Bavaria: Henry Regnery Company, 1954), 232.
13. Richter, *The Mad Monarch*, 233.
14. Ibid., 235.
15. McIntosh, *The Swan King*, 172.
16. Ibid., 170–71.
17. King, *The Mad King*, 259.
18. Desing, *King Ludwig II*, 35–36.
19. King, *The Mad King*, 259.
20. Frances A. Gerard, *The Romance of King Ludwig II of Bavaria* (Norwich: Jarrold, 1901), 272–73.
21. King, *The Mad King*, 261.
22. Ibid., 260–61.
23. Desing, *King Ludwig II*, 19–30.
24. King, *The Mad King*, 287–88.
25. Hans F. Nöhbauer, *Ludwig II* (New York: Taschen, 1998), 88.
26. Egon Caesar Corti, *Elizabeth, Empress of Austria* (New Haven: Yale University Press, 1936), 347.
27. King, *The Mad King*, 292–93.
28. Ibid., 287–88.
29. Norman, *A Brief History of Bavaria*, 96.
30. McIntosh, *The Swan King*, 173.
31. Desing, *King Ludwig II*, 44–46.
32. McIntosh, *The Swan King*, 201–4.

## Chapter 7

1.  Michael T. Kaufman, "Idi Amin, Murderous and Erratic Ruler of Uganda in the 70's, Dies in Exile," *New York Times*, August 17, 2003.
2.  Tony Avirgan and Martha Honey, "Dungeon Visit Yields Latest Amin Horrors," *Washington Post*, April 14, 1979.
3.  Avirgan and Honey, "Dungeon Visit Yields Latest Amin Horrors."

4.  David Gwyn, *Idi Amin: Death-Light of Africa* (Boston: Little, Brown, 1977), 207–8.
5.  "Idi Amin," *The Dictator's Playbook*, (television show), PBS, aired February 13, 2019, https://www.pbs.org/tpt/dictators-playbook/episodes/idi-amin/.
6.  Jonathon Green, *Morrow's International Dictionary of Contemporary Quotations* (New York: William Morrow & Co., 1982).
7.  Gwyn, *Idi Amin*, 24.
8.  Anton La Guardia, "Prayers but No Forgiveness for Idi Amin," *The Telegraph*, August 17, 2003.
9.  Gwyn, *Idi Amin*, 25–27.
10. Ibid., 29.
11. Michael Pollard, *Absolute Rulers* (Ada, Oklahoma: Garrett, 1992), 62.
12. Kaufman, "Idi Amin, Murderous and Erratic Dictator."
13. Gwyn, *Idi Amin*, 6.
14. Ibid., 84.
15. Ibid.
16. Kaufman, "Idi Amin, Murderous and Erratic Dictator."
17. Kim Wall, "Ghost Stories: Idi Amin's Torture Chambers," International Women's Media Foundation, December 27, 2016, https://www.iwmf.org/reporting/ghost-stories-idi-amins-torture-chambers/.
18. Wall, "Ghost Stories."
19. Ibid.
20. Gwyn, *Idi Amin*, 85.
21. Ibid., 7–8.
22. Pollard, *Absolute Rulers*, 63.
23. Gwyn, *Idi Amin*, 22–23.
24. Ibid., 5.
25. Ibid.
26. Kaufman, "Idi Amin, Murderous and Erratic Dictator."
27. Kaufman, "Idi Amin, Murderous and Erratic Dictator."
28. Gwyn, *Idi Amin*, 3–4.
29. Ibid., 126–29.
30. Ibid., 206.
31. Ibid., 207–8.
32. Ethan Bronner, "The Obscenely Easy Exile of Idi Amin," *New York Times*, August 19, 2003.

## Chapter 8

1. Paul Theroux, "The Golden Man," *New Yorker,* May 21, 2007.
2. Dilip Hiro, *Inside Central Asia: A Political and Cultural History of Uzbekistan, Turkmenistan, Kazakhstan, Kyrgyz Stan, Tajikistan, Turkey, and Iran* (Overlook, 2009), 215.
3. S. Peyrouse. "Berdymukhammedov's Turkmenistan: A Modest Shift in Domestic and Social Politics," *Journal of Central Asian Studies* 1 (2010): 78–80.
4. Polese and Horák, "Personality Cults and Nation-Building in Turkmenistan," in Rico Isaacs and Abel Polese, eds., *Nation-Building and Identity in the Post-Soviet Space: New Tools and Approaches* (Routledge, 2016): 169; Fabio De Leonardis, *Nation-Building and Personality Cult in Turkmenistan: The Türkmenbaşy Phenomenon* (Routledge, 2017), 3.
5. S. N. Eisenstadt, ed., *On Charisma and Institution Building: Max Weber and Modern Sociology* (Chicago and London, 1968: University of Chicago Press), 48.
6. De Leonardis, *Nation-Building and Personality Cult,* 77.
7. Anette Bohr, "Turkmenistan and the Turkmen," in Graham Smith, ed., *The Nationalities Question in the Post-Soviet States* (Longman: 1996), 356; De Leonardis, *Nation-Building and Personality Cult,* 79.
8. 88 Slavomir Horák, "The Ideology of the Türkmenbashy Regime," *Perspectives on European Politics and Society* 6, no. 2 (May 1, 2005): 309.
9. Alan Taylor, "The City of White Marble: Ashgabat, Turkmenistan," *The Atlantic,* June 5, 2013.
10. Saparmurat Niyazov, *Unity, Peace, Consensus* (Alma Ata: Noy Publications, 1994); De Leonardis, *Nation-Building and Personality Cult,* 81.
11. Martha Brill Olcott, *Central Asia's New States: Independence, Foreign Policy and Regional Security* (Washington, 1997: United States Institute of Peace Press).
12. Kort, 142–43.
13. De Leonardis, *Nation-Building and Personality Cult,* 86.
14. Bohr, "Turkmenistan and the Turkmen," 425.
15. Daniel Kalder, "The Madness of Turkmenbashi," *The Spectator,* February 17, 2010.
16. C. J. Chivers, "Saparmurat Niyazov, Turkmen Leader, Dies at 66," *New York Times,* December 21, 2006.

17. David Lewis, *The Temptations of Tyranny in Central Asia* (New York: Columbia University Press, 2008), 91–2.
18. De Leonardis, *Nation-Building and Personality Cult*, 89.
19. Theroux, "The Golden Man."
20. Suparmurat Niyazov, *Ruhnama. Reflections on the Spiritual Values of the Turkmen* (Ashgabat: The State Publishing Service of Turkmenistan. 2003), 24
21. De Leonardis, *Nation-Building and Personality Cult*, 89.
22. Rafis Abazov, *Historical Dictionary of Turkmenistan* (Oxford: Scarecrow Press, 2005), 68, 122, 134; De Leonardis, *Nation-Building and Personality Cult*, 90.
23. Niyazov, *Ruhnama*, 9.
24. Ibid., 144–45.
25. De Leonardis, *Nation-Building and Personality Cult*, 91–92.
26. Niyazov, *Ruhnama*, 9–10, 44, 179; De Leonardis, *Nation-Building and Personality Cult*, 92.
27. Felix Corley, "Turkmenistan: President's Personality Cult Imposed on Religious Communities," Forum 18, March 1, 2005, http://www.forum18.org/archive.php?article_id=522.
28. Niyazov, *Ruhnama*, 18; De Leonardis, *Nation-Building and Personality Cult*, 94.
29. Niyazov, *Ruhnama*, 73.
30. Ibid., 50, 99.
31. Daniel Sershen, "Turkmenistan's Natural Gas: Mixed Blessing," *Christian Science Monitor*, May 15, 2007.
32. 3232 Ilan Greenberg, "When a Kleptocratic, Megalomaniacal Dictator Goes Bad," *New York Times*, January 5, 2003.
33. De Leonardis, *Nation-Building and Personality Cult*, 103.
34. Annette Bohr, "Turkmenistan," Nations in Transit, Freedom House, June 30, 2009, https://www.refworld.org/docid/4a55bb45c.html; De Leonardis, *Nation-Building and Personality Cult*, 101–3.
35. Steven Lee Myers, "Turkmen Leader, Wishing to Be August, Settles for January," *New York Times*. August 11, 2002.

## Chapter 9

1. Barbara Demick, *Nothing to Envy: Ordinary Lives in North Korea* (New York: Spiegel & Grau, 2010), 2–4.
2. Demick, *Nothing to Envy*, 4.
3. Ibid., 8.

4. Andrei Lankov, *The Real North Korea: Life and Politics in the Failed Stalinist Utopia* (New York: Oxford University Press, 2014).
5. Demick, *Nothing to Envy*, 11–12.
6. "U.S. Department of State Country Report on Human Rights Practices 2001–Korea, Democratic People's Republic Of," Refworld, UNHCR.
7. "U.S. Department of State Country Report on Human Rights Practices 2001."
8. Ibid.
9. Demick, *Nothing to Envy*, 175.
10. Richard Worth, *Kim Jong Il* (New York: Chelsea House, 2008), 84–85.
11. Worth, *Kim Jong Il*, 93.
12. Demick, *Nothing to Envy*, 66–67.
13. Ibid., 67–68.
14. Worth, *Kim Jong Il*, 87.
15. "U.S. Department of State Country Report on Human Rights Practices 2001."
16. Ibid.
17. Ibid.
18. Demick, *Nothing to Envy*, 174.
19. "U.S. Department of State Country Report on Human Rights Practices 2001."
20. Ibid.
21. Ibid.
22. Ibid.
23. Christopher Hitchens, "Worse Than 1984: North Korea, Slave State," Slate, May 2, 2005.
24. Hitchens, "Worse Than 1984: North Korea, Slave State."
25. B. R. Myers, *The Cleanest Race: How North Koreans See Themselves—And Why It Matters* (Brooklyn, New York: Melville House, 2011).
26. Frederick L. Coolidge and Daniel L. Segal, "Is Kim Jong-Il like Saddam Hussein and Adolf Hitler? A Personality Disorder Evaluation," *Behavioral Sciences of Terrorism and Political Aggression* 1, no. 3 (September 1, 2009): 195–202.
27. Coolidge and Segal, "Is Kim Jong-Il like Saddam Hussein and Adolf Hitler?"
28. Worth, *Kim Jong Il*, 12–14.

29. Reuters, "Here Comes Trouble," *The Economist*, March 31, 2007.
30. Worth, *Kim Jong Il*, 14.
31. Demick, *Nothing to Envy*, 66.
32. Worth, *Kim Jong Il*, 86–87.
33. Ibid., 94.
34. Demick, *Nothing to Envy*, 14–15.
35. Simon Winchester, "There Are Lies on Both Sides of Korea's Border," *The Times*, December 20, 2011.

## Conclusion

1.  "North Korea Acclaims New 'Supreme' Leader at Memorial Service for Kim Jong-il," *New York Post*, December 29, 2011, https://nypost. com/2011/12/29/
    north-korea-acclaims-new-supreme-leader-at-memorial-service-for-kim-jong-il/.
2.  "North Korean Leader Kim Jong-il Dies 'of Heart Attack,'" BBC News, December 19, 2011, https://www.bbc.com/news/world-asia-16239693.
3.  Associated Press, Rafael Wober, "North Korea mourns Kim Jong Il; Son Is 'Successor,'" Deseret News, December 19, 2011, https://www.deseret. com/2011/12/20/20239254/
    north-korea-mourns-kim-jong-il-son-is-successor#in-this-image-made-from-associated-press-television-news-north-koreans-gather-to-mourn-the-death-of-north-korean-leader-kim-jong-il-in-front-of-a-mural-depicting-kim-jong-il-and-his-father-kim-sung-il-unseen-in-pyongyang-monday-dec-19-2011.
4.  Andrew Scull, "Madness and Meaning," *Paris Review*, April 22, 2015.
5.  Scull, "Madness and Meaning."
6.  Janna Levin, *How the Universe Got Its Spots: Diary of a Finite Time in a Finite Space* (New York: Anchor, 2003).
7.  Levin, *How the Universe Got Its Spots*.
8.  Maria Popova, "Madness and Genius: Cosmologist Janna Levin on the Vitalizing Power of Obsessiveness, from Newton to Einstein," *Brain Pickings* (blog), February 1, 2016, https://www.brainpickings. org/2016/02/01/janna-levin-how-the-universe-got-its-spots-madness/.
9.  Levin, *How the Universe Got Its Spots*.
10. Arthur Schopenhauer, *The World as Will and Representation*, vol. 1, trans. E. F. J. Payne (New York: Dover Publications, 1966).

11. Popova, "Arthur Schopenhauer on the Relationship Between Genius and Madness."
12. Schopenhauer, *The World as Will and Representation.*
13. William J. Dobson, *The Dictator's Learning Curve: Inside the Global Battle for Democracy* (Anchor, 2012).

# Index